Form 4715

1086085

Record your class number here.

SERVSAFE® COURSEBOOK

FIFTH EDITION

Updated with the *2009 FDA Food Code*

NATIONAL
RESTAURANT
ASSOCIATION®

Disclaimer

Copyright Permissions

National Restaurant Association

175 West Jackson Boulevard, Suite 1500

Chicago, IL 60604-2814

Email: permissions@restaurant.org

Coursebook, CBX5R (with exam answer sheet)   ISBN 978-1-58280-263-3

Coursebook, CBV5R (with online exam voucher)   ISBN 978-1-58280-262-6

Coursebook, CB5R (text only)   ISBN 978-1-58280-261-9

Printed in the USA

10 9 8 7 6 5 4 3 2

Introduction

Unit I The Food Safety Challenge

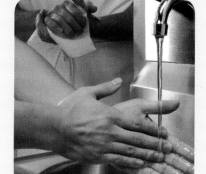

Unit II   The Flow of Food Through the Operation

Unit III   Sanitary Facilities and Pest Management

Unit IV   Food Safety Regulation and Employee Training

A Message From
The National Restaurant Association

The National Restaurant Association is pleased to bring you the fifth edition of *ServSafe® Coursebook,* updated with the *2009 FDA Food Code.*

By opening this book, you are taking the first step in your commitment to food safety. ServSafe training introduces you to the basic information you need to know to serve safe food. Training also helps you understand all the food safety risks faced by your operation. Once you're aware of these risks, you can find ways to reduce them, which will help you keep your operation, your customers, and your employees safe.

The ServSafe Training and Certification Program provides you with the knowledge, skills, and abilities you need to do your job. It leads the way in setting high food safety standards.

Created by Foodservice Industry Leaders　You can be confident knowing the ServSafe program was created by the foodservice industry, for the foodservice industry. Those who deal with the same food safety issues you face every day determined the topics you will learn in this book. From the basics of handwashing to more complex topics such as foodborne pathogens, your industry peers have provided you with the building blocks to keep food safe throughout your operation.

Delivered by Certified ServSafe Instructors　Your success in learning is important to us. That's why the Association has implemented higher standards for the people who train you, our Certified ServSafe Instructors.

Performed and Reinforced by You　Food safety doesn't stop once you've completed your ServSafe training and certification. It's only just begun. Training is a process, not an event. It is now your responsibility to take the knowledge you learned and share it with your employees. The information in chapter 15, Employee Food Safety Training, will help you find ways to train your staff. ServSafe also offers training materials to help you teach key food safety topics to hourly employees. Free materials are available in the Resource Center on *www.ServSafe.com.*

Thank you for investing your time in ServSafe training. We view your training as a critical piece of your success, and we are confident that you'll benefit greatly by applying what you learn to your own operation. For more information on all ServSafe programs, visit *www.ServSafe.com.*

About the National Restaurant Association

The National Restaurant Association, founded in 1919, is the leading business association for the restaurant industry, which is comprised of 935,000 restaurant and foodservice outlets and a workforce of 12.8 million employees—making it the cornerstone of the economy, career opportunities, and community involvement. Along with the National Restaurant Association Educational Foundation, the Association works to represent, educate, and promote the rapidly growing industry. For more information, visit our Web site at www.restaurant.org.

International Food Safety Council®

The International Food Safety Council's mission is to heighten the awareness of the importance of food safety education throughout the restaurant and foodservice industry. The council envisions a future in which foodborne illness no longer exists.

For more information about the International Food Safety Council, sponsorship opportunities, and initiatives, please call 312.261.5336, or visit *www.ServSafe.com*.

Active Founding Sponsors

American Egg Board

The Beef Checkoff

Ecolab Inc.

SYSCO Corporation

Campaign Sponsors

Cintas Corporation

Rubbermaid Commercial Products

<u>Acknowledgements</u>

The development of the *ServSafe Coursebook* text would not have been possible without the expertise of our many advisors and manuscript reviewers. Thanks to the following organizations for their time, effort, and dedication to creating this fifth edition.

3M

Boskovich Farms, Inc.

Centers for Disease Control and Prevention

Comark Instruments

The Cooking and Hospitality Institute of Chicago

Cooper-Atkins Corporation

Daydots

Fluke Corporation

Kendall College School of Culinary Arts, Chicago

Orkin Commercial Services

Washburne Culinary Institute, Chicago

How to Use *ServSafe Coursebook*

The plan below will help you study and retain the food safety principles in this textbook that are vital to keeping your establishment safe.

Beginning Each Chapter

Before you begin reading each chapter, you can prepare by:

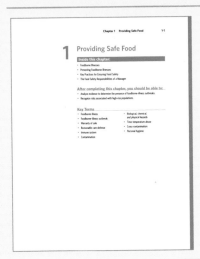

Reviewing the learning objectives.

Located on the front page of each chapter, the learning objectives identify tasks you should be able to do after finishing the chapter. They are linked to the essential practices for keeping your establishment safe.

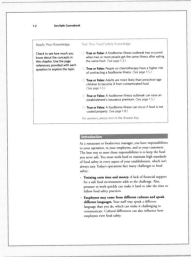

Completing the Test Your Food Safety Knowledge questions.

Five True or False questions at the beginning of each chapter will test your prior food safety knowledge. The questions include page references for you to explore the topics further. Answers are located in the Answer Key.

Throughout Each Chapter

Use the following learning tools to help you identify and reinforce the key principles as you read each chapter:

- **Key Terms.** These terms are important for a thorough understanding of the chapter content. They are highlighted throughout the chapter, where either they are explicitly defined or their meanings are made clear within the paragraphs in which they appear. Each key term is also defined in the Glossary.

- **Exhibits.** These are placed throughout each chapter to visually reinforce the key principles presented in the text. They include charts, photographs, illustrations, and tables.

- **Icons.** Two types of icons appear in *ServSafe Coursebook*.

  - In Chapters 5 through 10, an icon representing the various points in the flow of food appears in the left margin. As you read through these chapters, you will notice the highlighted portion of the icon changes according to the point within the flow of food being discussed.

The Flow of Food

  - Throughout the text you will see icons that reinforce critical food safety principles such as cross-contamination and proper cooling. While Key Point icons are the most common type, icons related to personal hygiene, cross-contamination, and time-temperature abuse are also included.

| Key Point | Health Alert | Cleaning & Sanitizing | Cross-Contamination | Bacterial Growth | Personal Hygiene |

- **Something to Think About.** Several food safety stories appear throughout the text to provoke discussion about various food safety topics. Some of these real-world stories focus on foodborne illnesses that have occurred when food was not handled safely. They emphasize the importance of following food safety practices and allow you to apply what you have learned by asking how the incident could have been prevented. Other stories showcase real-world solutions to food safety problems. These solutions may help you address similar problems in your own establishment.

At the End of Each Chapter

Several activities have been provided at the end of each chapter to test your knowledge. These include:

Case in Point Activities. These food safety case studies ask you to identify the errors made by the foodhandlers in each story and the proper practices that should have been followed.

Discussion Questions. These questions are designed to make you think about some of the important food safety concepts presented in the chapter. Answers to the questions are provided in the Answer Key.

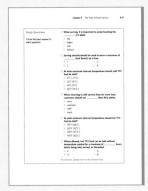

Study Questions. These multiple-choice questions are directly based on the learning objectives. If you have difficulty answering them, you should review the content further. Answers are located at the back of each chapter.

Additional Resources. In this section, you will find resources—books, articles, and Web sites—that will enable you to further explore the food safety concepts presented in each chapter.

Notes

The Food Safety Challenge

1 Providing Safe Food

Inside this chapter:

- Foodborne Illnesses
- Preventing Foodborne Illnesses
- Key Practices for Ensuring Food Safety
- The Food Safety Responsibilities of a Manager

After completing this chapter, you should be able to:

- Analyze evidence to determine the presence of foodborne-illness outbreaks.
- Recognize risks associated with high-risk populations.

Key Terms

- Foodborne illness
- Foodborne-illness outbreak
- Warranty of sale
- Reasonable care defense
- Immune system
- Contamination
- Biological, chemical, and physical hazards
- Time-temperature abuse
- Cross-contamination
- Personal hygiene

Apply Your Knowledge

Check to see how much you know about the concepts in this chapter. Use the page references provided with each question to explore the topic.

Test Your Food Safety Knowledge

① **True or False:** A foodborne-illness outbreak has occurred when two or more people get the same illness after eating the same food. *(See page 1-3.)*

② **True or False:** People on chemotherapy have a higher risk of contracting a foodborne illness. *(See page 1-5.)*

③ **True or False:** Adults are more likely than preschool-age children to become ill from contaminated food. *(See page 1-5.)*

④ **True or False:** A foodborne-illness outbreak can raise an establishment's insurance premium. *(See page 1-5.)*

⑤ **True or False:** A foodborne illness can occur if food is not cooled properly. *(See page 1-8.)*

For answers, please turn to the Answer Key.

Introduction

As a restaurant or foodservice manager, you have responsibilities to your operation, to your employees, and to your customers. The best way to meet those responsibilities is to keep the food you serve safe. You must work hard to maintain high standards of food safety in every aspect of your establishment, which is not always easy. Today's operations face many challenges to food safety:

- **Training costs time and money.** A lack of financial support for a safe food environment adds to the challenge. Also, pressure to work quickly can make it hard to take the time to follow food safety practices.

- **Employees may come from different cultures and speak different languages.** Your staff may speak a different language than you do, which can make it challenging to communicate. Cultural differences can also influence how employees view food safety.

- **Employees often have different levels of education.** This makes it more challenging to teach them food safety.

- **Illness-causing microorganisms are more frequently found on food that once was considered safe.** For example, *Salmonella* spp. is now found on produce more than in the past.

- **Food might be received from suppliers that are not practicing food safety.** This can cause a foodborne-illness outbreak.

- **The number of customers at high risk for getting a foodborne illness is increasing.** An example of this is the growing elderly population.

- **Training new staff leaves less time for food safety training.**

The ServSafe program will provide you with the tools you need to overcome the challenges in managing a good food safety program.

Foodborne Illnesses

Health Alert

A foodborne-illness outbreak is an incident in which two or more people experience the same illness after eating the same food.

A foodborne illness is a disease carried or transmitted to people by food. The Centers for Disease Control and Prevention (CDC) defines a foodborne-illness outbreak as an incident in which two or more people get the same illness after eating the same food. A foodborne illness is confirmed when laboratory analysis shows that a specific food is the source of the illness.

Each year, millions of people have foodborne illnesses. Most cases are not reported and do not occur at restaurants or foodservice establishments. But the cases that are reported and investigated help the industry learn about the causes of illnesses. The cases also raise awareness of what can be done to control them. Fortunately, all establishments, no matter how large or small, can take steps to ensure the safety of the food they prepare and serve.

The Costs of Foodborne Illnesses

Foodborne illnesses cost the United States billions of dollars each year. They cause lost productivity, hospitalization, long-term disability claims, and even death.

National Restaurant Association figures show that a foodborne-illness outbreak can cost an establishment thousands of dollars. From legal fees to loss of sales, the results can be devastating. It can even cause closure. See *Exhibit 1a* for many of the other costs an establishment can face.

Today, customers are very willing to sue because of injuries they feel they have suffered from the food they were served. Under the federal Uniform Commercial Code, a plaintiff bringing a lawsuit must prove all of the following:

- The food was unfit to be served.

- The food caused the plaintiff harm.

- In serving the food, the establishment violated the warranty of sale, which are the rules for how the food must be handled.

A plaintiff who has won can receive compensatory and punitive damages. Compensatory damages are awarded for lost work, lost wages, and medical bills. Punitive damages are awarded to punish the defendant for wanton and willful neglect. They are given in addition to compensatory damages.

An establishment can use a reasonable care defense against a food-related lawsuit if it has a food safety management system in place. A reasonable care defense must show that the establishment did everything that could be reasonably expected to keep its food safe. Documented standards, training practices, procedures, and positive inspection results are the keys to this defense.

Be aware that decisions in these suits follow the laws in their respective states. Check your state law to find out the appropriate defense in any action.

1a Costs of a Foodborne Illness to an Establishment

 Loss of customers and sales

 Loss of reputation

 Negative media exposure

 Lowered employee morale

 Lawsuits and legal fees

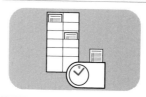 Employee absenteeism

 Increased insurance premiums

 Staff retraining

Populations at High Risk for Foodborne Illnesses

Studies of U.S. demographics show that certain groups of people have a higher risk of getting a foodborne illness than others, sometimes with serious results. (See *Exhibit 1b* on the next page.) They include:

- Infants and preschool-age children

- Pregnant women

- Elderly people

- Other people with compromised immune systems, such as people with cancer/on chemotherapy, people with HIV/AIDS, and transplant recipients

These groups of people are at a higher risk because they have issues with their immune systems—the body's defense system against illness. People at risk are more vulnerable to developing a foodborne illness and complications such as a lengthier illness, being hospitalized, or death.

1b   People at High Risk for Foodborne Illnesses

Young children

Pregnant women

Elderly people

Other people with compromised immune systems

Infants and Preschool-Age Children

Young children are at a higher risk for getting foodborne illnesses because they have not yet built up their immune systems.

Pregnant Women

Pregnant women are at a higher risk because their immune systems are compromised due to the pregnancy.

Elderly People

As people age, their immune systems weaken. Changes in the body's organs and systems can have an impact. For example, stomach-acid production decreases as people get older, allowing more ingested pathogens to enter the intestinal path. A change in the stomach and intestinal tract allows the body to keep food for longer periods, allowing more time for toxin formation. Additionally, their senses of taste and smell decline, leading to a change in their eating habits. The food they choose may not give them enough nutrients to maintain their immune systems.

Other People with Compromised Immune Systems

Immune-compromised people are at a higher risk for getting a foodborne illness because their bodies have damaged immune systems. Often, these people are on medication or chemotherapy, which weakens their ability to recover from a foodborne illness.

For example, people who have received an organ or bone-marrow transplant take medication to prevent the body from destroying the new organ or bone marrow—in the same way that the immune system works to clear infections from the body. The medication suppresses the immune system. This leaves the body vulnerable to infections, such as some of the illnesses caused by foodborne pathogens.

Preventing Foodborne Illnesses

Before you can prevent foodborne illnesses, you must know what conditions in your operation lead to them. You must recognize the hazards that can make food unsafe. You also need to understand the common factors that cause foodborne illnesses.

Potential Hazards to Food Safety

Unsafe food usually results from contamination, which is the presence of harmful substances in food. Some hazards are introduced in food by humans or the environment. Others occur naturally.

These hazards are divided into the following three categories (see *Exhibit 1c*):

- Biological hazards include illness-causing microorganisms. Other examples are certain plant, mushroom, and seafood toxins.

- Chemical hazards include cleaners, sanitizers, polishes, machine lubricants, and toxic metals.

- Physical hazards are foreign objects that accidentally get into food. Examples include hair, dirt, bandages, metal staples, and broken glass. Naturally occurring objects, such as bones in fillets, are also physical hazards.

By far, biological hazards are the greatest threat to food safety. Illness-causing microorganisms cause most foodborne-illness outbreaks.

How Food Becomes Unsafe

The CDC has identified the five most common risk factors that cause foodborne illnesses.

❶ Purchasing food from unsafe sources

❷ Failing to cook food adequately

❸ Holding food at incorrect temperatures

❹ Using contaminated equipment

❺ Poor personal hygiene

Each of these factors is discussed on the next two pages. Often, cases of foodborne illnesses involve several factors.

1c   Hazards to Food Safety

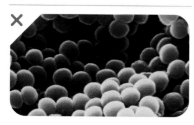

Biological

Chemical

Physical

1d　Time-Temperature Abuse

Food has been time-temperature abused any time it has been allowed to remain too long at temperatures favorable to the growth of microorganisms.

1e　Cross-Contamination

Cross-contamination occurs when microorganisms are transferred from one surface or food to another.

Time-Temperature Abuse

Food has been **time-temperature abused** any time it has been allowed to remain too long at temperatures that favor growth of foodborne microorganisms. (See *Exhibit 1d.*) A foodborne illness can result if food is time-temperature abused in any of these ways:

- It is not held or stored at required temperatures.

- It is not cooked or reheated to temperatures that kill microorganisms.

- It is not cooled properly.

Cross-Contamination

Cross-contamination occurs when microorganisms are transferred from one surface or food to another. (See *Exhibit 1e.*) A foodborne illness can result if cross-contamination occurs in any of these ways:

- Contaminated ingredients are added to food that receives no further cooking.

- Contaminated food touches or drips fluids onto ready-to-eat food.

- A foodhandler touches contaminated food and then touches ready-to-eat food.

- Ready-to-eat food touches contaminated surfaces.

- Contaminated cleaning towels touch food-contact surfaces.

Poor Personal Hygiene

Individuals with poor **personal hygiene** can offend customers, contaminate food or food-contact surfaces, and cause illness. A foodborne illness can result if employees do any of the following:

- Fail to wash their hands properly after using the restroom or whenever their hands have become contaminated

- Cough or sneeze on food

- Touch or scratch wounds and then touch food they are handling

- Come to work while sick

Purchasing Food from Unsafe Sources

Food can become contaminated at any point in the supply chain. It is your responsibility to purchase food only from approved suppliers. An approved food supplier is one that has been inspected and meets all applicable local, state, and federal laws.

A foodborne illness can result if food is purchased without considering the following:

- Shellfish should be purchased from sources that are listed in the Interstate Certified Shellfish Shippers List.

- Mushrooms picked in the wild should be bought from sources that use approved mushroom-identification experts to inspect each mushroom and find them to be safe.

- "Homemade" food items should not be purchased.

Contaminated Equipment

All food-contact surfaces in the establishment must be cleaned and sanitized on a scheduled basis to prevent foodborne illnesses. Foodborne illnesses can result when:

- Food-contact surfaces are not cleaned and sanitized before use.

- Dishwashing procedures do not adequately clean and sanitize equipment.

Something to Think About...	Turkey Trouble
	Many customers fell ill after eating at a buffet in a country club in New Mexico. Dozens required medical treatment. The culprit? Roast turkey, stuffing, and gravy contaminated with the bacteria *Staphylococcus aureus*.
	More than one factor led to the outbreak. Several of the foodhandlers had the bacteria. Poor personal hygiene practices led them to contaminate the turkey. The problem was made worse when the cooked turkey was not cooled properly. Finally, the bacteria spread when the foodhandlers used the same utensils to handle the turkey and other food.
	What should have been done to prevent this incident?

Key Practices for Ensuring Food Safety

To keep the food in your operation safe, you should focus on the following things:

- Controlling time and temperature
- Preventing cross-contamination
- Practicing good personal hygiene
- Purchasing food from approved, reputable suppliers
- Cleaning and sanitizing properly

It is important to establish standard operating procedures for each of these areas. The ServSafe program will provide you with the knowledge to properly design these procedures.

The Food Safety Responsibilities of a Manager

Managers have some basic food safety responsibilities. They must serve safe food and train employees in safe foodhandling practices. They must know about current regulations affecting the establishment. Most important, they must have a positive and supportive attitude toward food safety.

Meeting Food Safety Regulations

To stay open, your establishment must meet city, county, and state food regulations. The regulatory agency that inspects your establishment shares your commitment to food safety. They may be able to assess fines and close an establishment that serves unsafe food. Therefore, it is in your best interest to work with local authorities.

The Food and Drug Administration (FDA) recommends that state and local health departments hold the person in charge of a restaurant or foodservice establishment responsible for knowing and demonstrating the following information:

- Illnesses carried or transmitted by food and their symptoms
- Types of toxic materials used in the operation and how to safely store, dispense, use, and discard them
- Major food allergens and their symptoms

- Relationship between personal hygiene and the spread of illnesses, especially as it relates to cross-contamination, bare-hand contact with ready-to-eat food, and handwashing

- Reporting system that ensures employees inform their manager of illnesses

- How to keep injured or ill employees from contaminating food or food-contact surfaces

- Clear guidelines for excluding employees from the establishment or restricting them from handling food and equipment

- The need to control the length of time that TCS food is at temperatures that support microorganism growth

- Hazards associated with eating raw or undercooked meat, poultry, eggs, and seafood

- Safe times and temperatures for cooking TCS food, such as meat, poultry, eggs, and seafood

- Safe times and temperatures for storing, holding, cooling, and reheating TCS food

- Correct procedures for cleaning and sanitizing utensils and food-contact surfaces of equipment

- The need for equipment that is sufficient in number and capacity and is properly designed, constructed, located, installed, operated, maintained, and cleaned

- Approved sources of potable water and the importance of keeping it safe

- The principles of a food safety management system

- How the establishment's food safety procedures meet regulatory requirements

- Rights, responsibilities, and authorities that the local code assigns to employees, managers, and the local health department

Marketing Food Safety

Marketing your food safety efforts will help show employees and customers that your operation takes food safety seriously. Show employees through your actions that management is involved in and supports food safety policies. Emphasize that food safety training for all managers and employees is a priority.

There are several other things you can do to show your food safety commitment to your employees:

- Offer training courses, and evaluate and update them as needed.

- Discuss food safety expectations. Document foodhandling procedures, and update them as needed.

- Show employees that safe foodhandling is appreciated. Consider awarding certificates for training and giving out small rewards for good food safety records.

- Set a good example by following all food safety rules yourself.

You should also find ways to show customers that employees know and follow food safety rules. Make sure employees' appearances reflect your food safety focus. Consider using food safety place mats and posters to reinforce your message. Be sure your employees can answer simple food safety questions when asked by customers.

Summary

A foodborne illness is a disease carried or transmitted to people by food. Infants and preschool-age children, pregnant women, the elderly, people with cancer or on chemotherapy, people with HIV/AIDS, and transplant recipients are at a higher risk for getting foodborne illnesses.

An incident of foodborne illnesses can be very expensive for an establishment. Costs can include lawsuits, increased insurance premiums, and damage to the establishment's reputation.

The keys to food safety are controlling time and temperature throughout the flow of food, practicing good personal hygiene, preventing cross-contamination, purchasing from approved, reputable suppliers, and cleaning and sanitizing properly.

Apply Your Knowledge

Use these questions to
review the concepts
presented in this chapter.

Discussion Questions

① What are the potential costs associated with
foodborne-illness outbreaks?

② Why are the elderly at higher risk for getting
foodborne illnesses?

③ What are the three major types of hazards to
food safety?

For answers, please turn to the Answer Key.

Study Questions

Circle the best answer to each question.

① **Why are elderly people at a higher risk for foodborne illnesses?**

A Their immune systems have weakened with age.

B They are more likely to spend time in a hospital.

C They are more likely to suffer allergic reactions.

D Their appetites have decreased with age.

② **The three categories of food safety hazards are biological, physical, and**

A temporal.

B practical.

C chemical.

D thermal.

③ **For a foodborne illness to be considered an "outbreak," a minimum of how many people must experience the same illness after eating the same food?**

A 1

B 2

C 10

D 20

④ **According to the Centers for Disease Control and Prevention, the five most common risk factors that cause foodborne illnesses are failing to cook food adequately, holding food at incorrect temperatures, using contaminated equipment, practicing poor personal hygiene, and**

A reheating leftover food.

B serving ready-to-eat food.

C using single-use, disposable gloves.

D purchasing food from unsafe sources.

For answers, please turn to the Answer Key.

Additional Resources

Articles and Texts

Buzby, Jean C. 2001. Children and Microbial Foodborne Illness. *FoodReview.* 24 (2): 32.

Buzby, Jean C. 2002. Older Adults at Risk of Complications from Microbial Foodborne Illness. *FoodReview.* 25 (2): 30.

Hedberg, Craig W., S. Jay Smith, Elizabeth Kirkland, Vincent Radke, Tim F. Jones, and Carol A. Selman. 2006. Systematic Environmental Evaluations to Identify Food Safety Differences between Outbreak and Nonoutbreak Restaurants. *Journal of Food Protection.* 69 (11): 2697.

Woteki, Catherine E., and Brian D. Kineman. 2003. Challenges and Approaches to Reducing Foodborne Illness. *Annual Review of Nutrition.* 23:315.

Web Sites

Center for Infectious Disease Research & Policy
www.cidrap.umn.edu

Centers for Disease Control and Prevention
cdc.gov

Centers for Disease Control and Prevention Environmental Health Specialists Network (EHS-Net)
cdc.gov/nceh/ehs/EHSNet/default.htm

Conference for Food Protection
foodprotect.org

FDA Food Safety
www.fda.gov/Food/FoodSafety/default.htm

Foodborne Diseases Active Surveillance Network (Food Net)
cdc.gov/foodnet

Gateway to Government Food Safety Information
foodsafety.gov

National Restaurant Association
restaurant.org

Continued on next page ▶

► *Continued from previous page*

Documents and Other Resources

2009 FDA Food Code
www.fda.gov/Food/FoodSafety/RetailFoodProtection/FoodCode/
FoodCode2009/default.htm

*Centers for Disease Control and Prevention Endorses Certification of Food
Safety Kitchen Managers*
cdc.gov/nceh/ehs/EHSNet/certification.htm

FDA Enforcement Report Index
fda.gov/opacom/Enforce.html

FDA Foodborne Illness Resource Page
www.fda.gov/Food/FoodSafety/FoodborneIllness/default.htm

Foodborne Illness Cost Calculator
ers.usda.gov/data/foodborneillness

Notes

2 The Microworld

Inside this chapter:

- Pathogens
- Viruses
- Bacteria
- Parasites
- Fungi
- Biological Toxins
- Emerging Pathogens and Issues

After completing this chapter, you should be able to:

- Identify factors that affect the growth of foodborne bacteria (FAT TOM).
- Identify characteristics of TCS food.
- Identify major foodborne pathogens, their sources, resulting illnesses, and symptoms.
- Identify methods for preventing viral, bacterial, parasitic, and fungal contamination.
- Identify naturally occurring toxins and methods for preventing illness.

Key Terms

- Microorganisms
- Pathogens
- Toxins
- FAT TOM
- Temperature danger zone
- Water activity (a_w)
- Virus
- Bacteria
- Spore
- Parasite
- Fungi
- Mold
- Yeast

Apply Your Knowledge

Check to see how much you know about the concepts in this chapter. Use the page references provided with each question to explore the topic.

Test Your Food Safety Knowledge

1. **True or False:** Pathogens grow well at 155°F (68°C) *(See page 2-4.)*

2. **True or False:** A person with hepatitis A may experience double vision. *(See page 2-9.)*

3. **True or False:** *Bacillus cereus* is commonly linked with untreated garlic-and-oil mixtures. *(See page 2-15.)*

4. **True or False:** Purchasing fish from approved, reputable suppliers can help prevent anisakiasis. *(See page 2-22.)*

5. **True or False:** A person with ciguatera fish poisoning often sweats and experiences a burning sensation in the mouth. *(See page 2-27.)*

For answers, please turn to the Answer Key.

2a   Pathogens that Can Cause Foodborne Illness

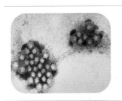
Viruses

Bacteria

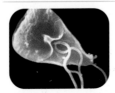
Parasites

Fungi

Courtesy of Centers for Disease Control and Prevention

Introduction

Microorganisms are small, living organisms that can be seen only through a microscope. While not all microorganisms cause illness, some do. These are called pathogens. Eating food contaminated with foodborne pathogens or their toxins (poisons) is the leading cause of foodborne illness.

In this chapter you will learn about specific pathogens and toxins that cause foodborne illness. Understanding them is the first step to preventing foodborne illness.

Pathogens

There are four types of pathogens that can contaminate food and cause foodborne illness: viruses, bacteria, parasites, and fungi. (See *Exhibit 2a*.) Many viruses, bacteria, and parasites cause illness but cannot be seen, smelled, or tasted. On the other hand, some fungi, like mold, change the appearance, smell, or taste of food, but they may not cause illness.

What Pathogens Need to Grow

Pathogens need six conditions to grow. These can be remembered by the acronym **FAT TOM.** (See *Exhibit 2b.*) A brief explanation of each condition follows.

2b Conditions Favoring the Growth of Foodborne Pathogens

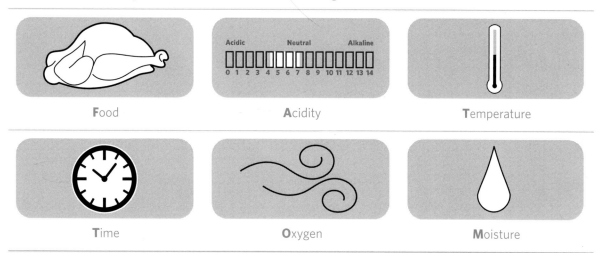

Food

Pathogens need an energy source to grow, such as carbohydrates or proteins. These are commonly found in food such as meat, poultry, dairy products, and eggs.

Acidity

pH is a measurement of how acidic or alkaline a food is. Food with a pH between 0.0 and 6.9 is acidic, while food with a pH between 7.1 and 14.0 is alkaline. Pathogens typically do not grow in alkaline food, such as crackers, or highly acidic food, such as lemons. They grow best in food that contains little or no acid (a pH of 4.6 to 7.5). (See *Exhibit 2c.*)

2c pH of Some Common Types of Food

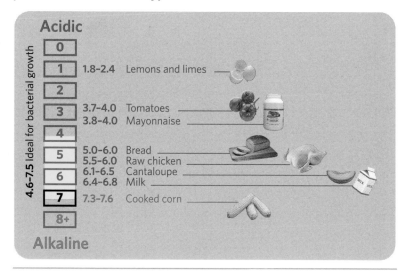

2d Temperature and Bacterial Growth

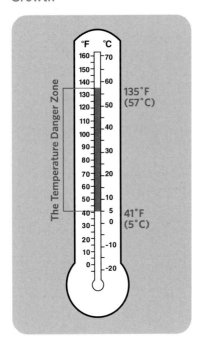

Pathogens grow well in food held between 41°F and 135°F (5°C and 57°C).

Temperature

Pathogens grow well in food held between the temperatures of 41°F and 135°F (5°C and 57°C). (See *Exhibit 2d.*) This range is known as the temperature danger zone.

Time

Pathogens need time to grow. When food is in the temperature danger zone, pathogens grow. After four hours, they will grow to a level high enough to cause illness.

Oxygen

Some pathogens require oxygen to grow, while others grow when oxygen is absent. Pathogens that grow without oxygen can occur in cooked rice, untreated garlic-and-oil mixtures, and temperature-abused baked potatoes.

Moisture

Pathogens require moisture in food to grow. The amount of moisture available in food for this growth is called its water activity (a_w). It is measured on a scale of 0.0 to 1.0, with water having a water activity of 1.0. Food with a water activity of .85 or higher is ideal for the growth of pathogens.

Food Most Likely to Become Unsafe

Any type of food can be contaminated. But some types are better able to support the growth of pathogens. (See *Exhibit 2e.*)

These types of food have the right FAT TOM conditions that pathogens need to grow. They have a natural potential for contamination because of the way they are grown, produced, or processed. They are also commonly involved in foodborne-illness outbreaks.

2e Food Most Likely to Become Unsafe

- Milk and dairy products

- Eggs (except those treated to eliminate *Salmonella* spp.)

- Meat: beef, pork, and lamb

- Poultry

- Fish

- Shellfish and crustaceans

- Baked potatoes

- Heat-treated plant food, such as cooked rice, beans, and vegetables

- Tofu or other soy protein
- Synthetic ingredients, such as textured soy protein in meat alternatives

- Sprouts and sprout seeds

- Sliced melons
- Cut tomatoes
- Cut leafy greens (fresh leafy greens that have been cut, shredded, sliced, chopped, or torn)

- Untreated garlic-and-oil mixtures

Controlling the Growth of Pathogens

Refrigerating food after preparing it will help keep food out of the temperature danger zone and prevent the growth of pathogens.

Controlling the Growth of Pathogens

You can help keep food safe by controlling FAT TOM. In your operation, however, you will most likely be able to control only time and temperature. These two conditions are so important that the food listed on the previous page is known as food that needs time and temperature control for safety, or TCS food for short.

To control temperature, you must do your best to keep TCS food out of the temperature danger zone. To control time, you must limit how long the TCS food spends in the temperature danger zone. (See *Exhibit 2f.*)

Like TCS food, ready-to-eat food also needs careful handling to prevent contamination. Ready-to-eat food is food that can be eaten without further preparation, washing, or cooking and includes:

- Washed fruit and vegetables, both whole and cut

- Deli meat

- Bakery items

- Sugar, spices, and seasonings

- Cooked food

Viruses

Viruses are the leading cause of foodborne illness. As a manager, you must understand what viruses are and the major foodborne illnesses they can cause. Most important, you must learn how to prevent them from causing illness.

Viruses share some basic characteristics:

- They can survive refrigeration and freezer temperatures.

- They cannot grow in food, but once eaten, they grow inside a person's intestines.

- They can contaminate both food and water.

- They can be transmitted from person to person, from people to food, and from people to food-contact surfaces.

When customers get sick from food contaminated with viruses, it is usually because their food was handled by an employee who has a virus. This might be the operation's employee, an employee of the manufacturer, or anyone who has the virus and

Key Point

Viruses can be transmitted from person to person, from people to food, and from people to food-contact surfaces.

2g   Preventing Viruses from Contaminating Food

Handwashing can prevent the transfer of viruses to food.

then handles the food. People carry viruses in their feces and can transfer them to their hands after using the restroom. Ready-to-eat food can then become contaminated if hands are not washed properly. To prevent the spread of viruses in your operation, do the following:

- Keep foodhandlers who are vomiting or have diarrhea or jaundice from working.

- Make sure foodhandlers wash their hands. (See *Exhibit 2g.*)

- Minimize bare-hand contact with ready-to-eat food.

Major Foodborne Illnesses Caused by Viruses

Hepatitis A and Norovirus gastroenteritis are two major foodborne illnesses caused by viruses. For each illness, you must understand the following characteristics:

- Common source

- Food commonly linked with it

- Most common symptoms

- Most important prevention measures

The table on page 2-8 is an overview of all the illnesses in this section. It will help you see similarities and differences that make it easier to remember each illness.

Throughout this chapter, you will also see that the illnesses have been grouped according to their most important prevention measure. Each illness will be grouped by one of the following measures:

- Controlling time and temperature

- Preventing cross-contamination

- Practicing personal hygiene

- Purchasing from approved, reputable suppliers

Note that this measure is not the only way to prevent each illness. Other measures are listed in the tables for each illness.

Practicing Personal Hygiene

These illnesses can be prevented by practicing personal hygiene:

- Hepatitis A   **page 2-9**

- Norovirus gastroenteritis   **page 2-9**

ServSafe Coursebook

Major Foodborne Illnesses Caused by Viruses

Most Important Prevention Measure			Controlling time and temperature	Preventing cross-contamination	Practicing personal hygiene		Purchasing from approved, reputable suppliers
Illness					Hepatitis A	Norovirus gastroenteritis	
Virus Characteristics	Commonly Linked Food	Poultry					
		Eggs					
		Meat					
		Fish					
		Shellfish			•	•	
		Ready-to-eat food			•	•	
		Produce					
		Rice/grains					
		Milk/dairy products					
		Contaminated water			•	•	
	Most Common Symptoms	Diarrhea				•	
		Abdominal pain/cramps			•	•	
		Nausea			•	•	
		Vomiting				•	
		Fever			•		
		Headache					
	Prevention Measures	Handwashing			•	•	
		Cooking					
		Holding					
		Cooling					
		Reheating					
		Approved suppliers			•	•	
		Excluding foodhandlers			•	•	
		Preventing cross-contamination					

Most Important Prevention Measure: Practicing personal hygiene

Illness	Hepatitis A (*HEP-a-TI-tiss*)
Virus	Hepatitis A

Hepatitis A is mainly found in the feces of people infected with it. The virus can contaminate water and many types of food. It is commonly linked with ready-to-eat food. However, it has also been linked with shellfish contaminated by sewage.

The virus is often transferred to food when infected foodhandlers touch food or equipment with fingers that have feces on them. Eating only a small amount of the virus can make a person sick. An infected person may not show symptoms for weeks but can be very infectious. Cooking does not destroy hepatitis A.

Food Commonly Linked with the Virus
- Ready-to-eat food
- Shellfish from contaminated water

Most Common Symptoms
- Fever (mild)
- General weakness
- Nausea
- Abdominal pain
- Jaundice (appears later)

Other Prevention Measures
- Keep employees who have jaundice out of the operation.
- Keep employees who have been diagnosed with hepatitis A out of the operation.
- Wash hands.
- Minimize bare-hand contact with ready-to-eat food.
- Purchase shellfish from approved, reputable suppliers.

Most Important Prevention Measure: Practicing personal hygiene

Illness	Norovirus gastroenteritis (*NOR-o-VI-rus GAS-tro-EN-ter-I-tiss*)
Virus	Norovirus

Like hepatitis A, Norovirus is commonly linked with ready-to-eat food. It has also been linked with contaminated water. Norovirus is often transferred to food when infected foodhandlers touch food or equipment with fingers that have feces on them.

Eating only a small amount of Norovirus can make a person sick. It is also very contagious. People become contagious within a few hours after eating it. The virus is often in a person's feces for days after symptoms have ended.

Food Commonly Linked with the Virus
- Ready-to-eat food
- Shellfish from contaminated water

Most Common Symptoms
- Vomiting
- Diarrhea
- Nausea
- Abdominal cramps

Other Prevention Measures
- Keep employees with diarrhea and vomiting out of the operation.
- Keep employees who have been diagnosed with Norovirus out of the operation.
- Wash hands.
- Minimize bare-hand contact with ready-to-eat food.
- Purchase shellfish from approved, reputable suppliers.

Bacteria

While most foodborne illnesses are caused by viruses, bacteria are also responsible for a large number of them. Knowing what bacteria are and how they grow can help you control them. Bacteria that cause foodborne illness have some basic characteristics:

- Most bacteria are controlled by keeping food out of the temperature danger zone.

- Most will grow rapidly, if FAT TOM conditions are right.

- Some change into a different form, called spores, to protect themselves.

- Some produce toxins in food as they grow and die. When the toxins are eaten, an illness can result. Cooking may not destroy these toxins.

Bacterial Growth

Bacterial growth can be broken into four progressive stages (phases): lag, log, stationary, and death. (See *Exhibit 2h.*)

2h   Growth Stages of Bacteria

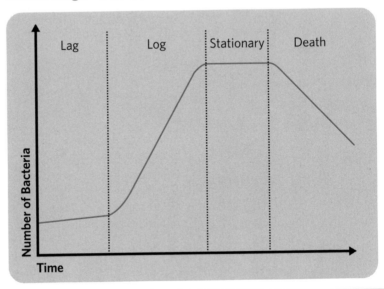

2i Rapid Bacterial Growth

Number of Cells	Time
1 cell	0 min.
2 cells	20 min.
4 cells	40 min.
8 cells	1 hr.
16 cells	1 hr. 20 min.
> 1 billion	10 hrs.

Bacteria can double their population every twenty minutes.

When bacteria are first introduced to food, they go through an adjustment period, called the lag phase. In this phase, their number is stable as they prepare for growth. To prevent food from becoming unsafe, it is important to prolong the lag phase as long as possible. You can accomplish this by controlling the conditions for growth: temperature, time, oxygen, moisture, and pH. As mentioned earlier, you have the most control over time and temperature in your operation. For example, by refrigerating food, you can keep bacteria in the lag phase.

Bacteria reproduce by splitting in two. As long as conditions are favorable, bacteria can grow very rapidly, doubling their number as often as every twenty minutes. (See *Exhibit 2i*.) This rapid growth occurs in the log phase. Food will rapidly become unsafe if it is allowed to enter the log phase.

Bacteria can continue to grow until nutrients and moisture become scarce or conditions otherwise become unfavorable. Eventually, the population reaches a stationary phase, in which just as many bacteria are growing as are dying. When the number of bacteria dying exceeds the number growing, the population declines. This is called the death phase.

The time required for bacteria to adapt to a new environment (lag phase) and to begin a rapid rate of growth (log phase) depends on whether FAT TOM conditions, such as temperature, are right. *Exhibit 2j* shows how different temperatures affect the growth rate of *Salmonella* spp. As the graph shows, *Salmonella* spp. grows more quickly at warmer temperatures (95°F [35°C]) than at colder temperatures (44°F and 50°F [7°C and 10°C]). At even colder temperatures (42°F [6°C]), *Salmonella* spp. does not grow at all—but notice that it does not die either (prolonging the lag phase). This is why refrigerating food properly helps keep it safe.

2j Growth of *Salmonella* spp. at Different Temperatures

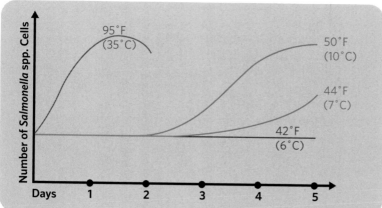

Spores

When nutrients are not available, certain bacteria can change into a different form—called spores—to keep from dying. Spores are commonly found in soil and can contaminate food grown there, such as potatoes, other vegetables, and rice. They can also contaminate meat, poultry, fish, and other food exposed to soil or dust.

A spore can resist heat, allowing it to survive cooking temperatures. Spores can also revert back to a form capable of growth. This can occur when food is not stored at the proper temperature or when it is not held or cooled properly. You must prevent this to keep food safe.

Major Foodborne Illnesses Caused by Bacteria

For each major foodborne illness caused by bacteria, you must understand these characteristics:

- Common source

- Food commonly linked with it

- Most common symptoms

- Most important prevention measures

The table on page 2-14 is an overview of all the illnesses in this section. It will help you see similarities and differences that make it easier to remember each illness.

Controlling Time and Temperature

These illnesses can be prevented through time and temperature control:

- *Bacillus cereus* gastroenteritis   **page 2-15**

- Listeriosis   **page 2-15**

- Hemorrhagic colitis   **page 2-16**

- *Clostridium perfringens* gastroenteritis   **page 2-16**

- Botulism   **page 2-17**

Preventing Cross-Contamination

These illnesses can be prevented by preventing cross-contamination:

- Salmonellosis   **page 2-17**

Practicing Personal Hygiene

These illnesses can be prevented by practicing personal hygiene:

- Shigellosis   **page 2-18**
- Staphylococcal gastroenteritis   **page 2-18**

Purchasing from Approved, Reputable Suppliers

These illnesses can be prevented by purchasing products from approved, reputable suppliers:

- *Vibrio vulnificus* primary septicemia/gastroenteritis   **page 2-19**

Major Foodborne Illnesses Caused by Bacteria

Most Important Prevention Measure

			Controlling time and temperature					Preventing cross-contamination	Practicing personal hygiene		Purchasing from approved, reputable suppliers
Illness			Bacillus cereus gastroenteritis	Listeriosis	Hemorrhagic colitis	Clostridium perfringens gastroenteritis	Botulism	Salmonellosis	Shigellosis	Staphylococcal gastroenteritis	Vibrio vulnificus primary septicemia/gastroenteritis
Bacteria Characteristics	Commonly Linked Food	Poultry				•		•			
		Eggs						•			
		Meat	•	•	•	•					
		Fish									
		Shellfish									•
		Ready-to-eat food		•					•	•	
		Produce	•		•		•	•	•		
		Rice/grains	•								
		Milk/dairy products	•	•				•			
		Contaminated water							•		•
	Most Common Symptoms	Diarrhea	•		•	•		•	•		
		Abdominal pain/cramps			•	•		•	•	•	•
		Nausea	•				•			•	•
		Vomiting	•				•	•		•	•
		Fever						•	•		
		Headache									
	Prevention Measures	Handwashing							•	•	
		Cooking	•	•	•			•			•
		Holding	•			•	•			•	
		Cooling	•					•		•	
		Reheating				•	•			•	
		Approved suppliers			•						•
		Excluding foodhandlers			•			•	•		
		Preventing cross-contamination		•	•			•			

Most Important Prevention Measure: Controlling time and temperature

Illness   *Bacillus cereus* gastroenteritis *(ba-SIL-us SEER-ee-us GAS-tro-EN-ter-I-tiss)*
Bacteria   *Bacillus cereus*

Bacillus cereus is a spore-forming bacteria found in soil. The bacteria can produce two different toxins when allowed to grow to high levels. The toxins cause different illnesses.

Food Commonly Linked with the Bacteria

Diarrhea illness

- Cooked vegetables
- Meat products
- Milk

Vomiting illness

- Cooked rice dishes, including fried rice and rice pudding

Most Common Symptoms

Diarrhea illness

- Watery diarrhea
- No vomiting

Vomiting illness

- Nausea
- Vomiting

Other Prevention Measures

- Cook food to minimum internal temperatures.
- Hold food at the right temperatures.
- Cool food correctly.

Most Important Prevention Measure: Controlling time and temperature

Illness   Listeriosis *(liss-TEER-ee-O-sis)*
Bacteria   *Listeria monocytogenes* *(liss-TEER-ee-uh MON-o-SI-TAHJ-uh-neez)*

Listeria monocytogenes is found in soil, water, and plants. Unlike other bacteria, it grows in cool, moist environments. The illness is uncommon in healthy people, but high-risk populations are especially vulnerable—particularly pregnant women.

Food Commonly Linked with the Bacteria

- Raw meat
- Unpasteurized dairy products
- Ready-to-eat food, such as deli meat, hot dogs, and soft cheeses

Most Common Symptoms

Pregnant women

- Miscarriage

Newborns

- Sepsis
- Pneumonia
- Meningitis

Other Prevention Measures

- Throw out any product that has passed its use-by or expiration date.
- Cook raw meat to minimum internal temperatures.
- Prevent cross-contamination between raw or undercooked food and ready-to-eat food.
- Avoid using unpasteurized dairy products.

Most Important Prevention Measure: Controlling time and temperature

Illness   Hemorrhagic colitis *(hem-or-RA-jik ko-LI-tiss)*
Bacteria   Shiga toxin-producing *Escherichia coli (ess-chur-EE-kee-UH KO-LI)*,
               including **O157:H7, O26:H11, O111:H8, and O158:NM**

Shiga toxin-producing *E. coli* can be found in the intestines of cattle. It can contaminate meat during slaughtering. Eating only a small amount of shiga toxin-producing *E. coli* can make a person sick. Once eaten, it produces toxins in the intestines, which cause the illness. The bacteria are often in a person's feces for weeks after symptoms have ended.

Food Commonly Linked with the Bacteria

- Ground beef (raw and undercooked)
- Contaminated produce

Most Common Symptoms

- Diarrhea (eventually becomes bloody)
- Abdominal cramps
- Kidney failure (in severe cases)

Other Prevention Measures

- Cook food, especially ground beef, to minimum internal temperatures.
- Purchase produce from approved, reputable suppliers.
- Prevent cross-contamination between raw meat and ready-to-eat food.
- Keep employees with diarrhea out of the operation.
- Keep employees who have been diagnosed with hemorrhagic colitis out of the operation.

Most Important Prevention Measure: Controlling time and temperature

Illness   *Clostridium perfringens* gastroenteritis *(klos-TRID-ee-um per-FRIN-jins GAS-tro-EN-ter-I-tiss)*
Bacteria   *Clostridium perfringens*

Clostridium perfringens is found in soil, where it forms spores that allow it to survive. It is also carried in the intestines of both animals and humans.

Clostridium perfringens does not grow at refrigeration temperatures, but it grows very rapidly in food in the temperature danger zone. Commercially prepared food is not often involved in outbreaks. People who get sick usually do not have nausea, fever, or vomiting.

Food Commonly Linked with the Bacteria

- Meat
- Poultry
- Dishes made with meat and poultry, such as stews and gravies

Most Common Symptoms

- Diarrhea
- Severe abdominal pain

Other Prevention Measures

- Cool and reheat food correctly.
- Hold food at the right temperatures.

Most Important Prevention Measure: Controlling time and temperature

Illness   Botulism *(BOT-chew-liz-um)*
Bacteria *Clostridium botulinum (klos-TRID-ee-um BOT-chew-LINE-um)*

Clostridium botulinum forms spores that are commonly found in water and soil. These spores can contaminate almost any food. The bacteria do not grow well in refrigerated or highly acidic food or in food with low moisture. However, *Clostridium botulinum* grows without oxygen and can produce a deadly toxin when food is time-temperature abused. Without medical treatment, death is likely.

Food Commonly Linked with the Bacteria

- Incorrectly canned food
- Reduced oxygen packaged (ROP) food
- Temperature-abused vegetables, such as baked potatoes
- Untreated garlic-and-oil mixtures

Most Common Symptoms

Initially

- Nausea and vomiting

Later

- Weakness
- Double vision
- Difficulty in speaking and swallowing

Other Prevention Measures

- Hold, cool, and reheat food correctly.
- Inspect canned food for damage.

Most Important Prevention Measure: Preventing cross-contamination

Illness   Salmonellosis *(SAL-men-uh-LO-sis)*
Bacteria *Salmonella* **spp.** *(SAL-me-NEL-uh)*

Many farm animals carry *Salmonella* spp. naturally. Eating only a small amount of these bacteria can make a person sick. How severe symptoms are depends on the health of the person and the amount of bacteria eaten. The bacteria are often in a person's feces for weeks after symptoms have ended.

Food Commonly Linked with the Bacteria

- Poultry and eggs
- Dairy products
- Produce

Most Common Symptoms

- Diarrhea
- Abdominal cramps
- Vomiting
- Fever

Other Prevention Measures

- Cook poultry and eggs to minimum internal temperatures.
- Prevent cross-contamination between poultry and ready-to-eat food.
- Keep foodhandlers who have been diagnosed with salmonellosis out of the operation.

Most Important Prevention Measure: Practicing personal hygiene

Illness   Shigellosis *(SHIG-uh-LO-sis)*
Bacteria   *Shigella* **spp.** *(shi-GEL-uh)*

Shigella spp. is found in the feces of humans with shigellosis. Most illnesses occur when people eat contaminated food or water. Flies can also transfer the bacteria from feces to food. Eating only a small amount of these bacteria can make a person sick. High levels of the bacteria are often in a person's feces for weeks after symptoms have ended.

Food Commonly Linked with the Bacteria

- Food that is easily contaminated by hands, such as salads containing TCS food (potato, tuna, shrimp, macaroni, and chicken)
- Food that has made contact with contaminated water, such as produce

Most Common Symptoms

- Bloody diarrhea
- Abdominal pain and cramps
- Fever (occasionally)

Other Prevention Measures

- Keep foodhandlers who have diarrhea out of the operation.
- Keep foodhandlers who have been diagnosed with shigellosis out of the operation.
- Wash hands.
- Control flies inside and outside the operation.

Most Important Prevention Measure: Practicing personal hygiene

Illness   Staphylococcal gastroenteritis *(STAF-ul-lo-KOK-al GAS-tro-EN-ter-I-tiss)*
Bacteria   *Staphylococcus aureus* *(STAF-uh-lo-KOK-us OR-ee-us)*

Staphylococcus aureus can be found in humans—particularly in the hair, nose, throat, and infected cuts. It is often transferred to food when people carrying it touch these areas on their bodies and then handle food without washing their hands. If allowed to grow to large numbers in food, the bacteria can produce toxins that cause the illness when eaten. Because cooking cannot destroy these toxins, preventing bacterial growth is critical.

Food Commonly Linked with the Bacteria

Food that requires handling during preparation, including:

- Salads containing TCS food (egg, tuna, chicken, and macaroni)
- Deli meat

Most Common Symptoms

- Nausea
- Vomiting and retching
- Abdominal cramps

Other Prevention Measures

- Wash hands, particularly after touching the hair, face, or body.
- Cover wounds on hands and arms.
- Hold, cool, and reheat food correctly.

Most Important Prevention Measure: Purchasing from approved, reputable suppliers

Illnesses	*Vibrio* **gastroenteritis** (*VIB-ree-o GAS-tro-EN-ter-I-tiss*)
	Vibrio vulnificus **primary septicemia** (*VIB-ree-o vul-NIF-ih-kus SEP-ti-SEE-mee-uh*)
Bacteria	*Vibrio vulnificus* and *Vibrio parahaemolyticus* (*VIB-ree-o PAIR-uh-HEE-mo-lit-ih-kus*)

 These bacteria are found in the waters where shellfish are harvested. They can grow very rapidly at temperatures in the middle of the temperature danger zone. People with chronic illnesses (such as diabetes or cirrhosis) who become sick from these bacteria may get primary septicemia, a severe illness that can lead to death.

Food Commonly Linked with the Bacteria

- Oysters from contaminated water

Most Common Symptoms

- Diarrhea
- Abdominal cramps and nausea
- Vomiting
- Low-grade fever and chills

Other Prevention Measures

- Cook oysters to minimum internal temperatures.

Parasites

Illnesses from parasites are not as common as those caused by bacteria or viruses. But it is still important to understand this group of pathogens to prevent the illnesses they cause. Parasites share some common characteristics:

- They cannot grow in food. They must be in the meat of another animal, called a host, to survive.

- They can use many animals as hosts, including cows, chickens, pigs, and fish.

- They can be found in the feces of animals and people.

- They contaminate both food and water—particularly water used to irrigate produce.

Key Point

Parasites can use many animals as hosts, including cows, chickens, pigs, and fish.

Major Foodborne Illnesses Caused by Parasites

For each major foodborne illness caused by parasites, you must understand these characteristics:

- Common source

- Food commonly linked with it

- Most common symptoms

- Most important prevention measures

The table on page 2-21 is an overview of all the illnesses in this section. It will help you see similarities and differences that make it easier to remember each illness.

Purchasing from Approved, Reputable Suppliers

These illnesses can be prevented by purchasing products from approved, reputable suppliers:

- Anisakiasis   **page 2-22**

- Cryptosporidiosis   **page 2-22**

- Giardiasis   **page 2-23**

Major Foodborne Illnesses Caused by Parasites

Most Important Prevention Measure			Controlling time and temperature	Preventing cross-contamination	Practicing personal hygiene	Purchasing from approved, reputable suppliers		
Illness						Anisakiasis	Cryptosporidiosis	Giardiasis
Parasite Characteristics	Commonly Linked Food	Poultry						
		Eggs						
		Meat						
		Fish				•		
		Shellfish						
		Ready-to-eat food						
		Produce					•	•
		Rice/grains						
		Milk/dairy products						
		Contaminated water					•	•
	Most Common Symptoms	Diarrhea					•	•
		Abdominal pain/cramps					•	•
		Nausea					•	•
		Vomiting						
		Fever						•
		Headache						
	Prevention Measures	Handwashing					•	•
		Cooking				•		
		Holding						
		Cooling						
		Reheating						
		Approved suppliers				•	•	•
		Excluding foodhandlers					•	•
		Preventing cross-contamination						

Most Important Prevention Measure: Purchasing from approved, reputable suppliers

Illness   Anisakiasis *(ANN-ih-SAH-KYE-ah-sis)*
Parasite   *Anisakis* simplex *(ANN-ih-SAHK-iss SIM-plex)*

People can get sick when they eat raw or undercooked fish containing this parasite.

Food Commonly Linked with the Parasite

Raw and undercooked fish, including:

- Herring
- Cod
- Halibut
- Mackerel
- Pacific salmon

Most Common Symptoms

- Tingling in throat
- Coughing up worms

Other Prevention Measures

- Cook fish to minimum internal temperatures.
- If serving raw or undercooked fish, purchase sushi-grade fish that has been frozen to the right time-temperature requirements.

Most Important Prevention Measure: Purchasing from approved, reputable suppliers

Illness   Cryptosporidiosis *(KRIP-TOH-spor-id-ee-O-sis)*
Parasite   *Cryptosporidium parvum* *(KRIP-TOH-spor-ID-ee-um PAR-vum)*

Cryptosporidium parvum can be found in the feces of people infected with it. Foodhandlers can transfer it to food when they touch food with fingers that have feces on them. Day-care and medical communities have been frequent locations of person-to-person spread of this parasite. Symptoms will be more severe in people with weakened immune systems.

Food Commonly Linked with the Parasite

- Contaminated water
- Produce

Most Common Symptoms

- Watery diarrhea
- Abdominal cramps
- Nausea
- Weight loss

Other Prevention Measures

- Use properly treated water.
- Keep foodhandlers with diarrhea out of the operation.
- Wash hands.

Photo courtesy of Boskovich Farms, Inc.

Most Important Prevention Measure: Purchasing from approved, reputable suppliers

Illness	**Giardiasis** (*JEE-are-DYE-uh-sis*)
Parasite	*Giardia duodenalis* (*jee-ARE-dee-uh do-WAH-den-AL-is*), also known as **G. lamblia** or **G. intestinalis**

Giardia duodenalis can be found in the feces of infected people. Foodhandlers can transfer the parasite to food when they touch food with fingers that have feces on them.

Food Commonly Linked with the Parasite

- Improperly treated water
- Produce

Most Common Symptoms

Initially

- Fever

Later

- Diarrhea
- Abdominal cramps
- Nausea

Other Prevention Measures

- Use properly treated water.
- Keep foodhandlers with diarrhea out of the operation.
- Wash hands.

Photo courtesy of Boskovich Farms, Inc.

Fungi

While **fungi** can cause illness, they mostly spoil food. They are found in air, soil, plants, water, and some food. Mold and yeast are examples.

Mold

Molds share some basic characteristics:

- They spoil food and sometimes cause illness.

- Some produce toxins, such as aflatoxins.

- They grow under almost any condition. But they grow well in acidic food with low water activity, such as jams, jellies, and cured salty meat such as ham, bacon, and salami.

- Cooler or freezer temperatures may slow their growth, but do not kill them.

Some molds produce toxins that can cause allergic reactions, nervous system disorders, and kidney and liver damage. For example, aflatoxin, produced by the molds *Aspergillus flavus* and *Aspergillus parasticus,* can cause liver disease. Food such as corn and corn products, peanuts and peanut products, cottonseed, milk, and tree nuts (such as Brazil nuts, pecans, pistachio nuts, and walnuts) have been associated with aflatoxins.

Throw out all moldy food, unless the mold is a natural part of the product (e.g., cheese such as Brie, Camembert, and Gorgonzola). The Food and Drug Administration (FDA) recommends cutting away moldy areas in hard cheese—at least one inch (2.5 centimeters) around them. You can also use this procedure on food such as salami and firm fruit and vegetables.

2k Yeast on Jelly

Yeast may look like a white or pink discoloration or slime.

Yeast

Yeasts share some basic characteristics:

- They can spoil food quickly. Signs of spoilage can include a smell or taste of alcohol. The yeast itself may look like a white or pink discoloration or slime. (See *Exhibit 2k.*)

- Like molds they grow well in acidic food with low water activity, such as jellies, jams, syrup, honey, and fruit or fruit juice.

Throw out any food that has been spoiled by yeast.

Biological Toxins

As you learned earlier, most foodborne illnesses are caused by pathogens, a form of biological contamination. But biological toxins can also cause illness. Some of these toxins are produced by pathogens, while others come from a plant or animal that was eaten. Seafood toxins, plant toxins, and mushroom toxins have all caused foodborne illness. You must understand what these toxins are, the illnesses they can cause, and the steps you can take to prevent them.

Seafood Toxins

Seafood toxins, including fish and shellfish toxins, cannot be smelled or tasted. They also cannot be destroyed by freezing or cooking once they form in food. Some fish toxins are systemic—produced by the fish itself. Pufferfish, moray eels, and freshwater minnows all produce systemic toxins. Cooking does not destroy them. Due to the extreme risk it poses, pufferfish should not be served unless the chef has been licensed to prepare it.

While some fish toxins are systemic, microorganisms on fish produce others. Some occur when predatory fish consume smaller fish that have eaten the toxin. Shellfish can be contaminated when they eat marine algae that have a toxin.

Major Foodborne Illnesses Caused by Seafood Toxins

For each major foodborne illness caused by seafood toxins, you must understand these characteristics:

- Common source
- Food commonly linked with it
- Most common symptoms
- Most important prevention measures

The table on page 2-26 is an overview of all the illnesses in this section. It will help you see similarities and differences that make it easier to remember each illness.

Purchasing from Approved, Reputable Suppliers

These illnesses can be prevented by purchasing products from approved, reputable suppliers:

- Scombroid poisoning   **page 2-27**
- Ciguatera fish poisoning   **page 2-27**
- Paralytic shellfish poisoning (PSP)   **page 2-28**
- Neurotoxic shellfish poisoning (NSP)   **page 2-28**
- Amnesic shellfish poisoning (ASP)   **page 2-29**

Major Foodborne Illnesses Caused by Seafood Toxins

Most Important Prevention Measure			Controlling time and temperature	Preventing cross-contamination	Practicing personal hygiene	Purchasing from approved, reputable suppliers				
Illness						Scombroid poisoning	Ciguatera fish poisoning	Paralytic shellfish poisoning (PSP)	Neurotoxic shellfish poisoning (NSP)	Amnesic shellfish poisoning (ASP)
Seafood Toxin Characteristics	Commonly Linked Food	Fish				•	•			
		Shellfish						•	•	•
	Most Common Symptoms	Diarrhea				•		•	•	•
		Abdominal pain/cramps								•
		Nausea						•	•	
		Vomiting				•		•	•	•
		Fever								
		Headache				•				
		Neurological symptoms				•	•	•	•	•
	Prevention Measures	Handwashing								
		Cooking								
		Holding				•				
		Cooling								
		Reheating								
		Approved suppliers				•	•	•	•	•
		Excluding foodhandlers								
		Preventing cross-contamination								

Most Important Prevention Measure: Purchasing from approved, reputable suppliers

| Illness | **Scombroid poisoning** (*SKOM-broyd*) |
| Toxin | **Histamine** (*HISS-ta-meen*) |

Scombroid poisoning is also known as histamine poisoning. It is an illness caused by eating high levels of histamine in scombroid and other species of fish. When the fish are time-temperature abused, bacteria on the fish make the toxin. It cannot be destroyed by freezing, cooking, smoking, or curing.

Food Commonly Linked with the Toxin

- Tuna
- Bonito
- Mackerel
- Mahi mahi

Most Common Symptoms

Initially

- Reddening of the face and neck
- Sweating
- Headache
- Burning or tingling sensation in the mouth or throat

Possibly later

- Diarrhea
- Vomiting

Other Prevention Measures

- Prevent time-temperature abuse during storage and preparation.

Most Important Prevention Measure: Purchasing from approved, reputable suppliers

| Illness | **Ciguatera fish poisoning** (*SIG-wa-TAIR-uh*) |
| Toxin | **Ciguatoxin** (*SIG-wa-TOX-in*) |

Ciguatoxin is found in certain marine algae. The toxin builds up in certain fish when they eat smaller fish that have eaten the toxic algae. Ciguatoxin cannot be detected by smell or taste. Cooking or freezing the fish will not eliminate it. Symptoms may last months or years depending on how severe the illness is.

Food Commonly Linked with the Toxin

Predatory tropical reef fish from the Pacific Ocean, the western part of the Indian Ocean, and the Caribbean Sea, including:

- Barracuda
- Grouper
- Jacks
- Snapper

Most Common Symptoms

- Reversal of hot and cold sensations
- Nausea
- Vomiting
- Tingling in fingers, lips, or toes
- Joint and muscle pain

Other Prevention Measures

- Purchase predatory tropical reef fish from approved, reputable suppliers.

Most Important Prevention Measure: Purchasing from approved, reputable suppliers

Illness	**Paralytic shellfish poisoning (PSP)** *(PAIR-ah-LIT-ik)*
Toxin	**Saxitoxin** *(SAX-ih-TOX-in)*

Some types of shellfish can become contaminated as they filter toxic algae from the water. People get sick with paralytic shellfish poisoning (PSP) when they eat these shellfish. Saxitoxin cannot be smelled or tasted. It is not destroyed by cooking or freezing. Death from paralysis may result if high levels of the toxin are eaten.

Food Commonly Linked with the Toxin

Shellfish found in colder waters, such as those of the Pacific and New England coasts, including:

- Clams
- Mussels
- Oysters
- Scallops

Most Common Symptoms

- Numbness
- Tingling of the mouth, face, arms, and legs
- Dizziness
- Nausea
- Vomiting
- Diarrhea

Other Prevention Measures

- Purchase shellfish from approved, reputable suppliers.

Most Important Prevention Measure: Purchasing from approved, reputable suppliers

Illness	**Neurotoxic shellfish poisoning (NSP)** *(NUR-o-TOX-ik)*
Toxin	**Brevetoxin** *(BREV-ih-TOX-in)*

Some types of shellfish can become contaminated as they filter toxic algae from the water. People get sick with neurotoxic shellfish poisoning (NSP) when they eat these shellfish. Brevetoxin cannot be smelled or tasted. It is not destroyed by cooking or freezing.

Food Commonly Linked with the Toxin

Shellfish found in the warmer waters of the west coast of Florida, the Gulf of Mexico, and the Caribbean Sea, including:

- Clams
- Mussels
- Oysters

Most Common Symptoms

- Tingling and numbness of the lips, tongue, and throat
- Dizziness
- Reversal of hot and cold sensations
- Vomiting
- Diarrhea

Other Prevention Measures

- Purchase shellfish from approved, reputable suppliers.

Most Important Prevention Measure: Purchasing from approved, reputable suppliers

Illness	**Amnesic shellfish poisoning (ASP)** *(am-NEE-zik)*
Toxin	**Domoic acid** *(duh-MO-ik)*

 Some types of shellfish can become contaminated as they filter toxic algae from the water. People get sick with amnesic shellfish poisoning (ASP) when they eat these shellfish. The severity of symptoms depends on the amount of toxin eaten and the health of the person. Domoic acid cannot be smelled or tasted. It is not destroyed by cooking or freezing.

Food Commonly Linked with the Toxin

Shellfish found in the coastal waters of the Pacific Northwest and the east coast of Canada, including:

- Clams
- Mussels
- Oysters
- Scallops

Most Common Symptoms

Initially

- Vomiting
- Diarrhea
- Abdominal pain

Possibly later

- Confusion
- Memory loss
- Disorientation
- Seizure
- Coma

Other Prevention Measures

- Purchase shellfish from approved, reputable suppliers.

2l   Mushrooms

Do not use mushrooms or mushroom products unless you have purchased them from approved, reputable suppliers.

Mushroom Toxins

Foodborne illnesses linked with mushrooms are almost always caused by eating toxic, wild mushrooms collected by amateur hunters. Most cases happen because toxic mushrooms are mistaken for edible ones. The symptoms of illness depend on the type of toxic mushrooms eaten.

Mushroom toxins are not destroyed by cooking or freezing. Do not use mushrooms or mushroom products unless you have purchased them from approved, reputable suppliers. (See *Exhibit 2l.*)

Plant Toxins

Plant toxins are another form of biological contamination. Illnesses from plant toxins usually happen because an operation has purchased plants from an unapproved source. Some illnesses, however, are caused by plants that have not been cooked properly. Here are some examples of items that have caused illness:

- Toxic plants, such as fool's parsley or wild turnips, mistaken for the edible version
- Honey from bees allowed to harvest nectar from toxic plants
- Undercooked kidney beans

To prevent plant toxins from getting into your operation's food, purchase plants and items made with plants only from approved, reputable suppliers. Then cook and hold dishes made from these items correctly.

Emerging Pathogens and Issues

Progress has been made in preventing foodborne illnesses in the United States. For example, waterborne illnesses such as typhoid fever (caused by *Salmonella* Typhi) and cholera (caused by *Vibrio cholerae*) were common in the early twentieth century. These illnesses are now almost forgotten due to improved methods of treating drinking water and sewage. In addition, processes such as milk sanitation and pasteurization and shellfish sanitation have virtually eliminated other once-common foodborne illnesses.

In the past, foodborne-illness outbreaks were often attributed to biological hazards in raw or inadequately cooked meat, poultry, and seafood. Today, new pathogens are being recognized and other hazards have come to the forefront. Some food items previously considered safe, such as produce, have become vehicles for pathogens. New chemical hazards, like acrylamide, have also become a concern. In addition, food is produced in greater quantities and is shipped from greater distances, across state and national borders.

To prevent these hazards from causing foodborne illness, it remains important for establishments to have sound food safety practices in place. This includes purchasing from approved, reputable suppliers and following proper storage, preparation, and serving practices.

Produce

Consumers are looking for healthy alternatives when they go out to eat. Year-round demand for convenient fresh fruit and vegetable options continues to increase. To meet this demand, many produce items are now imported from the global food supply and produce is processed into ready-to-use products. Produce, which was once considered safe, is now a potential vehicle for foodborne pathogens. Most produce is typically consumed raw, so there is virtually no step during preparation that can eliminate or reduce pathogens. To help ensure that the produce items you serve are safe, work only with an approved, reputable supplier, and ensure safe foodhandling practices in your establishment.

To address potential safety issues, many establishments are looking to local or organic farms as a safe source for produce. Managers must be aware that this will not guarantee the produce will be safer or more healthful than conventionally grown items. It is important, as you will learn in Chapter 6, to purchase produce from a supplier who has Good Agricultural Practices (GAPs) or Good Manufacturing Practices (GMPs) in place. Organically grown produce must contain the USDA Organic seal. USDA standards for organic crop production emphasize only the use of renewable resources and the conservation of soil and water to enhance environmental quality for future generations. These standards do not address food safety.

Avian Influenza

Recently, outbreaks of avian influenza, or "bird flu," have occurred in certain parts of the world. The H5N1 strain of avian influenza (AI) is very contagious to birds and can cause severe illness and death in them, particularly in poultry flocks. As a result of recent outbreaks, millions of birds were destroyed in Cambodia, China, Indonesia, Japan, Laos, South Korea, Thailand, and Vietnam.

Although the risk is low, public-health officials are concerned that the H5N1 strain has the potential to infect humans. Contact with the feces, saliva, or tissue of infected birds could potentially cause infection in humans. The population most at risk for illness has been poultry workers in areas where an outbreak has occurred. It is highly unlikely that the virus will infect persons working in non-agricultural jobs.

Although the H5N1 strain of AI has been found in the eggs and meat of infected poultry, the virus is destroyed by proper cooking and controlled through proper foodhandling procedures. Poultry and eggs from any country affected by the H5N1 outbreak are banned in the United States.

Acrylamide

In April 2002, Swedish scientists discovered people were being exposed to the chemical acrylamide in cooked, high-carbohydrate food. Their study showed that acrylamide forms as a result of high-temperature cooking methods, such as baking, frying, and roasting. There is concern that acrylamide is a human carcinogen, as it has been found to cause cancer in laboratory animals in high doses. Additionally, acrylamide has been shown to cause nerve damage and other adverse health affects in industrial settings.

The FDA has developed a plan for assessing the potential affects of acrylamide on humans. This plan includes:

- Researching the formation of acrylamide in food

- Determining the dietary exposure of consumers to acrylamide

- Gathering new information about the toxicology of acrylamide

- Assessing the potential risk of acrylamide exposure

- Evaluating options for reducing the potential risk

Summary

Microorganisms are small, living organisms that can be seen only through a microscope. Harmful microorganisms are called pathogens. Understanding how pathogens grow and contaminate food will help you understand how to prevent foodborne-illness outbreaks caused by them.

Pathogens need certain conditions to grow. These are best represented by the acronym FAT TOM. They include food, acidity, temperature, time, oxygen, and moisture. Any type of food can be contaminated. But some types, known as TCS food, are better for pathogen growth.

The four types of pathogens discussed in this chapter are viruses, bacteria, parasites, and fungi. Viruses are the leading cause of foodborne illness. They cannot grow in food, but they can survive refrigeration and freezer temperatures. The key to preventing the spread of viruses is good personal hygiene. Bacteria can usually be controlled by keeping food out of the temperature danger zone. Some bacteria can change into spores to keep from dying when they do not have enough nutrients. Others can produce toxins in food that can cause illness. Parasites need to be in the meat of another animal to survive. They can contaminate both food and water—particularly water used to irrigate produce. Purchasing products from approved, reputable suppliers is important for preventing foodborne illnesses caused by parasites.

Fungi, such as molds and yeasts, are generally responsible for spoiling food. Some molds, however, can produce harmful toxins. For this reason, food containing mold should always be discarded unless the mold is a natural part of the product. Yeasts can spoil food rapidly. Food spoiled by yeast should also be discarded.

Seafood toxins, plant toxins, and mushroom toxins also can cause foodborne illnesses. Fish toxins can be a natural part of the fish or produced by pathogens on it. Some occur when fish eat smaller fish that contain the toxin. Most shellfish toxins are caused by marine algae that have a toxin, which the shellfish then eats. Foodborne illnesses linked with mushrooms are almost always caused by eating toxic, wild mushrooms collected by amateur hunters. Similarly, foodborne illnesses caused by plant toxins usually happen because an operation has purchased plants from an unapproved supplier. Purchasing products from approved, reputable suppliers is important for preventing all these types of foodborne illnesses.

Apply Your Knowledge

① What pathogen caused the illness and why?

A Case in Point 1

A day-care center decided to prepare stir-fried rice to serve for lunch the next day. The rice was cooked to the right temperature at 1:00 p.m. It was then covered and placed on a countertop, where it was allowed to cool at room temperature. At 6:00 p.m., the cook placed the rice in the refrigerator. At 9:00 a.m. the following day, the rice was combined with the other ingredients for stir-fried rice and cooked to 165°F (74°C) for at least fifteen seconds. The cook covered the rice and left it on the stove until noon when she reheated it. Within an hour of eating the rice, several of the children complained that they were nauseous and began to vomit.

For answers, please turn to the Answer Key.

Apply Your Knowledge

① Why did the mahi-mahi steaks cause scombroid poisoning?

A Case in Point 2

Roberto received a shipment of frozen mahi-mahi steaks. The steaks were frozen solid at the time of delivery, and the packages were sealed but contained a large amount of ice crystals, indicating they had been time-temperature abused. Roberto accepted the mahi-mahi steaks and thawed them in the refrigerator at a temperature of 38°F (3°C). The thawed fish steaks were then held at this temperature during the evening shift and were cooked to order. The chefs followed the right guidelines for preparing, cooking, and serving the fish, monitoring time and temperature throughout the process. Unfortunately, the fish steaks caused an outbreak of scombroid poisoning.

For answers, please turn to the Answer Key.

Apply Your Knowledge

Use these questions to review the concepts presented in this chapter.

Discussion Questions

① What food items are better able to support the growth of pathogens?

② What two FAT TOM conditions are easiest for an establishment to control?

③ How can an outbreak of Norovirus be prevented?

④ What measures should be taken to prevent a seafood-specific foodborne illness?

⑤ How can plant toxins be prevented from getting into food?

For answers, please turn to the Answer Key.

Study Questions

Circle the best answer to each question.

① **Foodborne pathogens grow well at temperatures**
   A below 32°F (0°C).
   B between 1°F and 40°F (–17°C to 4°C).
   C between 41°F and 135°F (5°C and 57°C).
   D above 212°F (100°C).

② **FAT TOM stands for Food, Acidity, Temperature, Time, Oxygen and**
   A Meat.
   B Moisture.
   C Melatonin.
   D Management.

③ **Which pathogen is primarily found in the hair, nose, and throat of humans?**
   A *Giardia duodenalis*
   B *Bacillus cereus*
   C *Clostridium botulinum*
   D *Staphylococcus aureus*

Continued on next page ▶

► *Continued from previous page*

④ **While commonly linked with contaminated ground beef, what pathogen has also been linked with contaminated produce?**

A *Bacillus cereus*

B *Salmonella* spp.

C Shiga toxin-producing *E. coli*

D *Clostridium perfringens*

⑤ **Which practice can reduce *Salmonella* spp. in poultry to safe levels?**

A Storing food at 55°F (13°C) or higher

B Inspecting canned food for damage

C Cooking food to the right temperature

D Purchasing oysters from approved, reputable suppliers

⑥ **Covering wounds can help prevent the spread of which pathogen?**

A *Staphylococcus aureus*

B Norovirus

C *Vibrio vulnificus*

D *Salmonella* spp.

⑦ **Which foodborne illness has been linked with ready-to-eat food and shellfish contaminated by sewage?**

A Hepatitis A

B Anisakiasis

C Shigellosis

D Botulism

⑧ **Viruses such as Norovirus and hepatitis A can be spread when foodhandlers fail to**

A use pasteurized eggs.

B wash their hands.

C determine the correct moisture level.

D purchase beef from approved, reputable suppliers.

⑨ **What is the best way to prevent a foodborne illness caused by seafood toxins?**

A Freezing seafood prior to cooking it

B Purchasing smoked or cured seafood

C Purchasing seafood from approved, reputable suppliers

D Cooking seafood to the right minimum internal temperature

⑩ **A person who ate raw oysters later became disoriented and suffered memory loss. What illness was most likely the cause?**

A Amnesic shellfish poisoning

B Paralytic shellfish poisoning

C Neurotoxic shellfish poisoning

D Hemorrhagic shellfish poisoning

⑪ **Foodservice operations should not use mushrooms unless they have been**

A stored at 41°F (5°C) or lower.

B frozen before cooking or serving.

C purchased from an approved, reputable supplier.

D cooked to an internal temperature of 135°F (57°C).

For answers, please turn to the Answer Key.

Additional Resources

Articles and Texts

Balter, S., H. Hanson, L. Kornstein, L. Lee, V. Reddy, S. Sahl, F. Stavinsky, M. Fage, G. Johnson, W. Keene, J. Koepsell, M. Williams, K. MacDonald, N. Napolilli, J. Hofmann, C. Bopp, M. Lynch, K. Moore, J. Painter, N. Puhr, and P. Yu. 2006. *Vibrio parahaemolyticus* Infections Associated with Consumption of Raw Shellfish—Three States. *Morbidity and Mortality Weekly Report.* 55 (31): 854.

Batana, Luis M. *Seafood and Freshwater Toxins: Pharmacology, Physiology, and Detection.* New York: Marcel Dekker, Incorporated, 2000.

Bourn, Diane and John Prescott. 2002. A Comparison of the Nutritional Value, Sensory Qualities, and Food Safety of Organically and Conventionally Produced Food. *Critical Reviews in Food Science and Nutrition.* 42 (1): 1.

Corby, R., V. Lanni, V. Kistler, V. Dato, et. al. 2005. Outbreaks of *Salmonella* Infections Associated with Eating Roma Tomatoes—United States and Canada, 2004. *Morbidity and Mortality Weekly Report.* 54 (13): 325.

Doyle, Michael, Larry R. Buechat, and Thomas J. Montville, eds. *Food Microbiology: Fundamentals and Frontiers, 3rd edition revised.* Washington: ASM Press, 2007.

FDA Center for Food Safety and Applied Nutrition and USDA Food Safety and Inspection Service. *Quantitative Assessment of Relative Risk to Public Health from Foodborne* Listeria monocytogenes *among Selected Categories of Ready-to-Eat Foods.* 2003. Available at http://www.foodsafety.gov/~dms/lmr2-toc.html.

Gombas, David E., Chen Yuhan, Rocelle S. Clavero, and Virginia N. Scott. 2003. Survey of *Listeria monocytogenes* in Ready-to-Eat Foods. *Journal of Food Protection.* 66 (4): 559.

Heymann, David, ed. *Control of Communicable Disease Manual, 18th edition.* Washington: American Public Health Association Publication, 2004.

Hocking, Alisa D., J.I. Pitt, and Ulf Thrane. *Advances in Food Mycology.* Proceedings of the 5th International Workshop on Food Mycology. New York: Springer, 2006.

Hui, Y.H., Roy Smith, and David G. Spoerke. *Foodborne Disease Handbook. Volume 3, 2nd edition.* New York: Marcel Dekker, Incorporated, 2000.

Jay, James M., David A. Golden, and Martin J. Loessner. *Modern Food Microbiology, 7th edition.* New York: Springer, 2005.

Jenkins, P., S. Greene, J.P. Davis, J.R. Archer, D. Hoang-Johnson, M. Quinn, P. Duncan, G, Johnson, B.I. Rosen, P. Smith, V. Reddy, J. Schlegelmilch, J. Pendarvis, M. Donovan, J.E. Gunn, M.A. Barry, M. Davies, J. Vinjé, and M.A. Widdowson. 2007. Norovirus Activity: United States, 2006-2007. *Morbidity and Mortality Weekly Report.* 56 (33): 842.

Khodr, M., S. Hill, L. Perkins, S. Stiefel, C. Comer-Morrison, S. Lee, D.R. Patel, D. Peery, C.W. Armstrong, and G.B. Miller, Jr. 1994. Epidemiologic Notes and Reports *Bacillus cereus* Food Poisoning Associated with Fried Rice at Two Child Day Care Centers—Virginia, 1993. *Morbidity and Mortality Weekly Report.* 43 (10): 177.

Lee L.A., S.M. Ostroff, and H.B. McGee. 1991. An Outbreak of Shigellosis at an Outdoor Music Festival. *American Journal of Epidemiology.* 133: 608.

Ortega, Ynes R. and Michael P. Doyle. *Foodborne Parasites.* New York: Springer, 2006.

Ryser, Elliot T. and Elmer H. Marth. *Listeria, Listeriosis and Food Safety, 3rd edition.* New York: Marcel Dekker, Incorporated, 2006.

Samson, Robert A. *Food Mycology: A Multifaceted Approach to Fungi and Food.* Boca Raton: CRC Press, 2007.

Solomon, H.M. and D.A. Kautter. 1998. Growth and Toxin Production by *Clostridium botulinum* in Sautéed Onions. *Journal of Food Protection.* 49 (10): 618.

Solomon, H.M. and D.A. Kautter. 1998. Growth and Toxin Production by *Clostridium botulinum* in Bottled Chopped Garlic. *Journal of Food Protection.* 49 (10): 862.

Turner, Nancy J. and Adam F. Szczawinski. *Common Poisonous Plants and Mushrooms of North America, 2nd edition.* Portland, OR: Timber Press, Incorporated, 2003.

Zimomra, J., T. Wenderoth, A. Snyder, R. Russ, E.D. Peterson, R. French, T.J. Halpin, J.E. Florance, A. Adkins, J. Andrew, M. Burkgren, K. Crisler, T. Fagen, L. Fass, J.M. Galloway, S. Haines, R.H. Hinton, C. Jackson, N.S. Rivera, E.L. Testor, C. Williams, A.A. DiAllo, D.R. Patel, C.W. Armstrong, D. Woolard, and G.B. Miller. 1994. *Clostridium perfringens* gastroenteritis Associated with Corned Beef Served at St. Patrick's Day Meals—Ohio and Virginia, 1993. *Morbidity and Mortality Weekly Report.* 43 (08): 137.

Continued on next page ▶

► *Continued from previous page*

Web Sites

Acrylamide Infonet
acrylamide-food.org

AMS National Organic Program
ams.usda.gov/nop/indexIE.htm

Center for Infectious Disease Research & Policy
www.cidrap.umn.edu

Centers for Disease Control and Prevention
cdc.gov

FDA Food Safety
www.fda.gov/Food/FoodSafety/default.htm

*Foodborne Pathogenic Microorganisms and Natural Toxins Handbook -
The Bad Bug Book*
www.fda.gov/Food/FoodSafety/FoodborneIllness/FoodborneIllnessFoo
dbornePathogensNaturalToxins/BadBugBook/default.htm

Gateway to Government Food Safety Information
foodsafety.gov

International Food Information Center
ific.org

Documents and Other Resources

Avian Influenza
cdc.gov/flu/avian

Avian Influenza
who.int/csr/disease/avian_influenza/en

Emerging Infectious Diseases
cdc.gov/ncidod/eid/index.htm

FDA Acrylamide: Questions & Answers
www.fda.gov/Food/FoodSafety/FoodContaminantsAdulteration/
ChemicalContaminants/Acrylamide/ucm053569.htm

FDA Foodborne Illness Resources Pages
www.fda.gov/Food/FoodSafety/FoodborneIllness/default.htm

FDA Interstate Certified Shellfish Shippers List
www.fda.gov/Food/FoodSafety/Product-
SpecificInformation/Seafood/FederalStatePrograms/InterstateShellfish
ShippersList/default.htm

Guide for the Control of Molluscan Shellfish
www.fda.gov/Food/FoodSafety/Product-
SpecificInformation/Seafood/FederalStatePrograms/NationalShellfishS
anitationProgram/ucm046353.htm

FDA Seafood Information and Resources
www.fda.gov/Food/FoodSafety/Product-
SpecificInformation/Seafood/default.htm

Evaluation and Definition of Potentially Hazardous Foods
www.fda.gov/Food/ScienceResearch/ResearchAreas/
SafePracticesforFoodProcesses/ucm094141.htm

Morbidity and Mortality Weekly Report
cdc.gov/mmwr

Risk Assessment for Listeria monocytogenes *in Deli Meats*
www.fsis.usda.gov/OPPDE/rdad/FRPubs/97-013F/ListeriaReport.pdf

Seafood Inspection Program
seafood.nmfs.noaa.gov

3 Contamination, Food Allergens, and Foodborne Illness

After completing this chapter, you should be able to:

- Identify chemical and physical contaminants and methods of prevention.
- Identify the most common allergens, their associated symptoms, and methods for preventing allergic reactions.
- Recognize the need for food defense systems.

Key Terms

- Biological contaminants
- Chemical contaminants
- Toxic-metal poisoning
- Physical contaminants
- Food defense
- Food allergy
- Cross-contact

Apply Your Knowledge

Check to see how much you know about the concepts in this chapter. Use the page references provided with each question to explore the topic.

Test Your Food Safety Knowledge

1. **True or False:** Copper utensils and equipment can cause an illness when used to prepare acidic food. *(See page 3-3.)*

2. **True or False:** If you transfer a chemical to a new container, you must label it with the name of the chemical. *(See page 3-3.)*

3. **True or False:** Delivery people and service contractors are possible food defense risks. *(See page 3-4.)*

4. **True or False**: Milk is a common food allergen. *(See page 3-6.)*

5. **True or False:** A person with a shellfish allergy who unknowingly eats soup made with clam juice may experience a tightening in the throat. *(See page 3-6.)*

For answers, please turn to the Answer Key.

Introduction

You learned in Chapter 2 that biological contaminants, including viruses, bacteria, parasites, and fungi, are the leading cause of foodborne illnesses. But chemicals and physical contaminants can also be risks to the food you serve, as can people who would use these and other substances to deliberately contaminate food. Food allergens are also a concern for an increasing number of people. Fortunately, there are steps that you can take to reduce these risks and help keep food safe.

Chemical Contaminants

Chemical contaminants are responsible for many cases of foodborne illness. Contamination can come from a variety of substances normally found in the establishment.

3a   Toxic Metals

Acidic food prepared in equipment made from toxic metals, such as copper, can cause illness.

Toxic Metals

Some utensils and equipment contain toxic metals that can contaminate acidic food. These metals include:

- **Lead.** It is found in pewter, which can be used to make pitchers and other tableware.

- **Copper.** It is sometimes found in cookware, such as pots and pans (see *Exhibit 3a*).

- **Zinc.** This metal is found in galvanized items, which are coated with it. Some buckets, tubs, and other items may be galvanized.

If acidic food is stored in or prepared with this equipment, the metals can be transferred to the food and cause toxic-metal poisoning. For this reason, only food-grade utensils and equipment should be used to prepare and store food.

Carbonated-beverage dispensers that are improperly installed can also create a hazard. If carbonated water is allowed to flow back into the copper supply lines, it could leach copper from the line and contaminate the beverage. Beverage-dispensing systems should be installed and maintained by professionals who will ensure that a proper backflow-prevention device is installed.

Foodservice Chemicals

Chemicals can contaminate food if used or stored incorrectly. Chemicals such as cleaners, sanitizers, polishes, and machine lubricants can all be risks. To keep food safe, follow these guidelines:

- Store chemicals away from food, utensils, and equipment used for food. Keep them in a separate storage area in their original container. (See *Exhibit 3b.*)

- Follow manufacturers' directions when using chemicals.

- Be careful when using chemicals while food is being prepared.

- When transferring a chemical to a new container, label the container with the common name of the chemical.

- Only use lubricants that are made for food equipment.

3b   Chemicals

Store chemicals away from food, utensils, and equipment used for food.

3c   Physical Contamination

Metal shavings from the lid of a can might contaminate the food inside.

Physical Contaminants

Physical contamination results when objects get into food. It can also occur when natural objects are left in food, like bones in a fish fillet.

Here are some common **physical contaminants:**

- Metal shavings from cans (see *Exhibit 3c*)
- Staples from cartons
- Glass from broken lightbulbs
- Blades from plastic or rubber scrapers
- Fingernails, hair, and bandages
- Dirt
- Bones
- Jewelry
- Fruit pits

Closely inspect the food you receive. Take steps to make sure no physical contaminants can get into it.

The Deliberate Contamination of Food

While the food safety principles discussed in the ServSafe program help you address the accidental contamination of food, you must also be aware of how to prevent deliberate contamination. In addition to biological, chemical, and physical contaminants, radioactive materials are also a concern.

Those who would knowingly contaminate food include organized terrorists or activists, current or former employees, vendors, and competitors. Attacks might occur anywhere in the food supply chain, but they are usually focused on a food item, process, or business. The best way to protect food is to make it as hard as possible for someone to tamper with it. For this reason, a **food defense** program should deal with the points in your operation where food is at risk. These are highlighted in *Exhibit 3d.*

3d   Addressing Food Defense Threats in Your Operation

Human Elements

* Verify the identity of applicants—ask for references, verify them, and check identification.
* Train employees in food defense and establish food defense awareness in your establishment.
* Train employees to report suspicious activity.
* Establish a system to ensure that only on-duty employees are allowed in work areas.
* Establish rules for opening the back doors of the facility—determine who is authorized to open these doors and under what circumstances.
* Control access to food-production and food-storage areas by nonemployees.
* Allow employees to bring only essential items to work.
* Consider a two-employee rule during food preparation—employees should not be alone in food-preparation areas.
* Monitor preparation areas regularly via video cameras, windows, other employees, or management.

Interior Elements

* Limit access to doors, windows, roofs, and food-storage areas.
* Control entrances and exits to food displays, storage areas, and kitchens.
* Eliminate hiding places in all areas of the operation.
* Inspect all incoming food items; never accept suspect food.
* Restrict traffic in food-preparation and storage areas.
* Monitor self-service areas, and food items and equipment on display, such as salad bars, condiments, and exposed tableware.

Exterior Elements

* Ensure that the building's exterior is well lit.
* Control access to the ventilation system.
* Identify all food suppliers and consider using tamper-evident packages. Check the identification of the delivery person and the scheduled times of delivery, and document those deliveries.
* Tell suppliers that food defense is a priority and ask what steps they are taking to ensure their products are secure.
* Verify and preapprove all service personnel and providers.
* Prevent access to the facility by nonemployees after normal business hours.

3e   Common Food Allergens

Milk and dairy products

Eggs and egg products

Fish and shellfish

Wheat

Soy and soy products

Peanuts and tree nuts, such as pecans and walnuts

Food Allergens

The number of people in the United States with food allergies is increasing. A food allergy is the body's negative reaction to a particular food protein. Depending on the person, allergic reactions may occur immediately after the food is eaten or several hours later. The reaction could include some or all of the following symptoms:

- Itching in and around the mouth, face, or scalp
- Tightening in the throat
- Wheezing or shortness of breath
- Hives
- Swelling of the face, eyes, hands, or feet
- Abdominal cramps, vomiting, or diarrhea
- Loss of consciousness
- Death

If a customer is having an allergic reaction to food, call the emergency number in your area. Stay with the person or assign someone to do so. Always complete an incident report form.

You and your staff must be aware of the most common food allergens and the menu items that contain them, as listed in *Exhibit 3e.*

Preventing Allergic Reactions

Both service staff and kitchen staff need to do their part to avoid serving food that could cause an allergic reaction.

Service Staff

Your employees should be able to tell customers about menu items that contain potential allergens. At minimum, have one person available per shift to answer customers' questions about menu items. When customers say they have a food allergy, your staff should take it seriously. They must be able to do the following:

- **Describe dishes.** Tell customers how the item is prepared. (See *Exhibit 3f.*) Sauces, marinades, and garnishes often

3f   Describing Dishes

It is important to describe dishes to customers with food allergies.

contain allergens. For example, peanut butter is sometimes used as a thickener in sauces or marinades. This information is critical to a customer with a peanut allergy.

- **Identify ingredients.** Identify any "secret" ingredients. For example, your operation may have a house specialty that includes an allergen. While you may not want to share the recipe with the public, staff must be able to tell the secret ingredient to a customer who asks.

- **Suggest simple menu items.** Complex items such as casseroles, soups, and some desserts may contain many ingredients. These can be difficult to fully describe to customers.

Kitchen Staff

Kitchen staff must ensure that allergens are not transferred from food containing an allergen to the food served to the customer. This is called **cross-contact**. There are several ways in which it can occur:

- **Cooking different types of food in the same fryer oil.** One example of how this can happen is frying chicken in the same oil used to fry shrimp. (See *Exhibit 3g.*)

- **Putting food on surfaces that have touched allergens.** For example, putting chocolate chip cookies on the same parchment paper that was used for peanut butter cookies can transfer some of the peanut allergen.

To avoid cross-contact, do the following:

- **Wash, rinse, and sanitize cookware, utensils, and equipment before preparing food.**

- **Wash your hands and change gloves before preparing food.**

- **Assign specific equipment for preparing food for customers with allergens.** For example, if your operation serves fried chicken and fried clams, you could designate one piece of equipment for the seafood and another for the chicken.

3g   Allergen Cross-Contact

Avoid cooking allergens in the same oil used to fry other food.

Something to Think About...   Now That's a Bright Idea!

Ten years ago, a Midwestern restaurant group decided to review its food-allergy prevention policies. After looking at the entire operation, the group developed a system that uses brightly colored tickets to call out meals for guests with food allergies.

When a guest informs his or her server of a food allergy, the server records the individual's order on a separate, brightly colored ticket. The ticket includes the guest's table number, position at the table, the food allergy, and the order. The server then delivers the ticket to the kitchen and confirms it with the chef. The ticket stays with the meal and is signed by the manager before it is served.

Summary

Chemical contaminants can come from a variety of substances found in the establishment. These include toxic metals, cleaners, sanitizers, polishes, and machine lubricants. To prevent contamination, only use food-grade utensils and equipment to prepare and store food. Store chemicals away from food, utensils, and equipment used for food, and follow manufacturers' directions for use.

Physical contamination can occur when objects get into food or when naturally occurring objects, such as the bones in a fish fillet, pose a physical hazard. Closely inspect the food you receive, and take steps to ensure food will not become physically contaminated during its flow through your operation.

People may try to tamper with food using biological, chemical, physical, or even radioactive contaminants. As a manager, you must identify measures to prevent this. The key to protecting food is to make it as difficult as possible for tampering to occur.

Many people have food allergies. Managers and employees should be aware of the most common food allergens, which include milk and dairy products, eggs and egg products, fish and shellfish, wheat, soy and soy products, and peanuts and tree nuts. Both service staff and kitchen staff need to do their part to avoid serving food that can cause an allergic reaction.

Service staff must be able to tell customers about menu items that contain potential allergens. Kitchen staff must make sure that allergens are not transferred from food containing an allergen to the food served to the customer.

Apply Your Knowledge

Use these questions to review the concepts presented in this chapter.

Discussion Questions

① How can toxic-metal poisoning occur? What are some ways to prevent it?

② What are some ways to keep chemicals from contaminating food?

③ What measures can be taken to help ensure the safety of customers with food allergies?

For answers, please turn to the Answer Key.

Study Questions

Circle the best answer to each question.

① **Eggs and peanuts are dangerous for people with which condition?**
   A FAT TOM
   B Food allergies
   C Chemical sensitivity
   D Poor personal hygiene

② **Cooking tomato sauce in a copper pot can cause which foodborne illness?**
   A Hemorrhagic colitis
   B Foodborne infection
   C Toxic-metal poisoning
   D Staphylococcal gastroenteritis

Continued on next page ▶

► *Continued from previous page*

③ **To prevent chemical contamination, chemicals should be stored _____ food and utensils.**

  A next to

  B above

  C separate from

  D in the same area as

④ **Itching and tightening of the throat are symptoms of what?**

  A Hepatitis A

  B Food allergy

  C Hemorrhagic colitis

  D Ciguatera fish poisoning

⑤ **To prevent food allergens from being transferred to food,**

  A clean and sanitize utensils before use.

  B buy food from approved, reputable suppliers.

  C store cold food at 41°F (5°C) or lower.

  D avoid pewter tableware and copper cookware.

⑥ **What three points should a food defense program focus on to prevent possible threats to food?**

  A Inspection reports, HACCP program, invoices

  B Human elements, building interior, building exterior

  C Plant toxins, temperature logs, personal hygiene

  D Cleaning schedules, labeling procedures, FAT TOM

For answers, please turn to the Answer Key.

Additional Resources

Articles and Texts

Wilson, Robert. 2004. Restaurants and Food Allergies: A Dangerous Recipe. *Journal of Foodservice Business Research. 7 (3): 17.*

Web Sites

American Chemistry Council
americanchemistry.com/s_acc/index.asp

Center for Infectious Disease Research & Policy
www.cidrap.umn.edu

Centers for Disease Control and Prevention
cdc.gov

Department of Homeland Security
dhs.gov

Environmental Protection Agency
epa.gov

FDA Food Safety
www.fda.gov/Food/FoodSafety/default.htm

FDA Alert
www.fda.gov/Food/FoodDefense/Training/ALERT/default.htm

FDA Foodborne Illness Resource Page
www.fda.gov/Food/FoodSafety/FoodborneIllness/default.htm

Food Allergy & Anaphylaxis Network
foodallergy.org

Gateway to Government Food Safety Information
foodsafety.gov

National Food Service Security Council
nfssconline.org

National Institute for Occupational Safety and Health
cdc.gov/niosh

Occupational Safety and Health Administration
osha.gov

Risk and Insurance Management Society, Inc.
rims.org

Society for Risk Analysis
sra.org

Western Growers
wga.com

Continued on next page ▶

▶ *Continued from previous page*

Other Documents and Resources

2009 FDA Food Code
www.fda.gov/Food/FoodSafety/RetailFoodProtection/FoodCode/
FoodCode2009/default.htm

Food Allergens
www.fda.gov/Food/FoodSafety/FoodAllergens/default.htm

Food Defense and Emergency Response
www.fda.gov/Food/FoodDefense/default.htm

IRS Business Casualty, Disaster, and Theft Loss Workbook
www.irs.gov/publications/p584b/index.html

Morbidity and Mortality Weekly Report
cdc.gov/mmwr

Retail Food Stores and Food Service Establishments: Food Security Preventive Measures Guidance
www.fda.gov/Food/GuidanceComplianceRegulatoryInformation/Guida
nceDocuments/FoodDefenseandEmergencyResponse/ucm082751.htm

Notes

4 The Safe Foodhandler

Inside this chapter:

- How Foodhandlers Can Contaminate Food
- Diseases Not Transmitted Through Food
- Components of a Good Personal Hygiene Program
- Management's Role in a Personal Hygiene Program

After completing this chapter, you should be able to:

- Identify personal behaviors that can contaminate food.
- Identify proper handwashing procedures.
- Identify when hands should be washed.
- Identify appropriate hand antiseptics and when to use them.
- Identify hand maintenance requirements.
- Identify the proper procedure for covering wounds.
- Identify procedures that must be followed when using gloves.
- Identify jewelry that poses a hazard to food safety.
- Identify requirements for employee work attire.
- Identify the regulatory exceptions for allowing bare-hand contact with ready-to-eat food.
- Identify criteria for excluding employees from the establishment or restricting them from working with or around food.
- Identify criteria for excluding or restricting employees from working within establishments that serve high-risk populations.
- Identify illnesses that must be reported to the health agency.
- Identify policies that should be implemented regarding eating, drinking, and smoking while working with food.

Key Term

- Carriers
- Finger cot
- Hair restraint

4-2   ServSafe Coursebook

Apply Your Knowledge

Check to see how much you know about the concepts in this chapter. Use the page references provided with each question to explore the topic.

Test Your Food Safety Knowledge

① **True or False:** During handwashing, foodhandlers must vigorously scrub their hands and arms for five seconds. *(See page 4-5.)*

② **True or False:** Gloves should be changed before beginning a different task. *(See page 4-9.)*

③ **True or False:** Foodhandlers must wash their hands after smoking. *(See page 4-7.)*

④ **True or False:** A foodhandler diagnosed with shigellosis cannot continue to work at an establishment while he or she has the illness. *(See page 4-12.)*

⑤ **True or False:** Hand antiseptics should only be used before handwashing. *(See page 4-7.)*

For answers, please turn to the Answer Key.

Introduction

At every step in the flow of food through the operation—from receiving through service—foodhandlers can contaminate food and cause customers to become ill. Good personal hygiene is a critical protective measure against foodborne illness, and customers expect it.

You can minimize the risk of foodborne illness by establishing a personal hygiene program for your operation that spells out specific hygiene policies. You must also train your employees on these policies and enforce them. When employees have the proper knowledge, skills, and attitudes toward personal hygiene, you are one step closer to keeping food safe.

How Foodhandlers Can Contaminate Food

In previous chapters, you learned that foodhandlers can cause illness by transferring microorganisms to food they touch. Many times these microorganisms come from the foodhandlers themselves. Foodhandlers can contaminate food when they:

- Have a foodborne illness

- Have symptoms such as diarrhea, vomiting, or jaundice— a yellowing of the eyes or skin

- Have wounds that contain a pathogen

- Have contact with a person who is ill

- Touch anything that may contaminate their hands and then don't wash them

Key Point

With some illnesses, a person may infect others before showing any symptoms.

With some illnesses, a person may infect others before showing any symptoms. For example, a person could spread hepatitis A for weeks before having any symptoms. With other illnesses, a person may infect others for days or even months after symptoms are gone. Norovirus can be spread for days after symptoms have ended.

Some people carry pathogens and infect others without ever getting sick themselves. These people are called **carriers.**

The next three paragraphs will help illustrate some of the routes by which employees can contaminate food.

❶ A deli foodhandler who was diagnosed with salmonellosis failed to inform his manager that he was ill for fear of losing wages. It was later determined that he was the cause of an outbreak that involved more than two hundred customers through twelve different products.

❷ A foodhandler suffering from diarrhea, a symptom of gastrointestinal illness, did not wash his hands after using the restroom. He made approximately five thousand people ill when he mixed a vat of buttercream frosting with his bare hands and arms. Another large foodborne-illness outbreak was caused by a foodhandler who scratched an infected facial lesion and then handled a large amount of sliced pepperoni.

3 A foodborne-illness outbreak was traced to a woman who prepared food for a dinner party. The investigation revealed that the woman was caring for her infant son, who had diarrhea. The woman could not recall washing her hands after changing the infant's diaper. As a result, twelve of her dinner guests became violently ill with symptoms that included diarrhea and vomiting.

Key Point

Simple acts such as rubbing an ear or scratching the scalp can contaminate food.

Simple acts such as running fingers through the hair, wiping or touching the nose, rubbing an ear, scratching the scalp, or touching a pimple or an infected wound can contaminate food. *Staphylococcus aureus* is carried in the nose of 30 to 50 percent of healthy adults. About 20 to 35 percent of healthy adults carry it on their skin. If these microorganisms contaminate a foodhandler's hands that then touch food, the consequences can be severe. For this reason, foodhandlers must pay close attention to what they do with their hands and maintain good personal hygiene.

Diseases Not Transmitted Through Food

Key Point

Diseases such as AIDS, hepatitis B and C, and tuberculosis are not spread through food.

In recent years, the public has expressed growing concern over communicable diseases spread through intimate contact or by direct exchange of bodily fluids. Diseases such as Acquired Immune Deficiency Syndrome (AIDS), hepatitis B and C, and tuberculosis are not spread through food.

As a manager, you should be aware of the following laws concerning employees who have tested positive for the Human Immunodeficiency Virus (HIV) or have tuberculosis or hepatitis B or C:

- The Americans with Disabilities Act (ADA) provides civil-rights protection to individuals who are HIV positive or have hepatitis B, and thus prohibits employers from firing people or transferring them out of foodhandling duties simply because they have these diseases.

- Employers must maintain the confidentiality of employees who have any nonfoodborne illness.

4a   Good Personal Hygiene

Good personal hygiene is the key to the prevention of foodborne illness.

Components of a Good Personal Hygiene Program

Good personal hygiene is key to the prevention of foodborne illness. (See *Exhibit 4a*.) Good personal hygiene includes:

- Following hygienic hand practices
- Maintaining personal cleanliness
- Wearing clean and appropriate uniforms and following dress codes
- Avoiding certain habits and actions
- Maintaining good health
- Reporting illnesses

Hygienic Hand Practices

Handwashing

Handwashing is the most critical aspect of personal hygiene. While it may appear fundamental, many foodhandlers fail to wash their hands properly and as often as needed. As a manager, it is your responsibility to train your foodhandlers and then monitor them. Never take this simple action for granted.

Thorough handwashing only takes about twenty seconds. To ensure proper handwashing in your establishment, train your foodhandlers to follow these five steps (see *Exhibit 4b* on the next page):

1 **Wet your hands and arms with running water as hot as you can comfortably stand (at least 100°F [38°C]).**

2 **Apply soap.** Apply enough soap to build up a good lather.

3 **Scrub hands and arms vigorously for ten to fifteen seconds.** Lather well beyond the wrists, including the exposed portions of the arms. Clean under fingernails and between fingers. A nailbrush might be helpful.

4 **Rinse hands and arms thoroughly under running water.**

5 **Dry hands and arms with a single-use paper towel or hand dryer.** When leaving the restroom, consider using a paper towel to turn off the faucet and to open the door.

4b   Proper Handwashing Procedure

The whole process should take approximately twenty seconds.

❶ Wet your hands and arms with running water as hot as you can comfortably stand (at least 100°F [38°C]).

❷ Apply soap.

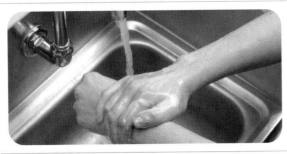

❸ Vigorously scrub hands and arms for ten to fifteen seconds. Clean under fingernails and between fingers.

❹ Rinse hands and arms thoroughly under running water.

❺ Dry hands and arms with a single-use paper towel or hand dryer. When leaving the restroom, consider using a paper towel to turn off the faucet and to open the door.

4c   Hand Care for Foodhandlers

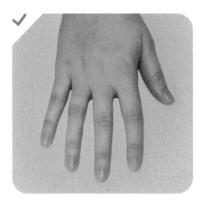

Keep fingernails short and clean.

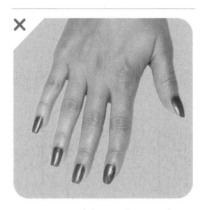

Do not wear false nails or nail polish.

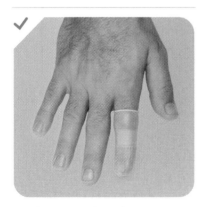

Bandage wounds and cover bandages.

Hand antiseptics are liquids or gels that are used to lower the number of pathogens on skin. If used, these substances must comply with Food and Drug Administration (FDA) standards and should only be used after proper handwashing—never in place of it. Once an antiseptic is applied, foodhandlers should not touch food or equipment until the substance has dried.

Foodhandlers must wash their hands before they start work and after:

- Using the restroom
- Handling raw meat, poultry and seafood (before *and* after)
- Touching the hair, face, or body
- Sneezing, coughing, or using a tissue
- Smoking, eating, drinking, or chewing gum or tobacco
- Handling chemicals that might affect the safety of food
- Taking out the garbage
- Clearing tables or busing dirty dishes
- Touching clothing or aprons
- Touching anything else that may contaminate hands, such as dirty equipment, work surfaces, or wiping towels
- Handling money

Bare-Hand Contact with Ready-to-Eat Food

Proper handwashing minimizes the risk of contamination associated with bare-hand contact with ready-to-eat food. If your jurisdiction allows bare-hand contact with ready-to-eat food, your establishment must have policies for employee health and train employees in handwashing and personal hygiene practices.

Hand Maintenance

In addition to washing, hands need other regular care to ensure they will not contaminate food. To keep food safe, make sure foodhandlers follow these guidelines (see *Exhibit 4c*):

- **Keep fingernails short and clean.** Long fingernails may be difficult to keep clean.

- **Do not wear false fingernails.** False and acrylic nails should not be worn while handling food because they can be difficult to keep clean and can break off into food. Some jurisdictions allow false nails if single-use gloves are worn. Check your local requirements.

- **Do not wear nail polish.** It can disguise dirt under nails and may flake off into food. Some jurisdictions allow nail polish if single-use gloves are worn. Check your local requirements.

Key Point

Wounds on hands should be covered with a clean bandage and a glove or finger cot.

- **Wear a bandage over wounds on hands and arms and make sure it keeps the wound from leaking.** You must wear a single-use glove or finger cot—a finger cover—over bandages on hands and fingers. These will protect the bandage and keep it from falling off into food.

Something to Think About...   More than They Bargained for

At a restaurant on the East Coast, the salad bar was a popular attraction. One afternoon while preparing the lettuce, an employee cut her finger. She immediately bandaged it and returned to work. Unfortunately, while she was tossing the salad, the bandage fell off the employee's finger and into the lettuce. A short time later, a customer notified the restaurant manager that she had found a used bandage in her salad. The manager made the necessary apologies and quickly comped her meal. Fortunately, the customer was very understanding, and the rest of the evening proceeded without incident.

What should have been done to prevent this situation?

Single-Use Gloves

Gloves can help keep food safe by creating a barrier between hands and food. (See *Exhibit 4d.*) When purchasing gloves for handling food, managers should:

- **Buy disposable gloves.** Gloves used to handle food are for single use only. They should never be washed and reused.

- **Buy gloves for different tasks.** Long gloves, for example, should be used for hand-mixing salads. Colored gloves can also be used to help prevent cross-contamination.

4d Gloves

Gloves can help keep food safe by creating a barrier between hands and food.

Key Point

Gloves must never be used in place of handwashing.

- **Provide different glove sizes.** Gloves that are too big will not stay on the hand, while those that are too small will tear or rip easily.

- **Consider providing gloves made from latex alternatives.** Some foodhandlers and customers may be sensitive to latex.

- **Focus on safety, durability, and cleanliness.** Make sure you purchase gloves specifically designed for food contact, which include gloves bearing the NSF International mark. (This mark is discussed in Chapter 11.)

Gloves must never be used in place of handwashing. Hands must be washed before putting gloves on and when changing to a new pair.

Foodhandlers should change their gloves:

- As soon as they become soiled or torn

- Before beginning a different task

- At least every four hours during continual use, and more often when necessary

- After handling raw meat and before handling ready-to-eat food

Often foodhandlers consider gloves more sanitary than bare hands. Because of this false sense of security, they might not change gloves as often as necessary. For this reason, it is critical to reinforce the importance of proper glove use with foodhandlers.

Other Good Personal Hygiene Practices

Personal hygiene can be a sensitive subject for some people, but because it is vital to food safety, managers must address the subject with every foodhandler.

4e   Hair Restraint

Foodhandlers should wear a clean hat or other hair restraint to keep hair away from food and to keep them from touching it.

General Personal Cleanliness

Foodhandlers must maintain personal cleanliness. This includes bathing or showering before work and keeping hair clean, since oily, dirty hair can harbor pathogens.

Proper Work Attire

A foodhandler's attire plays an important role in the prevention of foodborne illness. Dirty clothes may harbor pathogens, as well as give customers a bad impression of your establishment. Therefore, managers should make sure foodhandlers observe strict dress standards.

Foodhandlers should:

- **Wear a clean hat or other** hair restraint. A hair restraint will keep hair away from food and keep the foodhandler from touching it. (See *Exhibit 4e.*) Foodhandlers with facial hair should also wear beard restraints.

- **Wear clean clothing daily.** The type of clothing chosen should minimize contact with food and equipment, and should reduce the need for adjustments. If possible, foodhandlers should change into work clothes at the establishment. Dirty clothing that is stored in the establishment must be kept away from food and prep areas. This includes dirty aprons, chef coats, and uniforms.

- **Remove aprons when leaving food-preparation areas.** For example, aprons should be removed and properly stored prior to taking out the garbage or using the restroom.

- **Remove jewelry from hands and arms prior to preparing food and when working around food-preparation areas.** (See *Exhibit 4f.*) Jewelry may contain microorganisms, and foodhandlers may be tempted to touch it. Wearing jewelry may also pose a hazard when working around equipment. Remove rings (except for a plain band), bracelets (including medical information jewelry), and watches. Your company may also require you to remove other types of jewelry, including earrings, necklaces, and facial jewelry such as nose rings. Servers may wear jewelry if allowed by company policy.

4f   Jewelry

Remove jewelry from hands and arms prior to preparing food and when working around food-preparation areas.

Check with your local regulatory agency regarding requirements. These requirements should be reflected in written policies that are consistently monitored and enforced. All potential employees should be made aware of these policies prior to employment.

Policies Regarding Eating, Drinking, Smoking, and Chewing Gum and Tobacco

Small droplets of saliva can contain thousands of disease-causing microorganisms. In the process of eating, drinking, chewing gum or tobacco, or smoking, saliva can be transferred to a foodhandler's hands or directly to the food the person is handling. For this reason, foodhandlers must not smoke, chew gum or tobacco, or eat or drink while preparing or serving food, while working in food-preparation areas, or while working in areas used to clean utensils and equipment.

Some jurisdictions allow employees to drink from a covered container with a straw while in these areas. Check with your local regulatory agency. Foodhandlers should eat, drink, chew gum, or use tobacco products only in designated areas, such as an employee break room. Employees should never be allowed to spit in the establishment.

If food must be tasted during preparation, it must be placed in a separate dish and tasted with a clean utensil. (See *Exhibit 4g.*) The dish and utensil should then be removed from the food-preparation area for cleaning and sanitizing.

Policies for Reporting Illness and Injury

Foodhandlers must be encouraged to report health problems to the manager of the establishment before working. If they become ill while working, they must immediately report their condition. There are several instances when a foodhandler must either be *restricted* from working with or around food or *excluded* from working within the establishment. (See *Exhibit 4h* on the next page.)

If a foodhandler must refrigerate medication while working and it will be stored with food, he or she must store it inside a covered, leak-proof container that is clearly labeled.

4g   Safe and Unsafe Food-Testing Practices

To taste food during preparation, place it in a separate dish and taste it with a clean utensil.

Handling Employee Illnesses

If	Then
The foodhandler has a sore throat with a fever.	Restrict the foodhandler from working with or around food. Exclude the foodhandler from the operation if you primarily serve a high-risk population.
The foodhandler has at least one of these symptoms: • Vomiting • Diarrhea • Jaundice	Exclude the foodhandler from the operation. Before returning to work, foodhandlers who vomited or had diarrhea must meet one of these requirements. • Have had no symptoms for at least twenty-four hours • Have a written release from a medical practitioner Foodhandlers with jaundice must have a written release from a medical practitioner before they can go back to work.
The foodhandler has been diagnosed with a foodborne illness caused by one of these pathogens: • *Salmonella* Typhi • *Shigella* spp. • Shiga toxin-producing *E. coli* • Hepatitis A • Norovirus	Exclude the foodhandler from the operation. Notify the local regulatory authority. Work with the foodhandler's medical practitioner and/or the local regulatory authority to decide when the person can go back to work.

Any wounds on hands or arms should be covered with a bandage. Bandages should be clean and dry and must prevent leakage from the wound. As previously mentioned, disposable gloves or finger cots should be worn over bandages on hands.

4i   Modeling Proper Personal Hygiene

Managers must model proper behavior for foodhandlers at all times.

Management's Role in a Personal Hygiene Program

Management plays a critical role in the effectiveness of a personal hygiene program. Responsibilities include:

- Establishing proper personal hygiene policies

- Training foodhandlers on personal hygiene policies and retraining them when necessary

- Modeling proper behavior for foodhandlers at all times (see *Exhibit 4i*)

- Supervising food safety practices continuously and retraining foodhandlers as necessary

- Revising policies when laws and regulations change and when changes are recognized in the science of food safety

Job Assignments

As you write job descriptions and assign tasks, consider the risk of cross-contamination and plan tasks to prevent it. The risk may be higher if foodhandlers must perform several duties than if specific foodhandlers are assigned to a single duty. For example, an employee expected to prepare and wrap food, clear off tables, and then return to food-preparation duties could more easily contaminate food than an employee who is assigned to just one of these tasks. By planning tasks to prevent cross-contamination, you will minimize the supervision needed and enable employees to follow food safety rules more easily.

Something to Think About...   Who's Game?

A restaurant chain on the East Coast was looking for ways to increase its employees' knowledge of general food safety principles and the importance of handwashing. Management decided that, in addition to traditional training, they would hold a voluntary competition. Spurred by a chance to win a cash prize, employees formed teams and competed against each other in a test of handwashing basics and food safety knowledge. The program was a success, with most employees scoring better than 90 percent on the food safety quiz. The competition is now an annual event.

Summary

Foodhandlers can contaminate food at every step in its flow through the establishment. Good personal hygiene is a critical protective measure against contamination and foodborne illness. A successful personal hygiene program depends on trained foodhandlers who possess the knowledge, skills, and attitude necessary to keep food safe.

Foodhandlers have the potential to contaminate food when they have been diagnosed with a foodborne illness, are vomiting or have diarrhea, have wounds that contain a pathogen, or touch anything that might contaminate their hands and do not wash them. Foodhandlers must pay close attention to what they do with their hands since simple acts such as running fingers through their hair can contaminate food. Proper handwashing must always be practiced. This is especially important before starting work; after using the restroom; after sneezing, coughing, smoking, eating, or drinking; and before and after handling raw meat, poultry, and seafood. It is up to the manager to monitor handwashing to make sure it is thorough and frequent. In addition, hands need other care to ensure they will not transfer contaminants to food. Fingernails should be kept short and clean. Wounds on hands or arms should be covered with clean bandages. Hand wounds should also be covered with gloves or finger cots.

Single-use gloves can create a barrier between hands and food; however, they should never be used in place of handwashing. Hands must be washed before putting on gloves and when changing to a new pair. Gloves used to handle food are for single use and should never be washed and reused. They must be changed when they become soiled or torn, when beginning a new task, and whenever contamination occurs.

Personal hygiene can be a sensitive subject for some people, but, because it is vital to food safety, it must be addressed with every employee. All employees must maintain personal cleanliness. They should bathe or shower before work and keep their hair clean.

Prior to handling food or when working in food-preparation areas, foodhandlers must put on clean clothing and a clean hair restraint. They must also remove jewelry from hands and arms.

Servers may wear jewelry if allowed by company policy. Aprons should always be removed and properly stored when the employee leaves food-preparation areas.

Establishments should implement strict policies regarding eating, drinking, smoking, and chewing gum and tobacco. These activities should not be allowed when the foodhandler is preparing or serving food or working in food-preparation areas.

Employees must be encouraged to report health problems to management before working with food. Managers must not allow foodhandlers to work if they have been diagnosed with a foodborne illness caused by *Salmonella* Typhi, *Shigella* spp., shiga toxin-producing *E. coli,* hepatitis A, or Norovirus. Foodhandlers must also be excluded from the establishment if they have symptoms that include diarrhea, vomiting, or jaundice. Managers must restrict them from working with or around food if they have a sore throat with a fever.

Management plays a critical role in the effectiveness of a personal hygiene program. By establishing a program that includes specific policies and by training and enforcing those policies, managers can minimize the risk of causing a foodborne illness. Most important, managers must set a good example by modeling proper personal hygiene practices.

Apply Your Knowledge

Randall and his manager made several errors. Identify as many as you can on a separate piece of paper.

- If you can identify only eight to twelve errors, you may need to reread this chapter.

- If you can identify thirteen to sixteen errors, you have a good understanding of this chapter.

- If you can identify more than sixteen errors, you are on your way to becoming a food safety expert.

A Case in Point 1

Randall is a foodhandler at a deli. It is 7:47 a.m., and he has just woken up. He is scheduled to be at work and ready to go by 8:00 a.m. When he gets out of bed, his stomach feels queasy. He blames that on the beer he had the night before. Fortunately, Randall lives only five minutes from work. Despite this, he doesn't have enough time to take a shower. He grabs the same uniform he wore the day before when prepping chicken. He also puts on his watch and several rings.

Randall does not have luck on his side today. On the way to the restaurant, his oil light comes on. He is forced to pull off the road and add oil to his car. When he gets to work, he realizes he has left his hat at home. Randall is greeted by an angry manager. The manager puts Randall to work right away, loading the rotisserie with raw chicken. Randall then moves to serving a customer who orders a freshly made salad. Randall is known for his salads and makes the salad to the customer's approval.

The manager asks Randall to take out the garbage and then make potato salad for the lunch-hour rush. On the way back from the garbage run, Randall tells the manager that his stomach is bothering him. The manager, thinking of his staff shortage, asks Randall to stick it out as long as he can. Randall agrees and gets out the ingredients for the potato salad. Then he heads to the restroom in hope of relieving his symptoms. After quickly rinsing his hands in the restroom, he finds that the paper towels have run out. Short of time, he wipes his hands on his apron.

Later, Randall cuts his finger while making the potato salad. He bandages the cut and continues his prep work. The manager then tells Randall to clean the few tables in the deli that are available for customers. He puts on a pair of single-use gloves and cleans and sanitizes the tables. When finished, Randall grabs a piece of chicken from the rotisserie for a snack. He takes the chicken with him to the prep area, so he can get back to making the potato salad.

Randall and his manager made several errors. Identify as many as you can on a separate piece of paper.

For answers, please turn to the Answer Key.

Apply Your Knowledge	A Case in Point 2
What could have been done to prevent this outbreak?	Sixteen people became sick and four were hospitalized after drinking milk shakes contaminated with shiga toxin-producing *E. coli* at a drive-in restaurant. The outbreak was started by an employee who came to work despite being ill. The employee made a milk-shake mix that was served over a five-day period. She had diarrhea and severe abdominal cramps prior to making the shake mix. However, the employee continued to work until she was found to have a possible case of shiga toxin-producing *E. coli* five days later.
	Fourteen of the sixteen people who became ill had consumed milk shakes. Three people were briefly hospitalized. A fourth, a fifteen-year-old girl, required dialysis due to kidney failure resulting from the illness. The drive-in was temporarily closed, but it was cleaned and reopened a few days later.
	For answers, please turn to the Answer Key.

Apply Your Knowledge	Discussion Questions
Use these questions to review the concepts presented in this chapter.	① What are some basic work-attire requirements for employees?
	② What personal behaviors can contaminate food?
	③ What is the proper procedure for handling employee wounds on hands or arms?
	④ What procedures must foodhandlers follow when using gloves?
	⑤ What employee health problems pose a possible threat to food safety? What are the appropriate actions that should be taken?
	For answers, please turn to the Answer Key.

Study Questions

Circle the best answer to each question.

1. **What must foodhandlers do after touching their hair, face, or body?**
   A Wash their hands
   B Rinse their gloves
   C Change their aprons
   D Use a hand antiseptic

2. **What should foodhandlers do after prepping food and before using the restroom?**
   A Wash their hands
   B Take off their hats
   C Change their gloves
   D Take off their aprons

3. **Which piece of jewelry can be worn by a foodhandler?**
   A Diamond ring
   B Medical bracelet
   C Plain band ring
   D Watch

4. **When should hand antiseptics be used?**
   A Before washing hands
   B After washing hands
   C In place of washing hands
   D In place of wearing gloves

5. **When should foodhandlers who wear gloves wash their hands?**
   A After putting on the gloves
   B Before taking off the gloves
   C After applying a hand antiseptic
   D Before putting on the gloves

6. **Foodhandlers should keep their fingernails**
   A short and unpolished.
   B long and unpolished.
   C long and painted with nail polish.
   D short and painted with nail polish.

⑦ **A cook wore single-use gloves while forming raw ground beef into patties. The cook continued to wear them while slicing hamburger buns. What mistake was made?**

A   The cook did not wear reusable gloves while handling the raw ground beef and hamburger buns.

B   The cook did not clean and sanitize the gloves before handling the hamburger buns.

C   The cook did not wash hands before putting on the same gloves to slice the hamburger buns.

D   The cook did not wash hands and put on new gloves before slicing the hamburger buns.

⑧ **When a foodhandler has been diagnosed with shigellosis, what steps must be taken?**

A   The foodhandler must be told to not come in to work.

B   The foodhandler must be given a nonfoodhandling position.

C   The foodhandler can work, but must wear gloves when handling food.

D   The foodhandler can work, but must wash hands every fifteen minutes.

⑨ **Foodhandlers cannot work in their operation if they have an illness caused by which pathogen?**

A   *Vibrio vulnificus*

B   *Salmonella* Typhi

C   *Clostridium botulinum*

D   *Clostridium perfringens*

⑩ **Foodhandlers who work in a nursing home cannot work in the operation if they have which symptom?**

A   Thirst with itching

B   Sore throat with fever

C   Soreness with fatigue

D   Headache with soreness

Continued on next page ▶

► *Continued from previous page*

11 **Foodhandlers should not eat, drink, smoke, or chew gum or tobacco while**

A bare handed.

B on their break.

C prepping food.

D counting money.

12 **What should foodhandlers do if they cut their fingers while preparing food?**

A Cover the wound with a bandage.

B Stay away from food and prep areas.

C Cover the hand with a glove or a finger cot.

D Cover the wound with a bandage and a glove or a finger cot.

13 **What should a manager at a nursing home do if a cook calls in with a headache, nausea, and diarrhea?**

A Tell the cook to stay away from work and see a doctor.

B Tell the cook to rest for a couple of hours and then come to work.

C Tell the cook to come in for a couple of hours and then go home.

D Tell the cook to go to the doctor and then immediately come to work.

For answers, please turn to the Answer Key.

Additional Resources

Articles and Texts

Courtenay, Monique, Lina Ramirez, Beth Cox, Inyee Han, Xiupink Jiang, and Paul Dawson. 2005. Effects of Various Hand Hygiene Regimes on Removal and/or Destruction of *Escherichia coli* on Hands. *Food Service Technology.* 5 (2-4): 77.

Fendler, Eleanor J., Michael J. Dolan and Ronald A. Williams. 1998. Handwashing and Gloving for Food Protection Part I: Examination of the Evidence. *Dairy, Food and Environmental Sanitation.* 18 (12): 814.

Fendler, Eleanor J., Michael J. Dolan, Ronald A. Williams, and Daryl S. Paulson. 1998. Handwashing and Gloving for Food Protection Part II: Effectiveness. *Dairy, Food and Environmental Sanitation.* 18 (12): 824.

Paulson, Daryl S. 2000. Handwashing, Gloving, and Disease Transmission by the Food Preparer. *Dairy, Food and Environmental Sanitation.* 20 (11): 838.

Pragle, Aimee S., Anna K. Harding, James C. Mack. 2007. Food Workers' Perspectives on Handwashing Behaviors and Barriers in the Restaurant Environment. *Journal of Environmental Health.* 69 (10): 27.

Taylor, Anne K. 2000. Food Protection: New Developments in Handwashing. *Dairy, Food and Environmental Sanitation.* 20 (2): 114.

Yamamoto, Yukiko, Kazuhiro Ugai, and Yasuko Takahashi. 2005. Efficiency of Hand Drying for Removing Bacteria from Washed Hands: Comparison of Paper Towel Drying with Warm Air Drying. *Infection Control and Hospital Epidemiology.* 26:316.

Web Sites

Centers for Disease Control and Prevention
cdc.gov

FDA Food Safety
www.fda.gov/Food/FoodSafety/default.htm

Gateway to Government Food Safety Information
FoodSafety.gov

National Institute for Occupational Safety and Health
cdc.gov/niosh/homepage.html

Continued on next page ▶

▶ *Continued from previous page*

Documents and Other Resources

2009 FDA Food Code
www.fda.gov/Food/FoodSafety/RetailFoodProtection/FoodCode/
FoodCode2009/default.htm

CDC Vessel Sanitation Program
cdc.gov/nceh/vsp

Emerging Infectious Diseases
cdc.gov/ncidod/eid/index.htm

FDA Foodborne Illness Resource Page
www.fda.gov/Food/FoodSafety/FoodborneIllness/default.htm

Morbidity and Mortality Weekly Report
cdc.gov/mmwr

Notes

II The Flow of Food Through the Operation

Chapters in This Unit

5 The Flow of Food: An Introduction

Inside this chapter:

- Preventing Cross-Contamination
- Time and Temperature Control

After completing this chapter, you should be able to:

- Identify methods for preventing cross-contamination.
- Identify methods for preventing time-temperature abuse.
- Identify different types of temperature-measuring devices and their uses.
- Calibrate and maintain different temperature-measuring devices.
- Properly measure the temperature of food at each point in the flow of food.

Key Terms

- Flow of food
- Bimetallic stemmed thermometer
- Time-temperature indicator (TTI)
- Calibration

Apply Your Knowledge

Check to see how much you know about the concepts in this chapter. Use the page references provided with each question to explore the topic.

Test Your Food Safety Knowledge

① **True or False:** Chicken held at an internal temperature of 125°F (52°C) has been temperature abused. *(See page 5-4.)*

② **True or False:** Infrared thermometers are best for measuring the internal temperature of food. *(See page 5-7.)*

③ **True or False:** When checking the temperature of a roast using a bimetallic stemmed thermometer, only the tip of the thermometer stem should be inserted into the product. *(See page 5-10.)*

④ **True or False:** A thermometer calibrated by the boiling-point method must be set to 135°F (57°C), after being placed in the boiling water. *(See page 5-8.)*

⑤ **True or False:** Washing and rinsing a cutting board will prevent it from cross-contaminating the next product placed on it. *(See page 5-3.)*

For answers, please turn to the Answer Key.

5a The Flow of Food

Receiving

Purchasing

Storing

Preparing

The Flow of Food

Cooking

Serving

Reheating

Cooling

Holding

Introduction

Your responsibility for the safety of the food in your establishment starts long before any food is actually served to the customer. Many things can happen to a product on its path through the establishment, from purchasing and receiving through storing, preparing, cooking, holding, cooling, reheating, and serving. This path is known as the **flow of food**. (See *Exhibit 5a.*) A frozen product that leaves the processor's plant in good condition, for example, may thaw on its way to the distributor's warehouse and go unnoticed during receiving. Once in your establishment, the product might not be stored properly or cooked to the proper internal temperature. These mistakes could cause a foodborne illness.

The safety of the food served at your establishment will depend largely on how well you apply food safety concepts presented in this program throughout the flow of food. To be effective, you must have a good understanding of how to prevent cross-contamination and time-temperature abuse. You must also develop a system that prioritizes, monitors, and verifies the most important food safety practices. This will be discussed in Chapter 10.

Preventing Cross-Contamination

A major hazard in the flow of food is cross-contamination, which is the transfer of microorganisms from one food or surface to another. (See *Exhibit 5b*.) Microorganisms move around easily in a kitchen. They can be transferred from food or unwashed hands to prep tables, equipment, utensils, cutting boards, or other food.

Cross-contamination can occur at almost any point in an operation. When you know how and where microorganisms can be transferred, cross-contamination is fairly simple to prevent. It starts with the creation of barriers between food products. These barriers can be physical or procedural.

Physical Barriers for Preventing Cross-Contamination

- **Assign specific equipment to each type of food product.** For example, use one set of cutting boards, utensils, and containers for raw poultry; another set for raw meat; and a third set for produce. Some manufacturers make colored cutting boards and utensils with colored handles. Color-coding can tell employees which equipment to use with what products, such as green for produce, yellow for raw chicken, and red for raw meat. (See *Exhibit 5c*.) Although color-coding minimizes the risk of cross-contamination, it does not eliminate the need to practice other methods for preventing it.

- **Clean and sanitize all work surfaces, equipment, and utensils after each task.** After cutting up raw chicken, for example, it is not enough to simply rinse the cutting board. Wash, rinse, *and* sanitize cutting boards and utensils. Make sure employees know which cleaners and sanitizers to use for each job. (See Chapter 12 for more information on cleaning and sanitizing.)

5b Cross-Contamination

Cross-contamination is the transfer of microorganisms from one food or surface to another.

5c Color-Coded Equipment

Color-coded equipment can help prevent cross-contamination by making it easier to assign specific equipment to specific food.

Procedural Barriers for Preventing Cross-Contamination

- **When using the same prep table, prepare raw meat, seafood, and poultry and ready-to-eat food at different times.** For example, establishments with limited prep space can prepare lunch salads in the morning, clean and sanitize the utensils and surfaces, and then debone chicken for dinner entrées in the same space in the afternoon.

- **Purchase ingredients that require minimal preparation.** For example, an establishment can switch from buying raw chicken breasts to purchasing precooked chicken breasts.

Time and Temperature Control

One of the biggest factors responsible for foodborne-illness outbreaks is time-temperature abuse. Remember, food has been time-temperature abused when it has been allowed to remain at temperatures favorable to the growth of microorganisms. Foodborne microorganisms grow at temperatures between 41°F and 135°F (5°C and 57°C), which is why this range is known as the temperature danger zone. Microorganisms grow much faster in the middle of the zone, at temperatures between 70°F and 125°F (21°C and 52°C). (See *Exhibit 5d.*) Whenever food is held in the temperature danger zone, it is being abused.

As you learned in Chapter 2, time also plays a critical role in food safety. The longer food stays in the temperature danger zone, the more time microorganisms have to grow and make food unsafe. To keep food safe throughout the flow of food, you must minimize the amount of time it spends in the temperature danger zone. (See *Exhibit 5e.*) If food is held in this dangerous range for more than four hours, you must throw it out.

TCS food can be time-temperature abused as it flows through your establishment. This can occur when food is *not:*

- Cooked to the required minimum internal temperature

- Cooled properly

- Reheated properly

- Held at the proper temperature

5d Temperature and Bacterial Growth

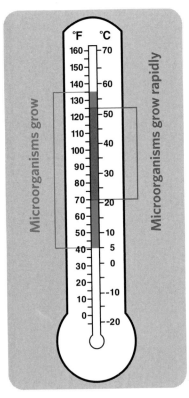

Foodborne microorganisms grow most rapidly at temperatures between 70°F and 125°F (21°C and 52°C).

5e   Preventing Time-Temperature Abuse

To keep food safe, you must minimize the amount of time it spends in the temperature danger zone.

5f   Time and Temperature Control

Print simple forms employees can use to record temperatures.

The best way to avoid time-temperature abuse is to establish procedures employees must follow and then monitor them. Make time and temperature control part of every employee's job. To be successful, you should:

- **Determine the best way to monitor time and temperature in your establishment.** Determine which food items should be monitored, how often, and by whom. Then assign responsibility to employees in each area. Make sure they understand exactly what you want them to do, how to do it, and why it is important.

- **Make sure the establishment has the right kinds of thermometers available in the right places.** Give employees their own calibrated thermometers. Have them use timers in prep areas to monitor how long food is being kept in the temperature danger zone.

- **Make sure employees regularly record temperatures and the times they are taken.** (See *Exhibit 5f.*) Print simple forms employees can use to record times and temperatures throughout the shift. Post these forms on clipboards outside of refrigerators and freezers, near prep tables, and next to cooking and holding equipment.

- **Incorporate time and temperature controls into standard operating procedures for employees.** This might include:

  ○ Removing from the refrigerator only the amount of food that can be prepared in a short period of time

  ○ Refrigerating utensils and ingredients before preparing certain recipes, such as tuna or chicken salad

  ○ Cooking TCS food to required minimum internal temperatures

- **Develop a set of corrective actions.** Decide what action should be taken if time and temperature standards are not met. For example, if you hold soup on a steam table and its temperature falls below 135°F (57°C) after two hours, you might reheat it to the correct temperature.

Choosing the Right Thermometer

To manage time and temperature, you need to monitor and control them. The thermometer may be the single most important tool you have to protect your food.

There are many types of thermometers used in an establishment. Each is designed for a specific purpose. Some are used to measure the temperature of refrigerated or frozen storage areas. Others measure the temperature of equipment, such as ovens, hot-holding cabinets, and dishwashing machines. Perhaps the most important type are thermometers that measure the temperature of food. The most common types used in establishments are the bimetallic stemmed thermometer, the thermocouple, and the thermistor. Infrared thermometers are also becoming increasingly popular.

Bimetallic Stemmed Thermometers

A common type of thermometer used in the restaurant and foodservice industry is the bimetallic stemmed thermometer. This type of thermometer measures temperature through a metal probe with a sensor toward the end. Bimetallic stemmed thermometers often have scales measuring temperatures from 0°F to 220°F (–18°C to 104°C). This makes them useful for measuring the temperatures of everything from incoming shipments to the internal temperature of food in hot-holding units. If you select this type of thermometer, make sure it has (see *Exhibit 5g*):

- An adjustable calibration nut to keep it accurate

- Easy-to-read, numbered temperature markings

- A dimple to mark the end of the sensing area (which begins at the tip)

- Accuracy to within ±2°F (±1°C)

5g Components of a Bimetallic Stemmed Thermometer

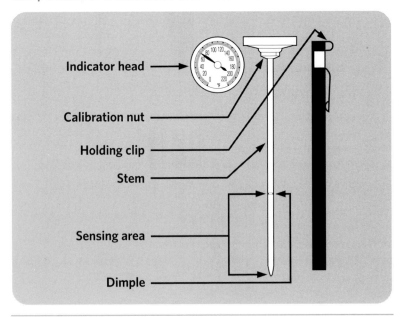

Indicator head

Calibration nut

Holding clip

Stem

Sensing area

Dimple

5h Thermocouple

5i Types of Temperature Probes

Immersion probe

Surface probe

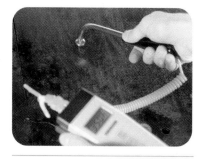

Penetration probe

Thermocouples and Thermistors

Thermocouples and thermistors measure temperatures through a metal probe or sensing area and display results on a digital readout. They come in a wide variety of styles and sizes, from small pocket models to panel-mounted displays. (See *Exhibit 5h.*) Many come with interchangeable temperature probes designed to measure the temperature of equipment and food.

Basic types of probes include immersion, surface, penetration, and air probes. (See *Exhibit 5i.*) Immersion probes are designed to measure temperatures of liquids, such as soups, sauces, or frying oil. Surface probes measure temperatures of flat cooking equipment like griddles. Penetration probes are used to measure the internal temperature of food. Air temperature probes measure temperatures inside refrigerators or ovens.

Infrared (Laser) Thermometers

Infrared thermometers use infrared technology to produce accurate temperature readings of food and equipment surfaces. They are quick and easy to use. Infrared thermometers can reduce the risk of cross-contamination and damage to food products because they do not require contact with food. However, they should not be used to measure air temperature or the internal temperature of food.

When using infrared thermometers, remember the following:

- **Hold the thermometer as close as possible to the product without touching it.**

- **Remove any barriers between the thermometer and the product being checked.** Do not take temperature measurements through glass or shiny or polished-metal surfaces, such as stainless steel or aluminum.

- **Always follow the manufacturer's guidelines.** They can provide tips on obtaining the most accurate temperature reading with the infrared thermometer you are using.

Time-Temperature Indicators (TTI) and Other Time-Temperature Recording Devices

Some instruments are designed to monitor both time and product temperature. The time-temperature indicator (TTI) is one example.

5j   Time and Temperature Indicator (TTI)

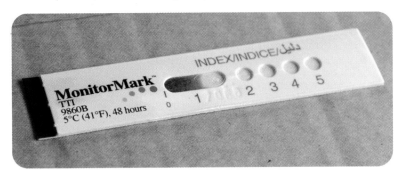

A change in color in the windows of this TTI alerts the receiver that time-temperature abuse has occurred.

Some suppliers attach these self-adhesive tags to a food shipment to determine if the temperature has exceeded safe limits during shipment or later storage. If it has, the TTI provides an irreversible record of the incident. A change in color inside the TTI windows notifies the employee receiving the shipment that the product has been time-temperature abused. (See *Exhibit 5j*.)

More suppliers are using recording devices that continuously monitor temperatures in their delivery trucks. If delivered products appear to have been time-temperature abused, the recording device can be checked to see if the temperature in the delivery truck changed at any time during transit.

How to Calibrate Thermometers

A thermometer must be adjusted in order to give an accurate reading. This adjustment is called **calibration.** Thermometers can be calibrated by adjusting them to the boiling point of water or to the point at which water turns to ice—the ice point.

When calibrating thermometers using the boiling-point method, follow these steps:

❶ **Bring clean tap water to a boil in a deep pan.**

❷ **Put the thermometer stem or probe into the boiling water so the sensing area is completely submerged.** Wait thirty seconds, or until the indicator stops moving. The thermometer stem or probe must remain in the boiling water, but do not let it touch the pan's bottom or sides.

❸ **Hold the calibration nut securely with a wrench or other tool and rotate the head of the thermometer until it reads 212°F (100°C) or the appropriate boiling-point temperature for your elevation.** The boiling point of water is about 1°F (about 0.5°C) lower for every 550 feet (168 meters) above sea level. On some thermocouples or thermistors, you can press a reset button.

Thermometers are often calibrated using the ice-point method. *Exhibit 5k* illustrates how to use this method.

5k Ice-Point Method for Calibrating a Thermometer

❶ **Fill a large container with crushed ice.** Add clean tap water until the container is full.

Note: Stir the mixture well.

❷ **Put the thermometer stem or probe into the ice water so the sensing area is completely submerged.** Wait thirty seconds or until the indicator stops moving.

Note: Do not let the stem or probe touch the container's bottom or sides. The thermometer stem or probe must remain in the ice water.

❸ **Hold the calibration nut securely with a wrench or other tool and rotate the head of the thermometer until it reads 32°F (0°C).**

Note: On some thermocouples or thermistors, you can press a reset button.

General Thermometer Guidelines

It is important to know how to use and care for each type of thermometer found in your operation. When it comes to maintenance, always follow manufacturers' recommendations. Here are a few simple guidelines for using thermometers.

- **Keep thermometers and their storage cases clean.**
  Thermometers should be washed, rinsed, sanitized, and air-dried before and after each use to prevent cross-contamination. Always have an adequate supply of clean and sanitized thermometers on hand.

- **Calibrate thermometers regularly to ensure accuracy.**
  This should be done before each shift or before each day's

deliveries. Thermometers should also be recalibrated any time they suffer a severe shock—for example, after being dropped or after an extreme change in temperature. Thermometers that hang or sit in refrigerators or freezers can be damaged easily. To make sure these thermometers are accurate, use a thermocouple with an air probe to check the air temperature in the unit and compare it to the thermometer readout. Hanging thermometers usually cannot be recalibrated and must be replaced if they are not accurate.

- **Never use glass thermometers to monitor the temperature of food.** If they break, they can be a physical hazard.

- **Measure internal temperatures of food by inserting the thermometer stem or probe into the thickest part of the product (usually the center).** It is a good practice to take at least two readings in different locations because product temperatures may vary across the food portion. When checking the internal temperature of food using a bimetallic stemmed thermometer, insert the stem into the product so that it is immersed from the tip to the end of the sensing area. When measuring the internal temperature of thin food, such as meat or fish patties, small diameter probes should be used.

- **Wait for the thermometer reading to steady before recording the temperature of a food item.** Wait at least fifteen seconds from the time the thermometer stem or probe is inserted into the food.

Summary

The flow of food is the path that food takes through your establishment from purchasing and receiving through storing, preparing, cooking, holding, cooling, reheating, and serving. Many things can happen to food as it flows through the establishment, but the hazards that the manager has most control over are cross-contamination and time-temperature abuse.

Cross-contamination is the transfer of microorganisms from one food or surface to another. Prevention starts with the creation of physical or procedural barriers between food products. Physical barriers include assigning specific equipment to each type of food product, and cleaning and sanitizing all work

The Flow of Food

Receiving • Storing • Preparing • Cooking • Holding • Cooling • Reheating • Serving • Purchasing

surfaces, equipment, and utensils after each task. Procedural barriers include purchasing ingredients that require minimal preparation, and preparing raw meat, fish, and poultry and ready-to-eat food at different times.

Food has been time-temperature abused when it has been allowed to remain at temperatures between 41°F and 135°F (5°C and 57°C). This temperature range is known as the temperature danger zone. To keep food safe, you must minimize the amount of time food spends in this dangerous range. To prevent time-temperature abuse in your establishment, you should incorporate time and temperature controls into your standard operating procedures, make thermometers available to your employees, and regularly record temperatures and the times they were taken.

Thermometers are the most important tools managers have to prevent time-temperature abuse. Managers should make sure employees know what different thermometers are used for and how to calibrate and use them properly. Thermometers can be calibrated using either the boiling-point or the ice-point method. The boiling-point method requires the thermometer to be adjusted to 212°F (100°C) or the appropriate boiling point for the establishment's elevation, after the stem or probe is placed in boiling water. Using the ice-point method, the thermometer is submerged in ice water and adjusted to 32°F (0°C).

Thermometers should be washed, rinsed, sanitized, and air-dried before and after each use to prevent cross-contamination. They should also be calibrated regularly to ensure accuracy. When measuring the internal temperature of food, the thermometer stem or probe should be inserted in the thickest part of the product (usually the center). When using a bimetallic stemmed thermometer, the stem should be immersed in the product from the tip to the end of the sensing area. When measuring the internal temperature of thin food, use a small diameter probe. Always wait for the thermometer reading to steady before recording the temperature of the food. Never use glass thermometers to measure food temperatures.

Apply Your Knowledge

Use these questions to review the concepts presented in this chapter.

Discussion Questions

① What are some ways food can be time-temperature abused?

② How can cross-contamination be prevented in the establishment?

③ How is a thermometer calibrated using the ice-point method?

For answers, please turn to the Answer Key.

Study Questions

Circle the best answer to each question.

① **A foodhandler has finished trimming raw chicken on a cutting board and needs it to prep vegetables. What must be done to the cutting board?**

A It must be dried with a paper towel.

B It must be turned over to the other side.

C It must be washed, rinsed, and sanitized.

D It must be rinsed in hot water and air-dried.

② **Which of these practices can help prevent cross-contamination?**

A Using a designated cutting board when preparing meat

B Preparing small batches of food at one time

C Identifying minimum internal cooking temperatures

D Calibrating thermometers regularly

③ **Infrared thermometers should be used to measure the**

A air temperature in a cooler.

B internal temperature of a turkey.

C surface temperature of a grill.

D internal temperature of a batch of soup.

④ **At what temperatures do foodborne pathogens grow most quickly?**

A Between 0°F and 41°F (−17°C and 5°C)

B Between 45°F and 65°F (7°C and 18°C)

C Between 70°F and 125°F (21°C and 52°C)

D Between 130°F and 165°F (54°C and 74°C)

⑤ **Which thermocouple probe should be used to check the temperature of a large stockpot of soup?**

A Air probe

B Surface probe

C Immersion probe

D Penetration probe

⑥ **When a thermometer is calibrated using the ice-point method, it should be adjusted to _____ after the stem or probe has been placed in the ice water.**

A 0°F (-17°C)

B 32°F (0°C)

C 41°F (5°C)

D 212°F (100°C)

⑦ **What type of thermometer is NOT appropriate for use in a restaurant or foodservice operation?**

A Thermistor

B Thermocouple

C Glass thermometer

D Bimetallic stemmed thermometer

For answers, please turn to the Answer Key.

Additional Resources

Articles and Texts

Green, Laura, Carol Selman, Anyana Banerjee, Ruthanne Marcus, Carlota Medus, Frederick J. Angulo, Vince Radke, Sharunda Buchanan, and EHS-Net Working Group. 2005. Food Service Workers' Self-Reported Food Preparation Practices: An EHS-Net Study. *International Journal of Hygiene and Environmental Health.* 208:27.

Hague, M. A., K. E. Warren, M. C. Hunt, D. H. Kropf, C. L. Kastner, S. L. Stroda, and D. E. Johnson. 1994. Endpoint Temperature, Internal Cooked Color, and Expressible Juice Color Relationships in Ground Beef Patties. *Journal of Food Science.* 59(3): 465.

Trout, G. R. 1989. Effect of pH and Total Pigment Concentration on the Internal Color of Cooked Ground Beef Patties. *Journal of Food Science.* 54(1): 1.

USDA FSIS. 1998. *Premature Browning of Cooked Hamburger—An FSIS / ARS Study.* Washington, D.C.

Warren, K. E., M. C. Hunt, and D. H. Kropf. 1995a. Myoglobin Oxidative State Affects Internal Cooked Color Development in Ground Beef Patties. *International Congress of Meat Science and Technology.* 41:394.

Web Sites

FDA Food Safety
www.fda.gov/Food/FoodSafety/default.htm

Gateway to Government Food Safety Information
foodsafety.gov

NSF International
nsf.org

Underwriters Laboratories, Inc.
ul.com

Other Documents and Resources

2009 FDA Food Code
www.fda.gov/Food/FoodSafety/RetailFoodProtection/FoodCode/FoodCode2009/default.htm

Notes

EXETER-IVANHOE CITRUS ASSN.
(EXETER PLANT)
EXETER, CALIF. 93221

VARIETY		CONTENTS
NAVEL ORANGES	18-2 LB. BAGS	SUNKIST CITRUS in MESH BAGS
VALENCIA ORANGES	12-3 LB. BAGS	
SWEET ORANGES	10-4 LB. BAGS	SUNKIST CITRUS in NET BAGS
TANGELOS	12-4 LB. BAGS	
TANGERINES	8-5 LB. BAGS	SUNKIST CITRUS in POLY BAGS
MANDARINS	10-5 LB. BAGS	
GRAPEFRUIT	5-8 LB. BAGS	SK in MESH BAGS
MARSH WHITE GRAPEFRUIT	6-8 LB. BAGS	SK in NET BAGS
MARSH RUBY GRAPEFRUIT	5-10 LB. BAGS	SK in POLY BAGS
LEMONS	6-10 LB. BAGS	

FGS-4/95

6 The Flow of Food: Purchasing and Receiving

Inside this chapter:

- Choosing a Supplier
- Inspection Procedures
- Receiving and Inspecting Specific Food

After completing this chapter, you should be able to:

- Identify characteristics of an approved food source.
- Maintain required records of shellstock tags and parasite destruction.
- Identify accept or reject criteria for receiving:
  - Refrigerated food
  - Frozen food
  - Dry food
  - Hot food
  - Nonfood items with a food-contact surface

Key Terms

- Shellstock identification tags
- Modified atmosphere packaging (MAP)
- Vacuum-packed food
- *Sous vide* food
- Ultra-high temperature (UHT) pasteurization
- Aseptically packaged food

Apply Your Knowledge

Check to see how much you know about the concepts in this chapter. Use the page references provided with each question to explore the topic.

Test Your Food Safety Knowledge

① **True or False:** A delivery of fresh fish should be received at an internal temperature of 41°F (5°C) or lower. *(See page 6-8.)*

② **True or False:** Turkey should be rejected if the texture is firm and springs back when touched. *(See page 6-12.)*

③ **True or False:** You should reject a delivery of frozen steaks covered in large ice crystals. *(See page 6-16.)*

④ **True or False:** If a sack of flour is dry upon delivery, the contents may still be contaminated. *(See page 6-18.)*

⑤ **True or False:** A supplier that has been inspected and is in compliance with local, state, and federal laws can be considered an approved source. *(See page 6-2.)*

For answers, please turn to the Answer Key.

Introduction

The final responsibility for the safety of food entering your establishment rests with you. You can avoid many potential food safety hazards by using approved, reputable suppliers and properly inspecting products when they are delivered.

Choosing a Supplier

A number of factors go into selecting the right suppliers. While service needs to be considered, choosing a supplier who can deliver safe food is the ultimate goal. Make sure suppliers can meet or exceed your standards. Keep the following criteria in mind when making your selection:

- **Make sure suppliers are approved and reputable.** An approved food supplier is one that has been inspected and is in compliance with applicable local, state, and federal laws. Make sure your suppliers have good food safety practices. This applies to all suppliers along the supply chain. Your operation's supply chain can include growers, shippers, packers, manufacturers, distributors (trucking fleets and warehouses), and local markets.

Receiving · Storing · Preparing · Cooking · Holding · Cooling · Reheating · Serving · Purchasing

The Flow of Food

- **Develop a relationship with your suppliers, and get to know their food safety practices.** Consider reviewing their most recent inspection reports. These reports can be from the U.S. Department of Agriculture (USDA), the Food and Drug Administration (FDA) or a third-party inspector. They should be based on Good Manufacturing Practices (GMP) or Good Agricultural Practices (GAP). GMP are the FDA's minimum sanitation and processing requirements for producing safe food. They describe the methods, equipment, facilities, and controls used to process food. Both suppliers and their sources are subject to GMP inspections.

  Make sure an inspection report reviews the following areas:

  - Receiving and storage
  - Processing
  - Shipping
  - Cleaning and sanitizing
  - Personal hygiene
  - Employee training
  - Recall program
  - HACCP program or other food safety system

  GAP audits measure critical areas in which produce safety could be compromised. These audits typically focus on:

  - Worker health and hygiene
  - Field sanitation and animal control
  - Fertilizer and pesticide usage
  - Irrigation water
  - Harvest practices

- **Arrange deliveries so they arrive one at a time and during off-peak hours.** Suppliers must deliver products when staff has adequate time to do inspections.

Inspection Procedures

If you establish procedures for inspecting products, you can reduce hazards before they enter your establishment. Here are some general guidelines that can help you improve the way you receive deliveries:

- **Train employees to inspect deliveries properly.** Ideally, you should assign the responsibility for receiving and inspecting deliveries to specific employees. These employees should be trained to check products for proper temperatures, expired code dates, signs of thawing and refreezing, pest damage, and so on. They also should be authorized to accept, reject, and sign for deliveries.

- **Plan ahead for shipments.** Have clean hand trucks, carts, dollies, and containers available in the receiving area. Make sure enough space is available in walk-ins and storerooms prior to receiving a shipment. Some operations use a refrigerator and a freezer in the receiving area for temporary storage. If products need to be washed or broken down and rewrapped, make work space available as close to the receiving area as possible. This will prevent dirt and pests from being brought into storage areas or into the kitchen.

- **Plan a backup menu in case you have to return food items.** If food is not safe or does not meet your standards, you may have to take an item off the menu, substitute another menu item, or try to arrange delivery from another supplier.

- **Inspect and store each delivery before accepting another one.** This will prevent product abuse in the receiving area.

- **Have the right information available.** Receivers should have a purchase order or order sheet ready to check against the supplier's invoice. The sheet should list quantities, quality specifications, and agreed-upon prices. It should also have room to record the date and time of delivery, product temperatures, and other notes.

6a   Checking Temperatures during Receiving

Take sample temperatures of all refrigerated food.

- **Inspect deliveries immediately.** Do a thorough visual inspection to count quantities, check for damaged products, and look for items that might have been repacked or mishandled. Spot-check weights and take sample temperatures of all refrigerated food. (See *Exhibit 6a.*) There is always a possibility that food—even government-inspected products—may have been mishandled during shipment.

- **Correct mistakes immediately.** If any products are damaged, are not at the correct temperature, or have not been delivered to specifications, do not accept them.

- **Put products away as quickly as possible, especially products requiring refrigeration.**

- **Keep the receiving area clean and well lighted to discourage pests.**

Rejecting Shipments

You have the right to refuse any delivery that does not meet your standards. You should have a company policy about returns, and your suppliers should be aware of it and agree to it. When food does not meet your standards, your employees should know what to do.

To reject a product or shipment:

- **Set the rejected product aside.** Keep it separate from other food and supplies.

- **Tell the delivery person exactly what is wrong with the rejected product.** Use your purchase agreement and company standards to back up your decision to reject the product.

Key Point

You have the right to refuse any delivery that does not meet your standards.

- **Get a signed adjustment or credit slip from the delivery person before throwing the product away or letting the delivery person remove it.**

- **Log the incident on the invoice or receiving document.** Note the food involved, including lot number and expiration date if appropriate, the standard that was not met, and the corrective action taken.

How to Check Temperatures of Deliveries

Use the following guidelines when checking the temperature of various types of food (see *Exhibit 6b*):

- **Meat, poultry, and fish.** Insert the thermometer stem or probe into the thickest part of the product (usually the center). Additionally, you may want to check the surface temperature using an appropriate thermometer, because it can be a better indicator of potential temperature abuse.

- **Reduced oxygen packaged (ROP) and bulk food.** Insert the thermometer stem or probe between two packages. As an alternative, it may be possible to check product temperature by folding the packaging around the thermometer stem or probe. Be careful not to puncture the packaging.

- **Other packaged food.** Open the package and insert the thermometer stem or probe into the product. The sensing area must be fully immersed in the product. The stem or probe must not touch the package.

- **Live, molluscan shellfish.** Insert the thermometer stem or probe into the middle of the carton or case—between the shellfish—for an air temperature reading. Check the temperature of shucked shellfish by inserting the stem or probe into the container until the sensing area is immersed.

- **Eggs.** Check the air temperature of the delivery truck, as well as the truck's temperature chart recorder for extreme temperature fluctuations during transport. Temperature fluctuations, high humidity, and warm temperatures may result in the growth of harmful microorganisms.

Receiving
Storing
Purchasing
Preparing
The Flow of Food
Cooking
Serving
Holding
Reheating
Cooling

Always be sure to use a clean and sanitized thermometer each time you check a temperature. If you do not have extra thermometers, clean and sanitize your thermometer after each use. Keep a bucket of sanitizing solution in the receiving area, or use approved sanitizing wipes.

6b Checking the Temperature of Various Types of Food

Meat, Poultry, Fish

Insert the thermometer stem or probe directly into the thickest part of the product (usually the center).

ROP and Bulk Food

Insert the thermometer stem or probe between two packages, or fold the packaging around it.

Other Packaged Food

Open the package and insert the thermometer stem or probe into the product.

Receiving and Inspecting Specific Food

Every food product delivered to your establishment should be inspected carefully for damage, potential contamination, and proper temperature. While receiving temperatures for fresh food are product specific, frozen food should always be received frozen. In addition, note each food's appearance, texture, smell, and in some cases, taste. The packaging of food and nonfood items should be intact and clean, and it should protect items from contamination. An in-depth look at receiving criteria for specific products follows on the next several pages.

Fish

Fresh fish is very sensitive to time-temperature abuse and can deteriorate quickly if handled improperly. If it is received on ice, the ice should be crushed and the container should be self-draining. Upon delivery, it should be received at a temperature of 41°F (5°C) or lower.

To be acceptable, fresh fish must also meet the following criteria:

* **Color:** bright red gills; bright shiny skin
* **Texture:** firm flesh that springs back when touched
* **Odor:** mild ocean or seaweed smell
* **Eyes:** bright, clear, and full
* **Packaging:** product should be surrounded by crushed, self-draining ice

The following criteria are grounds for rejecting fish:

* **Color:** dull gray gills; dull dry skin
* **Texture:** soft flesh that leaves an imprint when touched
* **Odor:** strong fishy or ammonia smell
* **Eyes:** cloudy, red-rimmed, sunken
* **Product:** tumors, abscesses, or cysts on the skin

See *Exhibit 6c* for examples of acceptable and unacceptable fish.

Frozen fish should be received frozen. If there is any indication it has been allowed to thaw, do not accept it. Fish that has thawed and then refrozen before reaching your establishment

6c Acceptable versus Unacceptable Fish

The Flow of Food

may have a sour odor and be off-color. Fillets often turn brown at the edges when they have been refrozen. Other signs include large amounts of ice or liquid in the bottom of the shipping box and moist, discolored, or slimy wrapping paper.

A supplier must freeze fish that will be served raw or partially cooked, such as sushi-grade fish, for a specific period of time to kill any parasites that might be in the fish. Fish should be frozen to one of the following temperatures prior to shipment:

- −4°F (−20°C) or lower for seven days (168 hours) in a storage freezer

- −31°F (−35°C) or lower until solid and then stored at −31°F (−35°C) for fifteen hours

- −31°F (−35°C) or lower until solid and then stored at −4°F (−20°C) or lower for a minimum of twenty-four hours

Certain species of tuna and some farm-raised fish can be served raw or partially cooked without being frozen to eliminate parasites. To be served this way, farm-raised fish must be raised in a controlled environment with feed that is parasite free. The supplier should provide documentation verifying this, and the establishment must keep the documentation on file for ninety days.

Your supplier will provide you with records showing that the fish was frozen correctly. You must keep these records on file for ninety days from the date you served the fish.

Shellfish

Shellfish varieties include mollusks such as clams, oysters, and mussels. They can be shipped live, frozen, in the shell, or shucked. Interstate shipping is monitored by the state, the FDA, and the shellfish industry. Shellfish must be purchased from suppliers listed in the Interstate Certified Shellfish Shippers List.

Shucked shellfish must be packaged in nonreturnable containers clearly labeled with the name, address, and certification number of the packer. Containers smaller than one-half gallon (1.9 L) must have either a "best if used by" or "sell by" date. Containers bigger than one-half gallon (1.9 L) must have the date the shellfish were shucked.

6d Acceptable versus
Unacceptable Shellfish

✓

✗

Live shellfish must be received on ice or at an air temperature of 45°F (7°C) or lower. Shucked product must be received at an internal temperature of 41°F (5°C) or lower. The FDA requires that they carry shellstock identification tags—tags that document where the shellfish was harvested. These tags must remain attached to the delivery container until all of the shellfish have been used. Employees must write on the tags the date that the last shellfish was sold or served from the container. Operators must keep these tags on file for ninety days from the date written on them.

To be acceptable, shellfish must also meet the following criteria:

- **Odor:** mild ocean or seaweed smell
- **Shells:** closed and unbroken, which indicates shellfish are alive (see *Exhibit 6d*)
- **Condition:** if fresh, they are received alive

The following criteria are grounds for rejecting shellfish:

- **Texture:** slimy, sticky, or dry
- **Odor:** strong fishy smell
- **Shells:** excessively muddy or broken shells (see *Exhibit 6d*)
- **Condition:** dead on arrival (open shells that do not close when tapped)

Crustaceans

Crustaceans include shrimp, crab, and lobster. All processed crustaceans must be received at an internal temperature of 41°F (5°C) or lower. Live lobsters and crabs must be received alive. A live lobster in good condition will show signs of movement and will curl its tail when picked up, while a dead one will not. (See *Exhibit 6e*.) Those showing weak signs of life should be cooked right away, while dead ones must be discarded or returned to the vendor for credit.

To be acceptable, crustaceans must also meet the following criteria:

- **Odor:** mild ocean or seaweed smell
- **Condition:** shipped alive, packed in seaweed, and kept moist

6e Unacceptable Lobster

✗

If a lobster's tail does not curl when picked up, the lobster is dead and should be rejected.

The following criteria are grounds for rejecting crustaceans:

- **Odor:** strong fishy smell
- **Condition:** dead on arrival

Meat

Meat must be purchased from plants inspected by the USDA or the state department of agriculture. During the mandatory inspection process, USDA inspectors examine the animal carcass and viscera for possible signs of illness and check processing plants for sanitary conditions. *Inspected* does not mean the product is free of microorganisms but that the product and processing plant have met certain standards. Meat products that have been inspected will be stamped with abbreviations for "inspected and passed" by the inspecting agency, along with a number identifying the processing plant. (See *Exhibit 6f.*) These stamps will not appear on every cut of meat, but one should be present on every inspected carcass and on packaging.

Most meat also carries a stamp indicating its "grade," or palatability, and level of quality. Grading is a voluntary service offered by the USDA and is paid for by processors and packers. USDA grades are printed inside a shield-shaped stamp. (See *Exhibit 6f.*)

Meat must be delivered at 41°F (5°C) or lower. To be acceptable, it must also meet the following criteria:

- **Color**
  - **Beef:** bright cherry red; aged beef may be darker in color; vacuum-packed beef will appear purplish in color
  - **Lamb:** light red
  - **Pork:** light pink meat; firm, white fat
- **Texture:** firm flesh that springs back when touched
- **Odor:** no odor
- **Packaging:** intact and clean

6f   Inspection and Grading Stamps for Meat

USDA Inspection Stamp

USDA Grading Stamp

Meat inspection is mandatory.

The following criteria are grounds for rejecting meat:

- **Color**

  ○ **Beef:** brown or green

  ○ **Lamb:** brown, whitish surface covering the lean meat

  ○ **Pork:** excessively dark color; soft or rancid fat

- **Texture:** slimy, sticky, or dry

- **Odor:** sour odor

- **Packaging:** broken cartons; dirty wrappers; torn packaging; vacuum packaging with broken seals

Poultry

Poultry is inspected by the USDA or the state department of agriculture in much the same way as meat. As with meat, grading is voluntary and paid for by processors. See *Exhibit 6g* for examples of poultry inspection and grading stamps.

If received on ice, the ice should be crushed and the container should be self-draining. Fresh poultry should be delivered at a temperature of 41°F (5°C) or lower.

To be acceptable, poultry must also meet the following criteria:

- **Color:** no discoloration

- **Texture:** firm flesh that springs back when touched

- **Odor:** no odor

- **Packaging:** product should be surrounded by crushed, self-draining ice

The following criteria are grounds for rejecting poultry:

- **Color:** purple or green discoloration around the neck; dark wing tips (red tips are acceptable)

- **Texture:** stickiness under the wings and around joints

- **Odor:** abnormal, unpleasant odor

6g   Inspection and Grading Stamps for Poultry

USDA Inspection Stamp

USDA Grading Stamp

Poultry inspection is mandatory.

6h   Grading and Inspection Stamps for Eggs

USDA Grading Stamp

USDA Inspection Stamp

6i   Unacceptable Shell Eggs

Eggs that are dirty or cracked should be rejected.

Eggs

As with meat and poultry, egg grading is voluntary and is provided by the USDA. The grading stamp certifies that eggs have been graded for quality under federal and/or state supervision. *Exhibit 6h* provides an example of a grading stamp for eggs.

You should use suppliers who can deliver eggs within a few days of the packing date. Eggs must be delivered in refrigerated trucks capable of documenting air temperature during transport. When the eggs arrive, the truck's air temperature should be 45°F (7°C) or lower, and the eggs must be stored immediately in refrigeration units that will hold them at an air temperature of 45°F (7°C) or lower.

Consider using in-shell pasteurized eggs when preparing dishes for high-risk populations or dishes that will be served with undercooked eggs.

Liquid, frozen, and dehydrated eggs must be pasteurized as required by law and bear the USDA inspection mark. (See *Exhibit 6h.*) When delivered, liquid and frozen eggs should be refrigerated or frozen at the proper temperature. Check packages for damage or signs of refreezing, and note use-by dates to be sure the product is in good condition and still usable. Cases or cartons of eggs for direct sale to the consumer must display safe-handling instructions on them.

To be acceptable, shell eggs must also meet the following criteria:

- **Odor:** no odor
- **Shells:** clean and unbroken

The following criteria are grounds for rejecting shell eggs:

- **Odor:** sulfur smell or off odor
- **Shells:** dirty or cracked (see *Exhibit 6i*)

6j Acceptable versus
Unacceptable Cheese

✓

✗

Dairy Products

Purchase only pasteurized dairy products, because unpasteurized products are potential sources of foodborne pathogens such as *Listeria monocytogenes* and *Salmonella* spp. All milk and milk products should be labeled "Grade A." This means they meet standards for quality and sanitary processing methods set by the FDA and the U.S. Public Health Service. Dairy products with the Grade A label—such as cream, cottage cheese, butter, and ice cream—are made with pasteurized milk.

Milk and dairy products should be received at 41°F (5°C) or lower unless otherwise specified by law. Check with the proper regulatory agency for temperature requirements.

In the United States, all cheese must meet certain standards of identity. For a product to be called "cheddar" or "mozzarella," for example, the government specifies ingredients that must be used, maximum moisture content, minimum fat content, and general characteristics.

To be acceptable, dairy products must also meet the following criteria:

- **Milk:** sweetish flavor

- **Butter:** sweet flavor; uniform color; firm texture

- **Cheese:** typical flavor and texture; uniform color; clean and unbroken rind (see *Exhibit 6j*)

The following criteria are grounds for rejecting dairy products:

- **Milk:** sour, bitter, or moldy taste; off odor; expired sell-by date

- **Butter:** sour, bitter, or moldy taste; uneven color; soft texture; contains foreign matter

- **Cheese:** abnormal flavor or texture; uneven color; unnatural mold; unclean or broken rind (see *Exhibit 6j*)

Fresh Produce

Fresh fruit and vegetables have different temperature requirements for transportation and storage. No specific temperature is mandated by regulation with the exception of cut melons, cut tomatoes and cut leafy greens, which must be

Receiving   Storing
Purchasing   Preparing
The Flow of Food   Cooking
Serving   Holding
Reheating   Cooling

6k   Unacceptable Produce

Reject any produce with signs of spoilage.

received and stored at 41°F (5°C) or lower. When receiving fresh-cut produce, reject any items that have passed their expiration date.

Reject deliveries if there is evidence of mishandling or insect infestation (including insect eggs and egg cases). Produce should also be rejected if there are signs of spoilage, including:

*   Mold (see *Exhibit 6k*)

*   Cuts

*   Wilting and mushiness

*   Discoloration and dull appearance

*   Unpleasant odors and tastes

Keep in mind that what applies to one item may not apply to another. For example, peaches with cuts in them could be considered poor quality, but potatoes and carrots with cuts would be considered acceptable. Discoloration in produce may vary as well. For example, oranges may actually revert to a green color without affecting the quality of the orange or its juice.

If produce items are pinched, squeezed, or roughly handled, they will bruise and spoil more quickly. Bruised produce can pose a hazard because the bruises provide a potential entry point for pathogens.

Use smell and taste to help determine product quality. Unpleasant odors will tell you when a product is not acceptable. With fruit, sometimes taste is the best test. Outer peels or skins can be blemished without affecting flavor or quality. Be sure to wash or peel fruit and vegetables carefully before tasting them.

Since there are so many ways produce can show signs of spoilage, employees need to learn not only how to identify obviously unacceptable produce, but also how to identify produce that will spoil quickly in storage. Most produce should not sit out at room temperature. Fresh fruit and vegetables are highly perishable and should be put into storage quickly. In general, produce should not be washed before it is stored. While washing would not hurt leafy green items, many other products are likely to decay faster if washed before storage. This is especially true for mushrooms and berries. Produce should be washed correctly before preparing and serving it.

Prepackaged Juice

Prepackaged juice must be purchased from a supplier with a HACCP plan. The juice must be treated (e.g., pasteurized) to prevent, eliminate, or reduce pathogens or have a warning label.

Refrigerated Ready-to-Eat Food

6l Unacceptable Refrigerated Ready-to-Eat Food

Reject product with holes or tears in the packaging.

More and more establishments are purchasing ready-to-eat food items, such as precut meats, salads containing TCS food, and refrigerated entrées that only require heating. These items must be received at 41°F (5°C) or lower unless otherwise specified. Packaging must be intact and in good condition. Reject product with holes or tears in packaging (see *Exhibit 6l*) or expired use-by dates.

Frozen Processed Food

Many establishments receive processed food items that are frozen. These items should be delivered frozen. They should also be received in packaging that is intact and in good condition. It is important to check for signs of thawing and refreezing. Simply because a product is frozen upon receipt does not mean it did not thaw and refreeze during prior handling. Obvious signs are blocks of ice or liquid at the bottom of the case, water stains on the packaging, or large ice crystals on the packaging or the product itself. (See *Exhibit 6m.*) Other signs include product discoloration or dryness and stains on the outer packaging.

6m Unacceptable Frozen Processed Food

Reject product with signs of thawing and refreezing, such as large ice crystals on the product.

Reduced Oxygen Packaged (ROP) Food

As you will recall, some bacteria need oxygen to grow. Reducing the oxygen inside food packaging can prevent this growth. This type of packaging is often referred to as ROP, or reduced oxygen packaging. There are several methods used by manufacturers to do this. These include MAP, vacuum packaging, and *sous vide*.

MAP stands for **modified atmosphere packaging.** By this method, the air inside of a package is altered using gases such as carbon dioxide and nitrogen. Many fresh-cut produce items are packaged this way.

Vacuum-packed food, such as bacon, is processed by removing the air around the product sealed in a package.

6n   Unacceptable ROP Food

Reject product with torn or leaking packaging.

6o   Unacceptable Canned Food

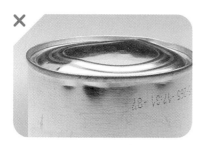

Reject cans with swollen ends, rust, or dents.

By the *sous vide* method, cooked or partially cooked food is vacuum packed in individual pouches and then chilled. This food is heated for service in the establishment. Frozen, precooked meals are typically packaged this way.

ROP food that is refrigerated should be received at 41°F (5°C) or lower unless otherwise specified by the manufacturer. Product that is frozen should be received frozen.

To be acceptable, ROP food must also meet the following criteria:

- **Packaging:** intact and in good condition; valid code dates

- **Product:** acceptable color

The following criteria are grounds for rejecting ROP food:

- **Packaging:** torn or leaking packages (see *Exhibit 6n*); expired code dates

- **Product:** unacceptable color; slime, bubbles, or excessive liquid

Canned Food

Canned products seem to pose little threat. Most have a fairly long shelf life and are usually used long before they have a chance to spoil. However, canned products provide a good environment for the microorganism that causes botulism. Always check cans for expired code dates and damage.

The following criteria are grounds for rejecting canned products (see *Exhibit 6o*):

- **Swollen ends.** One or both ends of a can may bulge from gas produced by the presence of chemicals or the growth of foodborne bacteria inside. If one end bulges out when the other is pressed, discard the can, because it has not gone through the proper heat-treating process to eliminate foodborne microorganisms.

- **Leaks and flawed seals.** If there are any leaks, flaws, or irregularities along the top or side seals, reject the can.

- **Rust.** If a can is rusted, it should be rejected because the contents may be too old or the rust may have eaten holes in the can. This can lead to contamination.

- **Dents.** Do not accept cans with dents along side or top seams. Reject cans with dents large enough to make it difficult to open them with a can opener because the seams may be broken. Check with your regulatory agency regarding dented cans. Some jurisdictions do not allow them.

- **Missing labels.** Any cans received without labels should be rejected.

Dry Food

Most microorganisms need moisture to grow, which is why dry food has a much longer shelf life than fresh food. In order to remain safe, dry food must remain dry and should be rejected when there are signs of wetness.

Because it can be stored at room temperature, dry food might not be sealed and stored as securely as other food. For this reason, it often attracts insects and rodents. Since these pests can easily get into packages, it is critical to check for signs. You can often spot insects or insect eggs in dry products such as cereal or flour by sprinkling some of the product on brown paper.

To be acceptable, dry food must also meet the following criteria:

- **Packaging:** intact and in good condition

- **Product:** normal color and odor

The following criteria are grounds for rejecting dry food:

- **Packaging:** holes, tears, or punctures; dampness or water stains on outer cases and inner packaging, which indicates it has been wet (see *Exhibit 6p*)

- **Product:** abnormal color or odor; spots of mold or slimy appearance; contains insects, insect eggs, or rodent droppings

6p   Unacceptable Dry Food

Reject dry food when packaging has holes or tears or shows signs of prior wetness.

6q   Unacceptable UHT Food

Reject UHT products if packaging is punctured or seals are broken.

Ultra-High Temperature (UHT) Pasteurized and Aseptically Packaged Food

Some food is heat-treated at very high temperatures to kill microorganisms in a process called ultra-high temperature (UHT) pasteurization. This food is often also aseptically packaged—sealed under sterile conditions to keep it from being contaminated. Examples include some puddings, juices, and creamers and milk products.

If food has been UHT pasteurized and aseptically packaged, it can be received at room temperature. If it has been UHT pasteurized but not aseptically packaged, it should be received at the temperature specified by the manufacturer or at 41°F (5°C) or lower. Packaging and seals must be intact. Reject the product if packaging is punctured or seals are broken. (See *Exhibit 6q*.)

Hot TCS Food

Occasionally, operators may receive a shipment of hot TCS food. It must be properly cooked as required by local or federal codes. If you purchase hot food, make sure suppliers have a HACCP plan or other means of documenting proper cooking methods and temperatures.

Hot TCS food must be received at 135°F (57°C) or higher. The shipping container must be able to maintain this temperature, and it must be undamaged. Reject the product if it does not meet these requirements.

Nonfood Items with a Food-Contact Surface

The packaging of nonfood items with a food-contact surface should protect the items from contamination. It should be intact and clean. Reject these items if packaging has any of the following problems:

- Tears, holes, or punctures

- Broken cartons or seals

- Dirty wrappers

- Leaks, dampness, or water stains

- Signs of pests or pest damage

- Expired code or use-by dates

Summary

Although federal and state agencies regulate and monitor the production and transportation of food such as meat, poultry, seafood, eggs, dairy products, and canned goods, it is your responsibility to check the quality and safety of food that comes into your establishment.

Make sure suppliers are getting their products from approved sources—those that have been inspected and are in compliance with local, state, and federal law. Develop a relationship with your suppliers, and get to know their food safety practices.

Operators must plan delivery schedules so products can be handled promptly and correctly. Employees assigned to receive deliveries should be trained to inspect food properly as well as to distinguish between products that are acceptable and those that are not. They should also be authorized to reject products that do not meet company standards and to sign for products that do.

All products arriving at the establishment should meet agreed-upon standards. Packaging should be clean and undamaged. Use-by dates should be current. Food should not show signs of mishandling.

Products must be delivered at the proper temperature. All food items—especially meat, poultry, and fish—should be checked for proper color, texture, and odor. Live, molluscan shellfish and crustaceans must be delivered alive. Eggs should be inspected for freshness and for dirty and cracked shells. Dairy products must be checked for freshness. Produce should be fresh and undamaged. Refrigerated ready-to-eat items should be received at 41°F (5°C) or lower unless otherwise specified. Packaging should be intact and in good condition. Frozen food should be inspected for signs of thawing and refreezing. ROP food should not bubble, appear slimy, or have excessive liquid. Canned food must be carefully examined for signs of damage. Dry food should be inspected for pest infestation and moisture. Hot TCS food must be delivered at 135°F (57°C) or higher.

Apply Your Knowledge

① **What was done incorrectly?**

A Case in Point 1

On Monday, a large food delivery arrived at the Sunnydale Nursing Home during the busy lunch hour. It included cases of frozen ground beef patties, canned vegetables, frozen shrimp, fresh tomatoes, a case of potatoes, and fresh chicken.

Betty, the new assistant manager, thought the best thing to do was to put everything away and check it later, since she was very busy. She told Ed, in charge of receiving, to sign for the delivery and put the food into storage. Ed asked her if it would be better to ask the delivery driver to come back later. Since she needed the chicken for dinner, Betty asked Ed to accept the delivery now, and then she went back to the front of the house.

Ed put the frozen shrimp and ground beef patties in the freezer and the fresh chicken in the refrigerator. Then he put the fresh tomatoes, potatoes, and canned vegetables in dry storage. When he was finished, he went back to work in the kitchen.

For answers, please turn to the Answer Key.

Apply Your Knowledge

① What was done wrong?

② What could be the result?

A Case in Point 2

ABC Seafood makes its usual Thursday afternoon delivery to The Fish House. John, a prep cook, is the only person in the kitchen when the driver rings the bell at the back door. The kitchen manager, who is in charge of receiving, is in a managers' meeting. The chef is out on an errand, and the rest of the kitchen staff are on break, although some are still in the restaurant.

John follows the driver onto the dock, where the driver unloads two crates of ice-packed fresh fish, bags of live mussels, two buckets of live oysters, a case of shucked oysters in plastic containers, and a case each of frozen shrimp and frozen lobster tails. John goes back into the kitchen to get a bimetallic stemmed thermometer and remembers to look in the chef's office for a copy of the order form. He takes both out to the dock and begins to inspect the shipment.

John checks the products against both the order sheet and the invoice, and then begins to check product temperatures. First, he checks the temperature of the shucked oysters by taking the cover off one container and inserting the thermometer stem into it. The thermometer reads 45°F (7°C).

After wiping the thermometer stem on his apron, John checks the internal temperature of a whole fish packed in ice. Finally, he reaches into one of the buckets of live oysters with his hand to see if it feels cold. He notices a few mussels and oysters with open and broken shells. He removes those with broken shells, knowing the chef will not use them.

John records all his findings on the order sheet he took from the chef's office, signs for the delivery, and starts putting the products away. He first puts away the live shellfish. Then he puts the shucked oysters and fresh fish in the refrigerator and the shrimp and lobster into the freezer.

For answers, please turn to the Answer Key.

Apply Your Knowledge

Use these questions to review the concepts presented in this chapter.

Discussion Questions

① What are some general guidelines for receiving food safely?

② What are proper methods for checking the temperatures of fresh poultry delivered on ice and bulk milk? What should the temperature be for each?

③ What are three conditions that would result in rejecting a shipment of fresh poultry?

④ What types of external damage to cans are cause for rejection?

For answers, please turn to the Answer Key.

Study Questions

Circle the best answer to each question.

① **What is the most important factor in choosing an approved food supplier?**

A   It has a HACCP program or other food safety system.

B   It has documented manufacturing and packing practices.

C   Its warehouse is close to the establishment, reducing shipping time.

D   It has been inspected and complies with local, state, and federal laws.

② **Raw, shucked shellfish that is received in a container bigger than one-half gallon (1.9 L) must have the packer's name, the packer's address, a certification number, and a**

A   shellstock identification tag.

B   shucked date.

C   harvest date.

D   USDA inspection mark.

Continued on next page ▶

> ► *Continued from previous page*

③ **What is the maximum acceptable receiving temperature for fresh beef?**

A 35°F (2°C)

B 41°F (5°C)

C 45°F (7°C)

D 50°F (10°C)

④ **What is the warmest acceptable receiving temperature for eggs?**

A 32°F (0°C)

B 41°F (5°C)

C 45°F (7°C)

D 50°F (10°C)

⑤ **Large ice crystals in a case of frozen food are evidence that the product may have been**

A received at 6°F to 10°F (–14°C to –12°C).

B stored at 6°F to 10°F (–14°C to –12°C).

C shipped correctly.

D thawed and refrozen.

⑥ **How should cartons of coleslaw be checked for correct receiving temperature?**

A Check the interior air temperature of the delivery truck.

B Open a carton and insert a thermometer stem into the food.

C Place a thermometer against the outside of the carton.

D Touch the carton to see if it is cold.

⑦ **A box of sirloin steaks carries a state department of agriculture inspection stamp. What does this stamp indicate?**

A   The steaks are free of disease-causing microorganisms.

B   The meat and processing plant have met USDA or a state department of agriculture's standards.

C   The meat wholesaler meets USDA or a state department of agriculture's quality-grading standards.

D   The farm that supplied the beef uses only certified animal feed.

⑧ **Which food should be rejected?**

A   Beef that is bright cherry red in color

B   Milk received at 41°F (5°C)

C   Prepackaged juice treated to reduce pathogens

D   Live shellfish received without shellstock tags

⑨ **Which food requires a USDA inspection stamp?**

A   Dry rice

B   Egg products

C   Fresh produce

D   Sushi-grade tuna

For answers, please turn to the Answer Key.

Additional Resources

Articles and Texts

Association of Food and Drug Officials. *A Pocket Guide to Can Defects.* Available online through http://afdo.org/afdo/publication/index.cfm.

Feinstein, Andrew H., and John M. Stefanelli. *Purchasing: Selection and Procurement for the Hospitality Industry,* 7th Edition. Hoboken, NJ: John Wiley & Sons, 2007.

National Restaurant Association Educational Foundation. *Inventory and Purchasing.* East Rutherford, NJ: Prentice Hall, 2006.

Reed, Lewis. Specs: *The Foodservice and Purchasing Specification Manual,* 2nd Edition. Hoboken, NJ: John Wiley & Sons, 2006.

Warfel, M.C., and Marion Cremer. *Purchasing for Food Service Managers,* 5th Edition. Richmond, CA: McCutchan Publishing, 2005.

Web Sites

American Egg Board
aeb.org

American Lamb Board
americanlambboard.org

American Mushroom Institute
americanmushroom.org

Association of Food, Beverage, and Consumer Products Companies
gmabrands.com

Conference for Food Protection
foodprotect.org

FDA Food Safety
www.fda.gov/Food/FoodSafety/default.htm

Gateway to Government Food Safety Information
foodsafety.gov

International Dairy Foods Association
idfa.org

Mushroom Council
mushroomcouncil.org

National Cattlemen's Beef Association: Beef for Foodservice Professionals
beeffoodservice.com

National Chicken Council
nationalchickencouncil.com

National Fisheries Institute
aboutseafood.com

National Frozen & Refrigerated Foods Association
nfraweb.org

National Pork Producers Council
nppc.org

National Turkey Federation
eatturkey.com

Produce Marketing Association
pma.com

United Fresh Produce Association
unitedfresh.org

USDA Food Safety and Inspection Service
www.fsis.usda.gov/

Western Growers
wga.com

Documents and Other Resources

2009 FDA Food Code
www.fda.gov/Food/FoodSafety/RetailFoodProtection/FoodCode/
FoodCode2009/default.htm

*Commodity-Specific Food Safety Guidelines for the Production and Harvest
of Lettuce and Leafy Greens Supply Chain*
www.fda.gov/downloads/Food/FoodSafety/Product-
SpecificInformation/FruitsVegetablesJuices/GuidanceComplianceRegul
atoryInformation/UCM169008.pdf

Commodity-Specific Food Safety Guidelines for the Melon Supply Chain
www.fda.gov/downloads/Food/FoodSafety/Product-
SpecificInformation/FruitsVegetablesJuices/
GuidanceComplianceRegulatoryInformation/UCM168625.pdf

Commodity-Specific Food Safety Guidelines for the Fresh-Tomato Supply Chain
www.fda.gov/downloads/Food/FoodSafety/Product-
SpecificInformation/FruitsVegetablesJuices/
GuidanceComplianceRegulatoryInformation/UCM171708.pdf

Current Good Manufacturing Practices
www.access.gpo.gov/nara/cfr/waisidx_06/21cfr110_06.html

Guide for the Control of Molluscan Shellfish
www.fda.gov/Food/FoodSafety/Product-
SpecificInformation/Seafood/FederalStatePrograms/
NationalShellfishSanitationProgram/ucm046353.htm

FDA Seafood Information and Resources
www.fda.gov/Food/FoodSafety/Product-SpecificInformation/Seafood/default.htm

Good Agricultural Practices: A Self-Audit for Growers and Handlers
ucgaps.ucdavis.edu

Interstate Certified Shellfish Shippers List
www.fda.gov/Food/FoodSafety/Product-
SpecificInformation/Seafood/FederalStatePrograms/InterstateShellfish
ShippersList/default.htm

7 The Flow of Food: Storage

Inside this chapter:

- General Storage Guidelines
- Types of Storage
- Storage Techniques
- Storing Specific Food

After completing this chapter, you should be able to:

- Store food to prevent contamination.
- Practice first-in-first-out (FIFO) product rotation.
- Ensure food is properly labeled and dated.
- Store food in appropriate storage containers.
- Store refrigerated, frozen, and dry food safely.

Key Terms

- First in, first out (FIFO)
- Refrigerated storage
- Frozen storage
- Dry storage
- Shelf life

Apply Your Knowledge

Check to see how much you know about the concepts in this chapter. Use the page references provided with each question to explore the topic.

Test Your Food Safety Knowledge

① **True or False:** Potato salad that has been prepared in-house and stored at 41°F (5°C) must be discarded after three days. *(See page 7-3.)*

② **True or False:** Food can be stored near chemicals as long as the chemicals are stored in sturdy, clearly labeled containers. *(See page 7-4.)*

③ **True or False:** Storing cans of stewed tomatoes at 65°F (18°C) is acceptable. *(See page 7-12.)*

④ **True or False:** Raw chicken must be stored below ready-to-eat food, such as pumpkin pie, if it is stored in the same walk-in refrigerator. *(See page 7-6.)*

⑤ **True or False:** If stored food has passed its expiration date, you should cook and serve it at once. *(See page 7-3.)*

For answers, please turn to the Answer Key.

Introduction

When food is stored improperly and not used in a timely manner, quality and safety suffer. Poor storage practices can cause food to spoil quickly, with potentially serious results.

General Storage Guidelines

Every facility has a wide variety of products that need to be stored. A few general rules can be applied to most storage situations:

- **Label food.** All ready-to-eat TCS food prepared on site that has been held for longer than twenty-four hours must be properly labeled. The label must include the name of the food and the date it should be sold, consumed, or discarded. If an item has been previously cooked and stored and is later mixed with another food item to make a new dish, the label on the new dish must indicate the discard date for the previously cooked item. For example, if ground beef has been cooked and stored at 41°F (5°C) or lower and later used to make

The Flow of Food

Receiving Storing
Purchasing Preparing
  Cooking
Serving Holding
Reheating Cooling

7a   Follow FIFO When Storing Food

One way to follow FIFO is to store products with the earliest use-by or expiration dates in front of products with later dates. Those stored in front are then used first.

meat sauce, the meat sauce must be labeled with the discard date of the ground beef.

- **Rotate products to ensure that the oldest inventory is used first.** The first in, first out (FIFO) method is commonly used to ensure that refrigerated, frozen, and dry products are properly rotated during storage. By this method, a product's use-by or expiration date is first identified. The products are then stored to ensure that the oldest are used first. One way to do this is to train employees to store products with the earliest use-by or expiration dates in front of products with later dates. Once shelved, those stored in front are used first. (See *Exhibit 7a.*)

- **Discard food that has passed its expiration date.** All ready-to-eat TCS food that has been prepared in-house can be stored for a maximum of seven days at 41°F (5°C) or lower before it must be thrown out.

- **Create a schedule to throw out stored food on a regular basis.** If a food item has not been sold or used by a specific date, throw it out, clean and sanitize the container, and refill the container with fresh product. For example, flour stored in plastic bins should be used within six to twelve months from the time it was placed in the bins. After that time period, discard the remaining flour, clean and sanitize the bins, and refill them with new flour.

- **Store food in containers intended for food.** The containers should be durable, leak-proof, and able to be sealed or covered. Never use empty food containers to store chemicals. Never put food in empty chemical containers.

- **Keep TCS food at 41°F (5°C) or lower, or at 135°F (57°C) or higher.** Store deliveries as soon as they have been inspected. Take out only as much food as you can prepare at one time, and put prepared food away until needed. Properly cool and store cooked food as soon as it is no longer needed. (See Chapter 8 for more information on cooling cooked food.)

- **Check temperatures of stored food and storage areas.** Temperatures should be checked at the beginning of the shift. Many establishments use a preshift checklist to guide employees through this process.

7b Improper Storage

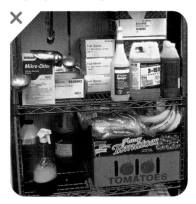

Never store food near chemicals or cleaning supplies.

Key Point
Store TCS food in refrigerators at an internal temperature of 41°F (5°C) or lower.

- **Store food, linens, and single-use items in designated storage areas.** These items should be stored away from walls and at least six inches (15 centimeters) off the floor. Do not store food near chemicals or cleaning supplies. (See *Exhibit 7b.*) Store dirty linens in a clean, washable container in a way that prevents the contamination of food.

- **Keep all storage areas clean and dry.** Floors, walls, and shelving in refrigerators, freezers, dry storerooms, and heated holding cabinets should be properly cleaned on a regular basis. Clean up spills and leaks right away to keep them from contaminating other food.

- **Clean dollies, carts, transporters, and trays often.**

Types of Storage

Most restaurants and foodservice establishments have several types of storage areas in their facilities. The most common include:

- **Refrigerated storage.** These areas are typically used to hold TCS food at 41°F (5°C) or lower. (Some TCS food might be held at a different temperature, as indicated by the food's manufacturer or your regulatory authority.) Refrigeration slows the growth of microorganisms and helps keep them from growing to levels high enough to cause illness.

- **Frozen storage.** These areas are used to hold frozen food at temperatures that will keep it frozen. Freezing does not kill all microorganisms, but it does slow their growth substantially.

- **Dry storage.** These areas are used to hold dry and canned food. To maintain the quality of this food, dry-storage areas should be kept at the appropriate temperature and humidity levels. Storerooms should be clean, well ventilated, and well lighted.

Managers should monitor storage areas because improper storage practices can affect food safety. For example, an overstocked refrigerator may not be able to hold the proper temperature and may not allow stock to be rotated properly.

Storage spaces should also be located to ease the flow of food through the operation and to prevent food contamination. They must be accessible to receiving, food-preparation, and cooking areas but located so that food is stored away from dishwashing and garbage areas.

Receiving · Storing · Preparing · Cooking · Holding · Cooling · Reheating · Serving · Purchasing

The Flow of Food

Storage Techniques

A few commonsense rules apply to each of these storage areas. Make sure employees follow these rules to keep food safe.

Refrigerated Storage

Keeping food as cold as possible without freezing extends its shelf life, the amount of time food will remain suitable for use. Ideal storage temperatures and shelf life will vary depending on the food. Fruit and vegetables will freeze if stored at temperatures ideal for seafood. Meat and poultry will have a shorter shelf life if stored at temperatures better suited for produce. If possible, store food such as meat and poultry in separate refrigerators to hold them at optimal temperatures. If this is impractical, store meat, poultry, seafood, and dairy products in the coldest part of the unit, away from the door.

While there are many types of refrigeration equipment available to operators, from walk-in refrigerators to refrigerated drawers, some general guidelines apply when using any of them:

- **Set refrigerators to the proper temperature.** The setting must keep the internal temperature of the food at 41°F (5°C) or lower unless otherwise indicated by the manufacturer or your regulatory authority. At least once during each shift, check the temperature of the unit. Use hanging thermometers in the warmest part of the refrigerator. Some units have a readout panel outside to check the temperature without opening the door. These should also be checked for accuracy.

- **Monitor food temperature regularly.** Randomly sample the internal temperature of stored food using a calibrated thermometer. (See *Exhibit 7c*.)

- **Schedule regular maintenance for refrigerators.** This will help keep food at the right temperatures.

- **Do not overload refrigerators.** Storing too many products prevents good airflow and makes units work harder to stay cold.

- **Use open shelving.** Lining shelves with aluminum foil, sheet pans, or paper restricts circulation of cold air in the unit.

7c   Monitor Refrigerated Food Temperatures Regularly

Randomly sample a food's internal temperature using a calibrated thermometer.

- **Keep refrigerator doors closed as much as possible.** Frequent opening lets warm air inside, which can affect food safety and make units work harder. Consider using cold curtains in walk-in refrigerators to help maintain temperatures.

- **Wrap or cover all food properly.** Leaving food uncovered can lead to cross-contamination.

7d   Improper Storage of Different Raw and Ready-to-Eat Food

Raw meat must never be stored above ready-to-eat food.

- **Store raw meat, poultry, and seafood separately from ready-to-eat food.** If raw and ready-to-eat food cannot be stored separately, store ready-to-eat food above raw meat, poultry, and seafood. This will prevent raw food juices from dripping onto ready-to-eat food. (See *Exhibit 7d.*) It is also recommended that raw meat, poultry, and seafood be stored in the following top-to-bottom order: seafood, whole cuts of beef and pork, ground meat and ground fish, whole and ground poultry. (See *Exhibit 7e.*) This order is based on the minimum internal cooking temperature of each food.

Frozen Storage

Following are some general guidelines for using freezers:

- **Set freezers to a temperature that will keep products frozen.** This temperature will vary from product to product. A temperature that is good for one product may affect the quality of another.

- **Check freezer temperatures regularly.** Use a calibrated thermometer to check the accuracy of hanging thermometers or unit readout.

7e   Refrigerator Storage

Recommended top-to-bottom order for storing different raw food in the same refrigerator

- **Place frozen food deliveries in freezers as soon as they have been inspected.** Never hold frozen food at room temperature. Raw meat, poultry, and seafood can be stored with or above ready-to-eat food in a freezer if all of the items have been commercially processed and packaged.

- **Ensure good airflow inside freezers.** This can be accomplished by using open shelving, keeping the door closed as much as possible, and keeping employees from overloading units.

- **Defrost freezer units on a regular basis.** They will operate more efficiently when free of frost. Move food to another freezer while defrosting.

- **Clearly label food prepared on site that is intended for frozen storage.**

- **Keep the unit closed as much as possible.** Frequent opening of the freezer doors allows warm air inside, which can affect food safety. Consider using cold curtains in walk-in freezers to help maintain temperatures.

Dry Storage

Dry food remains safe and retains quality if held in the right conditions. When storing dry food, follow these guidelines:

- **Keep storerooms cool and dry.** Moisture and heat are the biggest dangers to dry and canned food. For optimum quality and to assure safety, the temperature for the storeroom should be between 50°F and 70°F (10°C and 21°C).

- **Make sure storerooms are well ventilated.** This will help keep temperature and humidity constant throughout the storage area.

- **Store dry food away from walls and at least six inches (fifteen centimeters) off the floor.**

- **Keep dry food out of direct sunlight.**

Storing Specific Food

The general storage guidelines previously discussed apply to most food. However, certain types of food have special requirements.

Meat

- Store meat immediately after delivery and inspection in its own storage unit or in the coldest part of the refrigerator. Fresh meat must be held at an internal temperature of 41°F (5°C) or lower. Frozen meat should be stored at a temperature that will keep it frozen.

- If meat is removed from its original packaging, wrap it in airtight, moisture-proof material or place it in clean and sanitized containers.

- Primal cuts, quarters, sides of raw meat, and slab bacon can be hung on clean and sanitized hooks or can be placed on sanitized racks. To prevent cross-contamination, do not store meat above any other food.

Poultry

- Store fresh raw poultry at an internal temperature of 41°F (5°C) or lower. Frozen poultry should be stored at temperatures that will keep it frozen. If it has been removed from its original packaging, place it in airtight containers or wrap it in airtight material.

- Ice-packed poultry can be stored in a refrigerator as is. Use containers that are self-draining. Change the ice, and sanitize the container often.

Fish

Fresh fish is very sensitive to time-temperature abuse and can deteriorate quickly if handled improperly:

- Store fresh fish at an internal temperature of 41°F (5°C) or lower. Keep fillets and steaks in original packaging, or tightly wrap them in moisture-proof materials. Fresh, whole fish can be packed in flaked or crushed ice, and ice beds must be self-draining. Change the ice and clean and sanitize the container regularly.

- Store frozen fish at temperatures that will keep it frozen.

Key Point

Store fresh raw meat, poultry, and fish at an internal temperature of 41°F (5°C) or lower.

Receiving Storing Preparing Cooking Holding Cooling Reheating Serving Purchasing

The Flow of Food

Shellfish

Store live shellfish in its original container at an air temperature of 45°F (7°C) or lower. Shellstock identification tags must be kept on file for ninety days from the date the last shellfish was sold or served from the container.

Live, molluscan shellfish (clams, oysters, mussels, scallops) can be stored in a display tank under one of two conditions:

❶ The tank carries a sign stating that the shellfish are for display only.

❷ For shellfish to be served to customers, a variance must be obtained from the local health department. To obtain a variance, a HACCP plan must be submitted showing that:

○ Water from other tanks will not flow into the display tank.

○ Using the display tank will not affect product quality or safety.

○ Shellstock ID tags have been retained as required.

Store shucked shellfish at an internal temperature of 41°F (5°C) or lower.

Eggs

- Eggs received at an air temperature of 45°F (7°C), in compliance with laws governing their shipment from suppliers, must be placed immediately after inspection in refrigeration equipment capable of maintaining an air temperature of 45°F (7°C) or lower. Maintain constant temperature and humidity levels in refrigerators used to store eggs.

- Do not wash eggs before storing them, because they are washed and sanitized at the packing facility.

- Use the FIFO method of stock rotation. Plan to use all eggs within four to five weeks of the packing date.

- Keep shell eggs in cold storage right up until the time they are used. Take out only as many eggs as are needed for immediate use.

- Store frozen egg products at temperatures that will keep them frozen.

- Store liquid eggs according to the manufacturers' recommendations.

- Dried egg products can be stored in a cool, dry storeroom. Once they are reconstituted (mixed with water), store them in the refrigerator at 41°F (5°C) or lower. Do not reconstitute more dried egg product than is needed for immediate use.

Dairy Products

- Store dairy products at 41°F (5°C) or lower.

- Always use the FIFO method of stock rotation. Discard products if they have passed their use-by or expiration dates.

Fresh Produce

- Cut melons, cut tomatoes and cut leafy greens must be stored at 41°F (5°C) or lower, because they are TCS food.

Key Point

When soaking or storing produce in standing water or an ice-water slurry, do not mix different items or multiple batches of the same item.

- Other fruit and vegetables have various temperature requirements for storage. While many whole, raw fruit and vegetables can be stored at 41°F (5°C) or lower, not all will be stored at this temperature. Work with your produce supplier to determine the best storage temperature for the products you purchase. Whole, raw produce and raw, cut vegetables—such as celery, carrots, and radishes—delivered packed in ice can be stored as is. The containers must be self-draining, and ice should be changed regularly.

- Fruit and vegetables kept in the refrigerator can dry out quickly. Keep the relative humidity at 85 to 95 percent.

- Although most produce can be stored in the refrigerator, avocados, bananas, pears, and tomatoes ripen best at room temperature.

- Most produce should not be washed before storage. Moisture promotes the growth of mold in many instances. Instead, wash produce before preparing or serving it.

- When soaking or storing produce in standing water or an ice-water slurry, do not mix different items or multiple batches of the same item.

The Flow of Food

Receiving — Storing — Preparing — Cooking — Holding — Cooling — Reheating — Serving — Purchasing

- Store whole citrus fruit, hard-rind squash, eggplant, and root vegetables—such as potatoes, sweet potatoes, rutabagas, and onions—in a cool, dry storeroom. Temperatures of 60°F to 70°F (16°C to 21°C) are best. Make sure containers are well ventilated. Store onions away from other vegetables that might absorb odor.

ROP Food

Key Point

Always store ROP food at temperatures recommended by the manufacturer or at 41°F (5°C) or lower.

- Always store modified-atmosphere packaged (MAP), vacuum-packed, and *sous vide* food at temperatures recommended by the manufacturer or at 41°F (5°C) or lower. Frozen product should be stored at temperatures that will keep it frozen. Store and handle these products carefully.

- Vacuum packaging will not stop the growth of microorganisms that do not require oxygen to grow. ROP products are especially susceptible to the growth of *Clostridium botulinum*. Discard product if the package is torn or slimy, if it contains excessive liquid, or if the product bubbles, indicating the possible growth of *Clostridium botulinum*.

- Always check the expiration date before using MAP, vacuum-packed, and *sous vide* products. Labels should clearly list contents, storage temperature, preparation instructions, and a use-by date.

- Operators who package ROP food on site (such as sauces and soups) must follow specific rules for packaging and labeling. Consult your local regulatory authority for guidance.

UHT and Aseptically Packaged Food

- Food that has been pasteurized at ultra-high temperatures (UHT) and aseptically packaged (which means the packaging is free of microorganisms) can be stored at room temperature. Since much of this food is served cold, such as milk and pudding, you might want to store it in the refrigerator.

- Once opened, store UHT, aseptically packaged food in the refrigerator at 41°F (5°C) or lower.

- UHT products not aseptically packaged must be stored at an internal temperature of 41°F (5°C) or lower.

Canned Goods

- Store canned goods at a temperature between 50°F and 70°F (10°C to 21°C). Even canned food spoils over time. Higher storage temperatures may shorten shelf life. Acidic food, such as canned tomatoes, does not last as long as food low in acid. The acid can also form pinholes in the metal over time.

- Discard damaged cans.

- Keep storerooms dry. Too much moisture will cause cans to rust.

- Wipe cans clean with a sanitized cloth before opening them to help prevent dirt from falling into the contents of the can.

Dry Food

- Store dry food at a temperature between 50°F and 70°F (10°C to 21°C).

- Keep flour, cereal, and grain products such as pasta or crackers in airtight containers. They can quickly become stale in a humid room and can become moldy if there is too much moisture.

- Before using dry food, check containers or packages for damage from insects or rodents. Cereal and grain products are favorite targets for these pests.

- Salt and sugar, if stored in the right conditions, can be held almost indefinitely.

Summary

When food is stored improperly, quality and safety will suffer. Although different food has different storage needs, some common rules apply. Food should be stored in designated areas and rotated to ensure that the oldest product is used first. It should also be stored in its original packaging.

All ready-to-eat TCS food that is prepared on site and held for longer than twenty-four hours must be properly labeled. The label must include the name of the food and the date it should be sold, consumed, or discarded. It can be stored for a maximum of seven days at 41°F (5°C) or lower before it must be discarded. Throw out all food that has passed the manufacturers' use-by or expiration date. Check the temperatures of stored food and the storage area regularly, and keep these areas clean and dry to prevent contamination.

Refrigerators must be set to the proper temperature to slow the growth of microorganisms. The setting must keep the internal temperature of the food at 41°F (5°C) or lower. Do not line refrigerator shelves, overload units, or open doors too often. These practices make units work harder to maintain the temperature inside. If possible, store raw meat, poultry, and seafood separately from cooked and ready-to-eat food to prevent cross-contamination. If not, store these items below ready-to-eat food. Product temperatures should be checked periodically.

Freezers should be kept at a temperature that will keep product frozen. Unit temperatures should be checked often.

Dry-storage areas should be kept cool and dry and should be clean and well ventilated to maintain food quality. Food in dry storage should be stored away from walls and at least six inches (fifteen centimeters) off the floor. Do not store food products near chemicals or cleaning supplies, because food can easily become contaminated. Empty food containers should never be used to store chemicals.

Fresh meat, poultry, fish, and dairy products should be stored at 41°F (5°C) or lower. Fish and poultry can be stored under refrigeration in crushed ice as long as the containers are self-draining, the ice is changed, and the container is cleaned and sanitized regularly. Eggs should be refrigerated at an air temperature of 45°F (7°C) or lower, right up until they are used.

Live, molluscan shellfish should be stored in their original containers at an air temperature of 45°F (7°C). Fresh produce has various temperature requirements for storage. Produce should not be washed before storage because it can promote mold growth. ROP food should be stored at temperatures recommended by the manufacturer. Packages should be checked for signs of contamination, including bubbling, excessive liquid, tears, and slime. Once opened, UHT and aseptically packaged food should be stored in the refrigerator at 41°F (5°C) or lower. Dry and canned food should be stored at temperatures between 50°F and 70°F (10°C and 21°C).

Apply Your Knowledge

A Case in Point 1

① What storage errors were made?

② What food items are at risk?

Angie, a cook at the Sunnydale Nursing Home, began deboning chicken breasts that were stored earlier. When she finished, she put the chicken on an uncovered sheet pan and stored the pan in the refrigerator. She carefully placed the raw chicken on the top shelf, away from the hot soup. Next, Angie iced a carrot cake she had baked that morning. She put the carrot cake in the refrigerator on the shelf directly below the chicken breasts.

For answers, please turn to the Answer Key.

Apply Your Knowledge   A Case in Point 2

① What storage errors occurred?

A shipment was delivered to Enrico's Italian Restaurant on a warm summer day. Alyce, who was in charge of receiving for the restaurant, inspected the shipment and immediately proceeded to store the items. She loaded a case of sour cream on the dolly and wheeled it over to the reach-in refrigerator. When she opened the refrigerator, she noticed that it was tightly packed; however, she was able to squeeze the case into a spot on the top shelf. Next, Alyce wheeled several cases of fresh ground beef over to the walk-in refrigerator. She noticed that the readout on the outside of the walk-in indicated 39°F (4°C). Alyce pushed through the cold curtains and bumped into Mary, who had just cleaned the shelving in the unit and was lining it with new aluminum foil. Alyce returned to the receiving area and loaded several cases of pasta on the dolly. She was sweating as she stacked the boxes on the shelving unit and gave a quick glance at the thermometer in the dry-storage room, which read 85°F (29°C). When she was finished stacking the boxes, Alyce returned the dolly to the receiving area.

For answers, please turn to the Answer Key.

Apply Your Knowledge   Discussion Questions

Use these questions to review the concepts presented in this chapter.

① What is the recommended top-to-bottom order for storing the following food in the same refrigerator: raw trout, an uncooked beef roast, raw chicken, and raw ground beef?

② What are the storage requirements for live shellfish?

③ What can be done to help keep food safe in dry-storage areas?

④ Explain the FIFO method of stock rotation.

For answers, please turn to the Answer Key.

Study Questions

Circle the best answer to each question.

① In top-to-bottom order, how should a fresh pork roast, fresh salmon, a carton of lettuce, and a pan of fresh chicken breasts be stored in a cooler?

A Lettuce, fresh salmon, fresh pork roast, fresh chicken breasts

B Fresh salmon, fresh pork roast, fresh chicken breasts, lettuce

C Lettuce, fresh chicken breasts, fresh pork roast, fresh salmon

D Fresh salmon, lettuce, fresh chicken breasts, fresh pork roast

② Where should raw poultry be placed in a cooler?

A On the top shelf

B Next to produce

C On the bottom shelf

D Above ready-to-eat food

③ Why is first in, first out (FIFO) storage used?

A To ensure that the oldest food is used first

B To ensure that the newest food is used first

C To reduce the time it takes to store new shipments

D To use food that has passed its expiration date

④ When storing ready-to-eat TCS food that was prepared on site, what information must be included on the label?

A Potential allergens

B Product ingredients

C Nutritional information

D Sell-by or discard date

⑤ What is the warmest temperature at which ground beef can be safely stored?

A 0°F (-17°C)

B 32°F (0°C)

C 41°F (5°C)

D 60°F (16°C)

⑥ **At what temperature should dry-storage rooms be kept?**

  A   35°F to 40°F (2°C to 5°C)

  B   40°F to 60°F (5°C to 16°C)

  C   50°F to 70°F (10°C to 21°C)

  D   75°F to 90°F (21°C to 27°C)

⑦ **When storing food using the FIFO method, the food with the earliest use-by dates should be stored**

  A   below food with later use-by dates.

  B   behind food with later use-by dates.

  C   in front of food with later use-by dates.

  D   alongside food with later use-by dates.

⑧ **A restaurant that has prepared tuna salad can store it at 41°F (5°C) or lower for a maximum of how many days?**

  A   1

  B   3

  C   7

  D   9

⑨ **It is important to avoid lining cooler shelves with aluminum foil because the foil**

  A   can restrict the flow of cold air.

  B   can give food a metallic flavor.

  C   reduces visibility.

  D   prevents leaks from reaching the floor drain.

⑩ **Which storage practice is correct?**

  A   Storing chicken at 41°F (5°C)

  B   Storing fresh lamb at 45°F (7°C)

  C   Storing eggs at 50°F (21°C)

  D   Storing canned goods at 80°F (27°C)

For answers, please turn to the Answer Key.

Additional Resources

Articles and Texts

Cadwallader, Keith R., and Hugo Weenen. *Freshness and Shelf Life of Foods.* New York: Oxford University Press, 2002.

Chen, Y., W. H. Ross, V. N. Scott, and D. E. Gombas. 2003. *Listeria monocytogenes*: Low Levels Equal Low Risk. *Journal of Food Protection.* 66 (4): 570.

Rosso, L., S. Bajard, J. P. Flandrois, T. C. Lahellec, J. Fournaud, and P. Viet. 1996. Differential Growth of *Listeria monocytogenes* at 4 and 8°C: Consequences for the Shelf Life of Chilled Products. *Journal of Food Protection.* 59 (9): 944.

Ryser, Elliot T., and Elmer H. Marth. *Listeria, Listeriosis and Food Safety, 3rd edition.* New York: Marcel Dekker, 2006.

Web Sites

American Egg Board
aeb.org

American Lamb Board
americanlambboard.org

American Mushroom Institute
americanmushroom.org

Association of Food, Beverage and Consumer Products Companies
gmabrands.com

Conference for Food Protection
foodprotect.org

FDA Food Safety
www.fda.gov/Food/FoodSafety/default.htm

FDA Food Establishment Plan Review Guide
www.fda.gov/Food/FoodSafety/RetailFoodProtection/
ComplianceEnforcement/ucm101639.htm

Gateway to Government Food Safety Information
foodsafety.gov
This Web site provides links to selected government food safety-related information.

International Dairy Foods Association
idfa.org

Mushroom Council
mushroomcouncil.org

National Cattlemen's Beef Association: Beef for Foodservice Professionals
beeffoodservice.com

National Chicken Council
nationalchickencouncil.com

National Fisheries Institute
aboutseafood.com

National Frozen & Refrigerated Foods Association
nfraweb.org

National Pork Producers Council
nppc.org

National Turkey Federation
eatturkey.com

NSF International
nsf.org

Produce Marketing Association
pma.com

Underwriters Laboratories, Inc.
ul.com

United Fresh Produce Association
unitedfresh.org

USDA Food Safety and Inspection Service
www.fsis.usda.gov/

Other Documents and Resources

2009 FDA Food Code
www.fda.gov/Food/FoodSafety/RetailFoodProtection/FoodCode/
FoodCode2009/default.htm

Food Establishment Plan Review Guide
www.fda.gov/Food/FoodSafety/RetailFoodProtection/ComplianceEnfor
cement/ucm101639.htm

Risk Assessment for Listeria monocytogenes in Deli Meats
www.fsis.usda.gov/OPPDE/rdad/FRPubs/97-013F/ListeriaReport.pdf

Seafood Information and Resources
www.fda.gov/Food/FoodSafety/Product-SpecificInformation/Seafood/
default.htm

8 The Flow of Food: Preparation

Inside this chapter:

- Thawing Food
- Preparing Specific Food
- Cooking Food
- Cooking Requirements for Specific Food
- Cooling Food
- Reheating Food

After completing this chapter, you should be able to:

- Identify proper methods for thawing food.
- Identify the minimum internal cooking time and temperatures for TCS food.
- Identify the proper procedure for cooking TCS food in a microwave.
- Identify methods and time and temperature requirements for cooling cooked food.
- Identify time and temperature requirements for reheating cooked, TCS food.
- Identify methods for preventing contamination and time-temperature abuse when preparing food.
- Recognize the importance of informing consumers of risks when serving raw or undercooked food.

Key Terms

- Slacking
- Food additives
- Minimum internal temperature
- Ice-water bath
- Ice paddle

Introduction

Once food has been received and stored safely, it is essential that it be prepared, cooked, cooled, and reheated with just as much care. It is at these points in the flow of food that the risk of cross-contamination and time-temperature abuse is greatest.

Thawing Food

Freezing food does not kill microorganisms. If frozen food is exposed to the temperature danger zone during thawing, any foodborne microorganisms present will begin to grow. For this reason, food should never be thawed at room temperature. (See *Exhibit 8a.*)

For example, suppose a cook needs to quickly thaw a twenty-pound turkey. Because he is in a hurry, he places the turkey in a pan on a prep counter to thaw overnight. When the turkey begins to thaw, the skin and outer layers are exposed to the

8a Thawing Food

Food must never be thawed at room temperature, since any microorganisms present can grow to dangerous levels.

8b   Acceptable Methods for Thawing Food

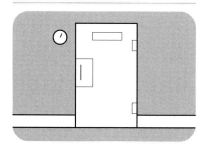

In refrigeration

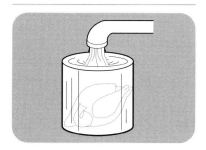

Submerged under running potable water

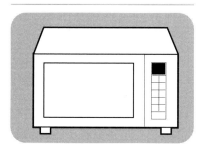

In a microwave oven

As part of cooking

temperature danger zone even though the core of the turkey is still frozen. This situation is hazardous because microorganisms present on the turkey may begin to grow.

To prevent this growth, there are only four acceptable methods for thawing TCS food (see *Exhibit 8b*):

- **Thaw food in a refrigerator at a product temperature of 41°F (5°C) or lower.** This method requires advance planning. Larger products, such as a turkey, can take several days to thaw completely in a refrigerator.

- **Submerge the food under running potable water at a temperature of 70°F (21°C) or lower.** Water flow must be strong enough to wash loose food particles into the overflow drain. Make sure the thawed product does not drip water onto other products or food-contact surfaces. Clean and sanitize the sink and work area before and after thawing food this way.

- **Thaw food in a microwave oven if it will be cooked immediately afterward.** Microwave thawing can actually start cooking the product, so do not use this method unless you intend to continue cooking the food immediately. Large items such as roasts or turkeys do not thaw well in the microwave.

- **Thaw food as part of the cooking process as long as the product reaches the required minimum internal cooking temperature.** Frozen hamburger patties, for example, can go straight from the freezer onto a grill without being thawed first. Frozen chicken can go straight into a deep fryer. These products cook quickly enough from the frozen state to pass through the temperature danger zone without harm. However, always make sure you verify the final internal cooking temperature with a thermometer.

Some frozen food may be slacked before cooking. Slacking is the process of gradually thawing frozen food in preparation for deep-frying, allowing even heating during cooking. For example, you might slack frozen, breaded chicken breasts by allowing them to warm from –10°F (–23°C) to 25°F (–4°C). Slack food just before you cook it. Do not let food get any warmer than 41°F (5°C). If slacking at room temperature is permitted in your jurisdiction, a system must be in place to ensure the product does not exceed 41°F (5°C).

Preparing Specific Food

Meat, Seafood, and Poultry

The sources of most cross-contamination in an operation are raw meat, poultry, and seafood. Your staff should use the following safe procedures when handling these products:

- **Use clean and sanitized work areas, cutting boards, knives, and utensils.** Prepare raw meat, poultry, and seafood separately or at a different time from fresh produce.

- **Wash hands properly.** If gloves are worn, hands should be washed, and the gloves changed before starting each new task.

- **Remove from refrigerated storage only as much product as can be prepared at one time.** When cubing beef for stew, for example, take out and cube one roast and refrigerate it before taking out another roast.

- **Return raw, prepared meat to refrigeration, or cook it as quickly as possible.** Store these items properly to prevent cross-contamination.

Salads Containing TCS Food

Chicken, tuna, egg, pasta, and potato salads all have been involved in foodborne-illness outbreaks. Because these salads are not typically cooked after preparation, there is no chance to eliminate microorganisms that may have been introduced during preparation. Therefore, care must be taken when preparing these salads. Follow these preparation guidelines:

- **Make sure leftover TCS food that will be used to make salads has been handled safely.** Leftover ingredients such as pasta, chicken, and potatoes should only be used if they have been cooked, held, and cooled properly. You should also make sure they have not been stored too long. Throw out items held at 41°F (5°C) or lower after seven days.

- **Prepare food in small batches so large amounts of food do not sit out at room temperature for long periods of time.** (See *Exhibit 8c*.)

8c Salads Containing TCS Food

Do not let large amounts of these types of food sit out at room temperature.

- **Consider chilling all ingredients and utensils before using them to make the salad.** For example, tuna, mayonnaise, and mixing bowls can be chilled before making tuna salad.

- **Leave food in the refrigerator until all ingredients are ready to be mixed.**

Eggs and Egg Mixtures

Historically, the contents of whole, clean, uncracked shell eggs were considered free of bacteria. It is now known that in rare cases a certain bacteria, *Salmonella* Enteritidis, can be found inside eggs. *Salmonella* Enteritidis can live inside a laying hen and can be deposited in an egg before the shell is formed. Although only a small number of eggs produced in the United States are likely to carry this type of bacteria, all untreated eggs are considered TCS food because they are able to support the rapid growth of microorganisms. When preparing eggs and egg mixtures, follow these guidelines:

8d Pooled Eggs

Containers used to hold pooled eggs must be washed and sanitized before being used for a new batch.

- **Handle pooled eggs (if allowed) with special care.** Pooled eggs are eggs that are cracked open and combined in a common container. They must be handled with care because bacteria in one egg can be spread to the rest. Pooled eggs must be cooked promptly after mixing, or stored at 41°F (5°C) or lower. Containers that have been used to hold pooled eggs must be washed and sanitized before being used for a new batch. (See *Exhibit 8d.*)

- **Consider using pasteurized shell eggs or egg products for egg dishes requiring little or no cooking.** Examples are hollandaise sauce, Caesar salad dressing, tiramisu, and mousse.

- **Operations that serve high-risk populations, such as hospitals and nursing homes, must take special care when using eggs.** Pasteurized eggs or egg products must be used when dishes containing eggs will be served raw or undercooked. If shell eggs will be pooled for a recipe, they must also be pasteurized. Unpasteurized shell eggs may be used if the dish will be cooked all the way through, such as in an omelet or a cake.

- **Promptly clean and sanitize all equipment and utensils used to prepare eggs.**

Key Point

Batters prepared with eggs or milk should be handled with care due to the risk of time-temperature abuse and cross-contamination.

Cross-Contamination

When preparing raw vegetables, start with a clean, sanitized work space. Prepare vegetables away from raw meat, poultry, and eggs, and from ready-to-eat food.

Batters and Breading

Batters prepared with eggs or milk should be handled with care. There is a risk of time-temperature abuse and cross-contamination when batters are made with these products. Breading must also be handled with care, since cross-contamination is a risk. In some cases, it may be better to buy frozen breaded items that can be taken directly from the freezer and then cooked thoroughly in the oven or fryer. If you prefer to make breaded or battered food from scratch, however, follow these guidelines:

- **Prepare batters in small batches.** Preparing small amounts prevents time-temperature abuse of both the batter and the food being coated. Store what you do not need at 41°F (5°C) or lower in a covered container.

- **When breading food that will be cooked at a later time, store it in the refrigerator as soon as possible.**

- **Create a plan to throw out unused batter or breading after a set amount of time.** This might be after using a batch or at the end of a shift.

- **Cook battered and breaded food thoroughly.** The coating acts as an insulator, which can prevent food from being thoroughly cooked. When deep-frying food, make sure the temperature of the oil recovers before loading each batch. Overloading the basket also slows cooking time, which means product could be removed from the fryer before it is thoroughly cooked. Be sure to monitor oil and food temperatures using calibrated thermometers, and watch cooking time.

Produce

Fresh produce must be handled carefully to prevent foodborne illness. Viruses such as hepatitis A, bacteria such as shiga toxin-producing *E. coli*, and parasites such as *Cryptosporidium parvum* can survive on produce, especially cut produce. The risk from such microorganisms can be minimized or eliminated by these simple preparation safeguards:

- **Make sure fruit and vegetables do not come in contact with surfaces exposed to raw meat and poultry.** Prepare produce away from raw meat, poultry, eggs, and ready-to-eat food. Clean and sanitize the work space and all utensils that will be used during preparation.

8e   Wash Fruit and Vegetables

Remove the outer leaves, and pull leafy greens completely apart and rinse thoroughly.

- **Wash fruit and vegetables thoroughly under running potable water to remove dirt and other contaminants before cutting, cooking, or combining with other ingredients.** The water should be slightly warmer than the temperature of the produce. Pay particular attention to leafy greens, such as lettuce and spinach. Remove the outer leaves, and pull lettuce and spinach completely apart and rinse thoroughly. (See *Exhibit 8e.*) Be sure to clean and sanitize surfaces that were used to prepare produce items for washing. Produce can be sanitized by washing it in water containing ozone. Check with your local regulatory authority to see if this is allowed in your area.

- **When soaking or storing produce in standing water or an ice-water slurry, do not mix different items or multiple batches of the same item.** Pathogens from contaminated produce can contaminate the water and the ice and spread to other produce.

- **Refrigerate and hold cut melons, cut tomatoes, and cut leafy greens at 41°F (5°C) or lower, because they are TCS food.**

- **If your establishment primarily serves high-risk populations, do not serve raw seed sprouts.**

Fresh Juice

If you package fresh fruit and vegetable juice on-site for sale at a later time, you must treat (e.g., pasteurize) the juice according to an approved HACCP plan. (You will learn about HACCP plans in Chapter 10.) As an alternative to manufacturing under a HACCP plan, the juice can be labeled with the following: *Warning: This product has not been pasteurized and therefore may contain harmful bacteria that can cause serious illness in children, the elderly, and people with weakened immune systems.*

Cross-Contamination

Store ice scoops outside of the ice machine in a clean, protected location.

Ice

People often forget that ice is also a food. It is used to chill beverages and to chill or dilute food. In Chapter 7, you learned how to store products on ice, such as poultry, seafood, and produce. Many establishments also use ice to chill food on display, such as canned beverages or fruit. Any time ice has been used to cool food in this way, you may not reuse it as a food.

Ice must be made from potable water (water that is safe to drink). Never use ice as an ingredient if it was used to keep food cold. Ice can become contaminated just as easily as other food. When transferring ice from an ice machine to an ice bin or to a display, use a clean, sanitized scoop and container. Never transfer ice in containers that have been used to store raw meat, poultry, or seafood, or chemicals. Store ice scoops outside the ice machine in a clean, protected location.

Preparation Practices That Require a Variance

You must get a variance when preparing food using certain methods. A variance is a document issued by your regulatory authority that allows a requirement to be waived or changed. When applying for a variance, you may have to submit a HACCP plan. It must address any food safety risks regarding the preparation method you will be using. The following methods for preparing food require a variance:

- Smoking food as a method of food preservation—not to enhance flavor.

- Using **food additives,** such as nitrates, nitrites, and sulfites, to preserve food—not to enhance flavor. Food additives are substances added to food to lengthen its shelf life. They are also used to alter food so it does not need time and temperature control. Some food additives are used to enhance flavor.

- Curing food.

- Custom-processing animals. For example, this may include dressing deer in the establishment for personal use.

- Packaging food using a reduced-oxygen packaging (ROP) method. This includes MAP, vacuum-packed, and *sous vide* food. *Clostridium botulinum* and *Listeria monocytogenes* are risks to food packaged in these ways.

- Sprouting seeds or beans.

- Offering live, mulluscan shellfish from a display tank.

The Flow of Food

Receiving · Storing · Preparing · Cooking · Holding · Cooling · Reheating · Serving · Purchasing

Cooking Food

The only way to reduce microorganisms in food to safe levels is to cook it to the required minimum internal temperature. This temperature varies from product to product. Minimum internal temperatures have been developed for most types of TCS food. They are listed in *Exhibit 8f.* However, your operation or jurisdiction might require different temperatures. These temperatures must be reached and held for the specified amount of time. A food's temperature should be checked in the thickest part of the food with a thermometer. At least two readings should be taken in different locations.

8f   Minimum Internal Cooking Temperatures

Product	Minimum Internal Cooking Temperature
Poultry (whole or ground duck, chicken, or turkey)	165°F (74°C) for 15 seconds
Stuffing and stuffed meat, fish, poultry, and pasta	165°F (74°C) for 15 seconds
TCS food cooked in a microwave (eggs, poultry, fish, and meat)	165°F (74°C)
Ground meat (beef, pork, and other meat)	155°F (68°C) for 15 seconds
Injected meat (including brined ham and flavor-injected roasts)	155°F (68°C) for 15 seconds
Mechanically tenderized meat	155°F (68°C) for 15 seconds
Pork, beef, veal, lamb	Steaks/Chops: 145°F (63°C) for 15 seconds Roasts: 145°F (63°C) for 4 minutes
Seafood (including fish, shellfish, and crustaceans)	145°F (63°C) for 15 seconds
Shell eggs for immediate service	145°F (63°C) for 15 seconds
Commercially processed, ready-to-eat food (hot held for service)	135°F (57°C)

Bacterial Growth

While cooking can reduce micro-organisms, it will not destroy the spores or toxins they may have produced. For this reason, it is critical to handle food safely before it is cooked.

While cooking can reduce to safe levels the number of microorganisms that may be present on food, it will not destroy spores or toxins that the microorganisms may have produced. For this reason, it is critical to handle food safely before it is cooked.

If your menu includes items that are raw or undercooked you must note it on the menu next to these items. Customers who order food that is raw or undercooked must be advised of the increased risk of foodborne illness. You can do this by posting a notice in your menu or through the use of brochures, table tents, or placards. Check your local requirements. The FDA also advises against offering raw or undercooked meat, poultry, seafood, or eggs to children. This is especially true for undercooked ground beef, which may be contaminated with shiga toxin-producing *E. coli* O157:H7.

Operations that primarily serve a high-risk population, such as nursing homes or day-care centers, cannot serve certain items. Never serve raw or undercooked eggs, meat, or seafood. Examples include over-easy eggs, raw oysters, and rare hamburgers. You also cannot serve raw seed sprouts.

Here are general guidelines to follow when cooking:

- **Specify cooking time and required minimum internal cooking temperature in all recipes.**

- **Use a thermometer with a probe that is the right size for the food.** Check the temperature in the thickest part of the food and take at least two readings in different locations. Clean and sanitize the thermometer after you are done using it.

- **Avoid overloading ovens, fryers, and other cooking equipment.** Overloading may lower the equipment or oil temperature, and the food might not cook properly.

- **Let the cooking equipment's temperature recover between batches.**

- **Use utensils or gloves to handle food after cooking.**

- **Taste food correctly to avoid cross-contamination.** The safest way to taste food is to ladle a small amount into a dish. Taste the food in the dish with a clean utensil. When finished, remove the dish and utensil from the area and have them cleaned and sanitized.

The Flow of Food

Receiving — Storing — Preparing — Cooking — Holding — Cooling — Reheating — Serving — Purchasing

8g   Checking the Temperature of Poultry

Poultry should be cooked to a minimum internal temperature of 165°F (74°C) for fifteen seconds.

Cooking Requirements for Specific Food

Poultry

Poultry should be cooked to a minimum internal temperature of 165°F (74°C) for fifteen seconds. (See *Exhibit 8g.*) Poultry has more types and higher counts of microorganisms than other meat because of the way it is processed. Therefore, it should be cooked more thoroughly.

Stuffing

Stuffing can pose a hazard, especially when it is made with TCS ingredients or when it is used in especially large birds or whole cuts of meat.

Stuffing Made with TCS Ingredients

Stuffing can be a TCS food when it is made with eggs, oysters, or other TCS ingredients. Since it is critical that these items are fully cooked, **stuffing made with TCS ingredients should be cooked to a minimum internal temperature of 165°F (74°C) for fifteen seconds.**

Stuffed Meat, Fish, Poultry, or Pasta

Stuffed meat, fish, poultry, or pasta should be cooked to a minimum internal temperature of 165°F (74°C) for fifteen seconds. Stuffing can be a hazard because it acts as insulation, preventing heat from reaching the center of the product. Always verify that both the stuffing and the product reach the required temperature.

Stuffing should be cooked separately, particularly when cooking whole large birds or large cuts of meat. Smaller cuts of meat, such as pork tenderloins or veal chops, may be stuffed before cooking as long as both the meat and the stuffing reach the required temperature.

Dishes That Include Previously Cooked, TCS Food

When cooking dishes that include previously cooked TCS ingredients, such as the ground beef in a meat sauce, **these ingredients must be cooked to a minimum internal temperature of 165°F (74°C) for at least fifteen seconds within two hours.**

When cooking dishes that include raw TCS ingredients, these ingredients must be cooked to their required minimum internal temperature. For example, when cooking jambalaya, you must ensure that the raw shrimp reaches its required minimum internal temperature of 145°F (63°C) for at least fifteen seconds.

Pork

Cook pork, such as chops or medallions of tenderloin, to a minimum internal temperature of 145°F (63°C) for fifteen seconds. (See *Exhibit 8h.*) Pork roasts, on the other hand, must hold the same minimum internal temperature for at least four minutes. Depending on the type of roast used, however, pork can be cooked at different internal temperatures. (See *Exhibit 8i.*)

8h   Checking the Temperature of Pork

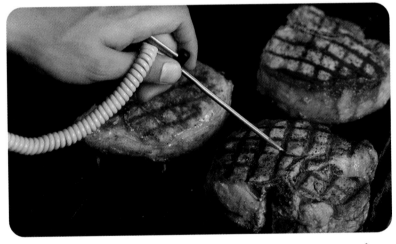

Pork chops should be cooked to a minimum internal temperature of 145°F (63°C) for fifteen seconds.

8i   Alternative Minimum Internal Temperatures for Cooking Beef and Pork Roasts

Temperature	Hold for (in minutes)
130°F (54°C)	112
131°F (55°C)	89
133°F (56°C)	56
135°F (57°C)	36
136°F (58°C)	28
138°F (59°C)	18
140°F (60°C)	12
142°F (61°C)	8
144°F (62°C)	5
145°F (63°C)	4

Chart adapted from the *FDA Food Code*

Beef

Steaks must reach and hold a minimum internal temperature of 145°F (63°C) for fifteen seconds. Roasts, on the other hand, must hold the same internal temperature for at least four minutes. Depending on the type of roast used, however, beef can be cooked at different internal temperatures. (See *Exhibit 8i.*)

Ground Meat

Ground beef, pork, and other meat must be cooked to a minimum internal temperature of 155°F (68°C) for fifteen seconds. It may also be cooked according to the alternative cooking temperatures indicated in *Exhibit 8j* on the next page. Most whole-muscle cuts of meat are likely to have microorganisms only on the surface. When meat is ground, such as for hamburger or sausage, microorganisms on the surface are mixed throughout the product. Check with your local regulatory authority for additional requirements.

8j Alternative Minimum Internal Temperatures for Cooking Ground, Mechanically Tenderized, and Injected Meat

Temperature	Hold for
145°F (63°C)	3 minutes
150°F (66°C)	1 minute
155°F (68°C)	15 seconds
158°F (70°C)	< 1 second

Chart adapted from the *FDA Food Code*

Mechanically Tenderized or Injected Meat

When meat is mechanically tenderized or injected, foodborne microorganisms on the surface can be carried into the interior. For this reason, **mechanically tenderized meat or injected meat, such as brined ham or flavor-injected roasts, must be cooked to a minimum internal temperature of 155°F (68°C) for fifteen seconds.** It may also be cooked according to the alternative cooking temperatures indicated in *Exhibit 8j*.

Game and Ratites

Commercially raised and inspected game animals, such as elk, deer, bison, and rabbit, can be cooked to the same minimum internal temperature as beef. Small cuts, such as steaks, can be cooked to a minimum internal temperature of 145°F (63°C) for fifteen seconds. Ground meat must be cooked to a minimum internal temperature of 155°F (68°C) for fifteen seconds. Stuffed meat should be cooked to a minimum internal temperature of 165°F (74°C) for fifteen seconds. Roasts can be cooked in the same way and to the same temperatures as beef and pork roasts.

Although they are birds, ratites (ostrich, emu, and rhea) are not cooked the same way as poultry. They will have a metallic taste if cooked to internal temperatures of 165°F (74°C) or higher. **Ratites are fully cooked when they reach a minimum internal temperature of 155°F (68°C) for fifteen seconds.** If portions or cutlets of these birds are stuffed, however, cook them to an internal temperature of 165°F (74°C) for fifteen seconds.

Receiving
Storing
Purchasing
Preparing
The Flow of Food
Cooking
Serving
Holding
Reheating
Cooling

8k   Checking the Temperature of Fish

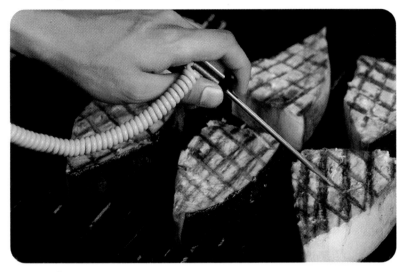

Cook fish to a minimum internal temperature of 145°F (63°C) for fifteen seconds.

Seafood

Cook seafood to a minimum internal temperature of 145°F (63°C) for fifteen seconds. (See *Exhibit 8k.*) If seafood has been ground, chopped, or minced, it should be cooked to a minimum internal temperature of 155°F (68°C) for fifteen seconds. Most whole-muscle cuts of fish are likely to have microorganisms only on their surface. When fish is ground, microorganisms on the surface are mixed throughout the product.

Key Point

Eggs for immediate service should be cooked to a minimum internal temperature of 145°F (63°C) for fifteen seconds.

Eggs and Egg Mixtures

In general, shell eggs cooked for immediate service should be cooked to a minimum internal temperature of 145°F (63°C) for fifteen seconds. When eggs are cooked this way, the white is set and the yolk begins to thicken. Properly cooked scrambled eggs or omelets are firm with no visible liquid egg remaining. Poached or fried eggs should be cooked until the white is firm and the yolk begins to thicken. To hold eggs for later service, cook them to a minimum internal temperature of 155°F (68°C) for fifteen seconds.

When cooking eggs, remove from storage only as many eggs as you need for immediate use. Never stack egg trays (flats) near the grill or stove.

Fruit and Vegetables

Although most fruit and vegetables can be eaten raw, many are cooked before they are served. **When cooking fruit, vegetables, grains (rice and pasta), and legumes (beans, refried beans) for hot holding, cook them to a minimum internal temperature of 135°F (57°C).** Cooked fruit and vegetables must never be left out or held at room temperature.

Commercially Processed, Ready-to-Eat Food

Commercially processed, ready-to-eat food that will be hot held for service must be cooked to a minimum internal temperature of 135°F (57°C). This includes items such as cheese sticks, deep-fried vegetables, etc.

Tea

Dry tea leaves contain low levels of bacteria, yeast, and mold (like most plant-derived food). Using improper brewing temperatures to prepare tea and storing it at room temperature for long periods of time can cause these microorganisms to grow to high levels. Improperly cleaned and sanitized equipment can also promote growth. When handling tea, follow these recommendations:

Key Point

Never hold brewed tea at room temperature for more than twelve hours.

- Brew only as much tea as you reasonably expect to sell within a few hours.

- Never hold brewed tea at room temperature for more than twelve hours. Discard any unused tea at the end of twelve hours.

- To protect tea flavor and avoid microbial contamination and growth, clean and sanitize tea brewing, storage, and dispensing equipment at least once a day. Equipment should be disassembled, washed, rinsed, and sanitized. Urn spigots should be replaced at the end of each day with freshly cleaned and sanitized ones.

- For any brewing method, use a thermometer to make sure brewing water in your equipment meets one of these specified temperatures:

    ○ 175°F (80°C) for automatic iced tea and automatic coffee machine equipment; tea leaves should remain in contact with the water for a minimum of one minute.

    ○ 175°F (80°C) minimum when using the traditional steeping method; tea leaves must be exposed to the water for approximately five minutes by this method.

Cooking TCS Food in a Microwave

Key Point

Eggs, poultry, seafood, and meat cooked in a microwave oven must be heated to a minimum internal temperature of 165°F (74°C).

Microwave ovens tend to cook food more unevenly than other methods of cooking. For this reason, there are special rules for using microwave ovens to cook eggs, poultry, seafood, and meat:

- Cover food to prevent the surface from drying out.

- Rotate or stir food halfway through the cooking process to distribute heat more evenly.

- Let the covered food stand for at least two minutes after cooking to let product temperature equalize.

Eggs, poultry, seafood, and meat cooked in a microwave oven must be heated to 165°F (74°C). Check the temperature of the food in several places to make sure it is cooked through.

Partial Cooking During Preparation

Some operations partially cook food during preparation and then finish cooking it just before service.

You must follow the steps below if you plan to partially cook meat, seafood, poultry, or eggs or dishes containing these items.

1. Do not cook the food for longer than sixty minutes during initial cooking.

2. Cool the food immediately after initial cooking.

3. Freeze or refrigerate the food after cooling it. If refrigerating the food, make sure it is held at 41°F (5°C) or lower.

4. Heat the food to at least 165°F (74°C) before selling or serving it.

5. Cool the food if it will not be served immediately or held for service.

Your local regulatory authority may require you to have written procedures that explain how the food cooked by this process will be prepared and stored. These procedures must be approved by the regulatory authority and describe the following.

- How the requirements will be monitored and documented

- Which corrective actions will be taken if requirements are not met

- How these food items will be marked after initial cooking to indicate that they need further cooking

- How these food items will be separated from ready-to-eat food during storage, once initial cooking is complete

8l Cooling Food

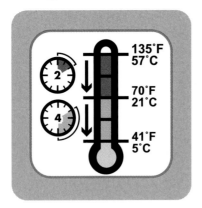

Food must be cooled from 135°F to 70°F (57°C to 21°C) within two hours and from 70°F to 41°F (21°C to 5°C) or lower in the next four hours.

8m Reducing the Size of Food

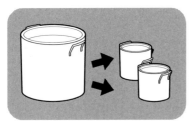

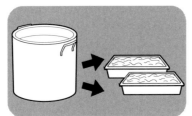

Before cooling food, start by dividing large containers of food into smaller containers.

Cooling Food

As you know, pathogens grow well in the temperature danger zone. But they grow much faster at temperatures between 125°F and 70°F (52°C and 21°C). Food must pass through this temperature range quickly to reduce this growth.

Cool TCS food from 135°F (57°C) to 41°F (5°C) or lower within six hours (see *Exhibit 8l*):

- First, cool food from 135°F to 70°F (57°C to 21°C) within two hours.

- Then cool it to 41°F (5°C) or lower in the next four hours.

If food has not reached 70°F (21°C) within two hours, it must be discarded or reheated and then cooled again.

If you can cool the food from 135°F to 70°F (57°C to 21°C) in less than two hours, you can use the remaining time to cool it to 41°F (5°C) or lower. However, the total cooling time cannot be longer than six hours. For example, if you cool food from 135°F to 70°F (57°C to 21°C) in one hour, you have the remaining five hours to get the food to 41°F (5°C) or lower. Check with your local regulatory authority for time and temperature requirements for cooling food in your jurisdiction.

Methods for Cooling Food

While common sense may suggest that the quickest way to cool food is to put it in the refrigerator, it is not. Refrigerators are designed to keep cold food cold. They usually do not have the capacity to cool hot food quickly. Never place large quantities of hot food in a refrigerator to cool.

In general, the thickness or density of food is the biggest factor in how quickly it cools. The denser the food product, the more slowly it cools. For example, refried beans take longer to cool than vegetable broth, since the beans are thicker.

The container in which food is stored also affects how fast it will cool. Stainless steel transfers heat from food faster than plastic. Shallow pans disperse heat faster than deep ones.

Before cooling food, you should start by reducing its size. This will allow it to cool faster. Cut large items into smaller pieces, or divide large containers of food into smaller containers or shallow pans. (See *Exhibit 8m*.)

There are a number of methods that can be used to cool food quickly and safely. These include (see *Exhibit 8n*):

- **Placing food in an ice-water bath.** After dividing food into smaller containers, place them into a clean prep sink or large pot filled with ice water. Stir the food frequently to cool it faster and more evenly.

- **Stirring food with an ice paddle.** Plastic paddles are available that can be filled with ice or with water and then frozen. Food stirred with these paddles will cool quickly. Food cools even faster when placed in an ice-water bath and stirred with an ice paddle.

- **Placing food in a blast chiller or tumble chiller.** Blast chillers blast cold air across food at high speeds to remove heat. They are typically used to cool large amounts of food. Tumble chillers tumble bags of hot food in cold water. Tumble chillers work well on thick food such as mashed potatoes.

8n   Safe Methods for Cooling Food

Ice-water bath   Ice paddle   Blast chiller

In addition to the methods identified in *Exhibit 8n,* food can be cooled by:

- **Adding ice or cold water as an ingredient.** This works for soups, stews, and other recipes that call for water as an ingredient. By this method, the recipe is prepared with less water than required. Cold water or ice is then added after cooking to cool the product and provide the remaining water.

Something to Think About...

That's Cool!

A small restaurant chain had noted a recurring problem at one of their facilities. The restaurant was having trouble cooling chili, which they packed in five-gallon buckets before storing it in the walk-in. Despite filling the buckets just over half full and using an ice paddle, the chili simply did not cool fast enough.

Management and the head chef set to work to find a solution. They determined that the best approach was to pour the chili into shallow hotel pans before placing it into the walk-in. The new system cooled the chili to 41°F (5°C) in a little less than two hours.

Once implemented, the new system even earned praise from employees. They had been using hotel pans to reheat the chili anyway, and the new system saved scraping and washing the buckets. The pans were also much easier to lift.

8o Reheating Temperatures
for Roasts

Temperature	Hold for
130°F (54°C)	112 minutes
131°F (55°C)	89 minutes
133°F (56°C)	56 minutes
135°F (57°C)	36 minutes
136°F (58°C)	28 minutes
138°F (59°C)	18 minutes
140°F (60°C)	12 minutes
142°F (61°C)	8 minutes
144°F (62°C)	5 minutes
145°F (63°C)	4 minutes

Reheating Food

Food reheated for immediate service to a customer, such as the beef in a roast beef sandwich, may be served at any temperature, as long as the food was properly cooked and cooled first.

Previously cooked, TCS food reheated for hot holding must be moved through the temperature danger zone as quickly as possible. Reheat it to an internal temperature of 165°F (74°C) for fifteen seconds within two hours.

Roasts can be reheated to the alternative temperatures listed in *Exhibit 8o,* depending on the type of roast and the oven used. Check your local regulatory requirements.

Summary

To protect food during preparation, you must handle it safely. The keys are time and temperature control and the prevention of cross-contamination.

Thaw frozen food in the refrigerator, under cool running potable water, in a microwave oven, or as part of the cooking process. Never thaw food at room temperature. Have employees prepare food in small batches, use chilled utensils and bowls, and record product temperatures and preparation times.

Cooking can reduce the number of microorganisms in food to safe levels. To ensure that microorganisms are destroyed, food must be cooked to minimum internal temperatures for a specific amount of time. These temperatures vary from product to product. Cooking does not kill the spores or toxins some microorganisms produce. That is why it is so important to handle food safely prior to cooking.

Once food is cooked, it should be served as quickly as possible. If it is going to be stored and served later, it must be cooled rapidly. TCS food must be cooled from 135°F to 70°F (57°C to 21°C) within two hours and from 70°F to 41°F (21°C to 5°C) or lower in the next four hours.

Before large quantities of food are cooled, they should be reduced in size to allow them to cool faster. Cut large food items into smaller pieces or divide large containers of food into smaller ones. There are several methods to cool food safely. They include using an ice-water bath, stirring food with ice paddles, or using a blast or tumble chiller.

Receiving
Storing
Purchasing
Preparing
The Flow of Food
Cooking
Serving
Holding
Reheating
Cooling

Previously cooked, TCS food that will be hot held must be reheated to an internal temperature of 165°F (74°C) for fifteen seconds within two hours before it can be served.

Apply Your Knowledge   A Case in Point 1

① **What did John do wrong?**

On Friday, John went to work at The Fish House knowing he had a lot to do. After changing clothes and punching in, he took a case of frozen raw shrimp out of the freezer. To thaw it quickly, he put the frozen shrimp into the prep sink and turned on the hot water. While waiting for the shrimp to thaw, John took several fresh, whole fish out of the walk-in refrigerator. He brought them back to the prep area and began to clean and fillet them. When he finished, he put the fillets in a pan and returned them to the walk-in refrigerator. He rinsed off the boning knife and cutting board in the sink, and wiped off the worktable with a dishtowel.

Next, John transferred the shrimp from the sink to the worktable using a large colander. On the cutting board, he peeled, deveined, and butterflied the shrimp using the boning knife. He put the prepared shrimp in a covered container in the refrigerator, and then started preparing fresh produce.

For answers, please turn to the Answer Key.

Apply Your Knowledge

① What did Angie do wrong?

A Case in Point 2

By 7:30 p.m., all the residents at Sunnydale Nursing Home had eaten dinner. As she began cleaning up, Angie realized she had a lot of chicken breasts left over. Betty, the new assistant manager, had forgotten to inform Angie that several residents were going to a local festival and would miss dinner.

"No problem," Angie thought. "We can use the leftover chicken to make chicken salad."

Angie left the chicken breasts in a pan on the prep table while she started putting other food away and cleaning up the kitchen. At 9:45 p.m., when everything else was clean, she put her hand over the pan of chicken breasts and decided they were cool enough to handle. She covered the pan with plastic wrap and put it in the refrigerator.

Three days later, Angie came in to work on the early shift. She decided to make chicken salad from the leftover chicken breasts. After she hung up her coat and put on her apron, Angie took all the ingredients she needed for chicken salad out of the refrigerator and put them on a worktable. Then she started breakfast.

First, she cracked three dozen eggs into a large bowl, added some milk, and set the bowl near the stove. Then she took bacon out of the refrigerator and put it on the worktable next to the chicken salad ingredients. She peeled off strips of bacon onto a sheet pan and put the pan into the oven. After wiping her hands on her apron, she went back to the stove to whisk the eggs and pour them onto the griddle. When they were almost done, Angie scooped the scrambled eggs into a hotel pan and put it in the steam table.

As soon as breakfast was cooked, Angie went back to the prep table to wash and cut up celery and cut up the chicken for chicken salad.

For answers, please turn to the Answer Key.

Apply Your Knowledge

Use these questions to review the concepts presented in this chapter.

Discussion Questions

① What are the minimum internal cooking temperatures for poultry, fish, pork, and ground beef?

② What are four proper methods for thawing food?

③ What methods can be used to cool cooked food?

④ What are the rules for properly cooking food in a microwave oven?

For answers, please turn to the Answer Key.

Study Questions

Circle the best answer to each question.

① **Beef stew must be cooled from 135°F to 70°F (57°C to 21°C) within _____ hours and from 70°F to 41°F (21°C to 5°C) or lower in the next _____ hours.**
   A 4, 2   C 2, 4
   B 3, 2   D 2, 3

② **What must you do to keep food safe after thawing it in a microwave?**
   A Hold it.   C Cool it.
   B Cook it.   D Freeze it.

③ **What is the minimum internal cooking temperature for stuffed pork chops?**
   A 135°F (57°C)
   B 145°F (63°C)
   C 155°F (68°C)
   D 165°F (74°C)

④ **What are the time and temperature requirements for reheating TCS food for hot holding?**
   A 135°F (57°C) for 15 seconds within 2 hours
   B 145°F (63°C) for 15 seconds within 2 hours
   C 155°F (68°C) for 15 seconds within 2 hours
   D 165°F (74°C) for 15 seconds within 2 hours

Continued on next page ▶

► *Continued from previous page*

⑤ **What is the minimum internal cooking temperature for eggs, meat, poultry, and seafood cooked in a microwave?**

A 135°F (57°C)   C 155°F (68°C)

B 145°F (63°C)   D 165°F (74°C)

⑥ **What is the minimum internal cooking temperature for eggs that will be hot-held for later service?**

A 135°F (57°C)   C 155°F (68°C)

B 145°F (63°C)   D 165°F (74°C)

⑦ **What is the danger of NOT cleaning and sanitizing a prep table between uses?**

A Off-flavors in food

B Poor personal hygiene

C Cross-contamination

D Time-temperature abuse

⑧ **What is the correct way to cool a stockpot of clam chowder?**

A Put the stockpot into a cooler.

B Put the stockpot into a freezer.

C Put the stockpot on a prep table.

D Put the stockpot into ice-water.

⑨ **What is the danger when thawing food at room temperature?**

A Cross-contamination

B Poor personal hygiene

C Physical contamination

D Time-temperature abuse

⑩ **What is the minimum internal cooking temperature for ground beef?**

A 135°F (57°C)   C 155°F (68°C)

B 145°F (63°C)   D 165°F (74°C)

For answers, please turn to the Answer Key.

Additional Resources

Articles and Texts

Baker, R. C., S. Hogarty, W. Poon, et al. 1983. Survival of *Salmonella typhimurium* and *Staphylococcus aureus* in eggs cooked by different methods. *Poultry Science.* 62: 1211.

Blankenship, L. C., S. E. Craven, R. G. Leffler, and C. Custer. 1988. Growth of *Clostridium perfringens* in Cooked Chili During Cooling. *Applied and Environmental Microbiology.* 54 (5): 1104-1108.

Buzby, Jean C. 2001. Children and Microbial Foodborne Illness. *FoodReview.* 24 (2): 32.

Buzby, Jean C. 2002. Older Adults at Risk of Complications from Microbial Foodborne Illness. *FoodReview.* 25 (2): 30.

Castellani, A.G., R. R. Clark, M. I. Gibson, and D. F. Meisner. 1952. Roasting Time and Temperature Required to Kill Food Poisoning Microorganisms Introduced Experimentally into Stuffing in Turkeys. *Food Research International.* 18 : 131-138.

Chia-Min, Lin and Cheng-I Wei. 1997. Transfer of *Salmonella montevideo* onto the Interior Surfaces of Tomatoes by Cutting. *Journal of Food Protection.* 60 (7): 858-863.

Doyle, M. P. and J. L. Schoeni. 1984. Survival and Growth Characteristics of *Escherichia coli* Associated with Hemorrhagic Colitis. *Applied and Environmental Microbiology.* 48 (4): 855-856.

Escartin, E. F., A. C. Ayala, and J. S. Lozano. 1989. Survival and growth of *Salmonella* and *Shigella* on Sliced Fresh Fruit. *Journal of Food Protection.* 52 (7): 471-472.

Golden, G. A., E. J. Rhodehamel, and D. A. Kautter. 1993. Growth of *Salmonella* spp. in Cantaloupe, Watermelon, and Honeydew Melons. *Journal of Food Protection.* 56 (3): 194-196.

Hague, M. A., K. E. Warren, M. C. Hunt, D. H. Kropf, C. L. Kastner, S. L. Stroda, and D. E. Johnson. 1994. Endpoint Temperature, Internal Cooked Color, and Expressible Juice Color Relationships in Ground Beef Patties. *Journal of Food Science.* 59 (3): 465-470.

Heddleson, R. A., S. Doores, R. C. Anantheswaran, and G. D. Kuhn. 1993. Viability Loss of *Salmonella* Species, *Staphylococcus aureus,* and *Listeria monocytogenes* in Complex Foods Heated by Microwave Energy. *Journal of Food Protection.* 59 (8): 813-818.

Heisick, J. E., D. E. Wagner, M. L. Nierman, and J. T. Peeler. 1989. *Listeria* spp. Found in Fresh Market Produce. *Applied and Environmental Microbiology.* 55 (8): 1925-1927.

Continued on next page ▶

▶ *Continued from previous page*

Humphrey, T. J., K. W. Martin, and A. Whitehead. 1994. Contamination of Hands and Work Surfaces with *Salmonella enteritidis* PT4 During the Preparation of Egg Dishes. *Epidemiology and Infection.* 113: 403-409.

Sawyer, C. A., S. A. Biglari, and S. S. Thompson. 1984. Internal End Temperature and Survival of Bacteria on Meats with and without a Polyvinylidene Chloride Wrap during Microwave Cooking. *Journal of Food Science.* 49 (3): 972-973.

Sawyer, C. A. 1985. Post-Processing Temperature Rise in Foods: Hot Air and Microwave Ovens. *Journal of Food Protection.* 48 (5): 429-434.

Scott, Elizabeth and Sally F. Bloomfield. 1990. The Survival and Transfer of Microbial Contamination via Cloths, Hands, and Utensils. *Journal of Applied Bacteriology.* 68: 271-278.

Steinbrugge, E. S., R. B. Maxcy, and M. B. Liewen. 1988. Fate of *Listeria monocytogenes* on Ready-to-Serve Lettuce. *Journal of Food Protection.* 51: 596-599.

Webster, R.C. and W.B. Esselen. 1956. Thermal Resistance of Food Poisoning Microorganisms in Poultry Stuffing. *Journal of Milk and Food Technology.* 19: 209-212.

Web Sites

American Egg Board
aeb.org

American Lamb Board
americanlambboard.org

Association of Food, Beverage, and Consumer Products Companies
gmabrands.com

Conference for Food Protection
foodprotect.org

FDA Food Safety
www.fda.gov/Food/FoodSafety/default.htm

Gateway to Government Food Safety Information
foodsafety.gov

National Cattlemen's Beef Association: Beef for Foodservice Professionals
beeffoodservice.com

National Chicken Council
nationalchickencouncil.com

National Fisheries Institute
aboutseafood.com

National Frozen & Refrigerated Foods Association
nfraweb.org

National Pork Producers Council
nppc.org

National Turkey Federation
eatturkey.com

Produce Marketing Association
pma.com

Tea Association of the USA, Inc.
teausa.com

United Fresh Produce Association
unitedfresh.org

USDA Food Safety and Inspection Service
www.fsis.usda.gov/

Documents and Other Resources

2009 FDA Food Code
www.fda.gov/Food/FoodSafety/RetailFoodProtection/FoodCode/
FoodCode2009/default.htm

*Assuring the Safety of Eggs and Menu and Deli Items Made From Raw,
Shell Eggs*
www.fda.gov/Food/FoodSafety/RetailFoodProtection/
IndustryandRegulatoryAssistanceandTrainingResources/ucm192177.htm

Recommendations for the Preparation of Iced and Hot Tea
teausa.com/general/teaassociation/foodbrewing/the_tea_manual.pdf

Seafood Information and Resources
www.fda.gov/Food/FoodSafety/Product-
SpecificInformation/Seafood/default.htm

9 The Flow of Food: Service

Inside this chapter:

- Holding Food for Service
- Serving Food Safely
- Off-Site Service

After completing this chapter, you should be able to:

- Identify time and temperature requirements for holding hot and cold TCS food.
- Identify procedures for preventing time-temperature abuse and cross-contamination when displaying and serving food.
- Identify the requirements for using time rather than temperature as the only method of control when holding ready-to-eat food.
- Implement methods for minimizing bare-hand contact with ready-to-eat food.
- Identify hazards associated with the transportation of food and methods for preventing them.
- Identify hazards associated with the service of food off site and methods for preventing them.
- Identify hazards associated with vending food and methods for preventing them.
- Prevent customers from contaminating self-service areas.
- Prevent employees from contaminating food.

Key Terms

- Food bar
- Sneeze guard
- Off-site service
- Mobile unit
- Temporary unit
- Vending machine

Apply Your Knowledge

Check to see how much you know about the concepts in this chapter. Use the page references provided with each question to explore the topic.

Test Your Food Safety Knowledge

① **True or False:** Cold TCS food must be held at an internal temperature of 41°F (5°C) or lower. *(See page 9-4.)*

② **True or False:** Hot TCS food must be held at an internal temperature of 120°F (49°C) or higher. *(See page 9-4.)*

③ **True or False:** Chicken salad can be held at room temperature if it has a label specifying it must be discarded after eight hours. *(See page 9-4.)*

④ **True or False:** When holding TCS food for service, the internal temperature must be checked at least every four hours. *(See page 9-3.)*

⑤ **True or False:** Servers can contaminate food simply by handling the food-contact surface of a plate. *(See page 9-6.)*

For answers, please turn to the Answer Key.

Introduction

The job of protecting food continues even after the food has been prepared and cooked properly, since microorganisms can still contaminate it before it is eaten. The key to serving safe food is to prevent time-temperature abuse and cross-contamination. Hold, display, and serve food at the correct temperature, and handle it safely. People do many things without knowing their actions can lead to contamination. Train employees to serve food properly, and make sure food safety rules are followed.

Holding Food for Service

In many establishments, food is cooked to order. If it has been stored, prepared, and cooked properly and then served immediately, it is less likely to cause illness. Even in facilities that cook food to order, many menu items are cooked and then held for service. A coffee shop might hold soup in a warming

Receiving Storing Preparing Cooking Holding Cooling Reheating Serving Purchasing

The Flow of Food

kettle. A steakhouse might keep prime rib warm on a steam table. Many establishments, such as cafeterias and buffets, hold almost all the food they serve.

Kitchen staff might be tempted to hold hot food at a lower temperature than required to maintain quality. However, employees must remember that microorganisms can grow at temperatures between 41°F and 135°F (5°C and 57°C). To ensure the safety of food that is held hot or cold, specific procedures must be followed.

General Rules for Holding Food

Follow these guidelines when holding food:

- **Check the internal temperature of food using a thermometer.** The temperature gauge on a holding unit may not provide an accurate indication of a food's internal temperature. Therefore, it is critical to use a thermometer to check temperature.

9a Checking Temperatures during Holding

Check the temperature of food at least every four hours.

- **Check the temperature of food at least every four hours.** (See *Exhibit 9a.*) Throw out food that is not at 135°F (57°C) or higher or at 41°F (5°C) or lower. As an alternative, check the temperature every two hours to leave time for corrective action.

- **Establish a policy to ensure that food being held for service will be discarded after a predetermined amount of time.** For example, a policy may state that a pan of veal on a buffet can be replenished all day as long as it is discarded at the end of the day.

- **Cover food and provide sneeze guards to protect food from contamination.** Covers also help maintain the internal temperature of food.

9b   Hot Holding

Hot TCS food must be held at an internal temperature of 135°F (57°C) or higher.

9c   Cold Holding

Cold TCS food must be held at an internal temperature of 41°F (5°C) or lower.

Hot Food

- **Hot TCS food must be held at an internal temperature of 135°F (57°C) or higher.** (See *Exhibit 9b*.)

- **Only use hot-holding equipment that can keep food at the proper temperature.**

- **Never use hot-holding equipment to reheat food if it is not designed to do so.** Most hot-holding equipment is not designed to pass food through the temperature danger zone quickly enough. Food should be properly reheated first and then transferred to the holding unit.

- **Stir food at regular intervals to distribute heat evenly.**

Cold Food

- **Cold TCS food must be held at an internal temperature of 41°F (5°C) or lower.** (See *Exhibit 9c*.)

- **Only use cold-holding equipment that can keep food at the proper temperature.**

Holding Food Without Temperature Control

Your operation may want to display or hold TCS food without temperature control. The following are some examples of when you might hold food without temperature control:

- **When displaying food for a short time, such as at an off-site catered event.**

- **When electricity is not available to power holding equipment.** If your operation displays or holds TCS food without temperature control, it must do so under certain conditions. Also note that the conditions for holding cold food are different from those for holding hot food.

Cold Food

You can hold cold food without temperature control for up to six hours if you meet the following conditions.

- **Hold the food at 41°F (5°C) or lower before removing it from refrigeration.**

- **Label the food with the time you removed it from refrigeration and the time you must discard it.** The discard

9d Holding Cold Food Without Temperature Control

In some jurisdictions, cold TCS food can be held without temperature control for up to six hours under certain conditions.

time on the label must be six hours from the time you removed the food from refrigeration. For example, if you remove potato salad from refrigeration at 3:00 p.m. to serve at a picnic, the discard time on the label should be 9:00 p.m. This equals six hours from the time you removed it from refrigeration. (See *Exhibit 9d*.)

- **Make sure the food does not exceed 70°F (21°C) while it is being served.** Throw out any food that exceeds this temperature.

- **Sell, serve, or discard the food within six hours.**

Hot Food

You can hold hot food without temperature control for up to four hours if you meet the following conditions.

- **Hold the food at 135°F (57°C) or higher before removing it from temperature control.**

- **Label the food with the time you must throw it out.** The discard time on the label must be four hours from the time you removed the food from temperature control.

- **Sell, serve, or discard the food within four hours.**

Before using time as a method of control, check with your local regulatory authority for specific requirements.

Serving Food Safely

After handling food safely and cooking it properly, you do not want to risk contamination when serving it.

Kitchen Staff

Train your kitchen staff in following these procedure.

- **Use clean and sanitized utensils for serving.** Use separate utensils for each food item, and properly clean and sanitize them after each serving task. Utensils should be cleaned and sanitized at least once every four hours during continuous use.

- **Store serving utensils properly.** Serving utensils can be stored in the food with the handle extended above the rim of the container. (See *Exhibit 9e*.) They can also be placed on a

9e Properly Stored Utensils

If stored in food, utensils should be stored with the handle extended above the rim of the container.

9f   Handling Ready-to-Eat Food

Minimize bare-hand contact with ready-to-eat food by using gloves or tongs to serve it.

clean, sanitized food-contact surface. Spoons or scoops used to serve food such as ice cream or mashed potatoes can be stored under running water that is 135°F (57°C).

- **Minimize bare-hand contact with ready-to-eat food.** Handle ready-to-eat food with tongs, deli sheets, or gloves. (See *Exhibit 9f.*) Bare-hand contact is allowed in some jurisdictions if the establishment has received prior approval. The establishment must outline policies for employee health and employee training in handwashing and personal hygiene. Check with your regulatory agency for requirements in your jurisdiction.

- **Practice good personal hygiene.** Proper handwashing is essential to keep food safe.

Servers

Food servers can contaminate food simply by handling the food-contact surfaces of glassware, dishes, and utensils. The following guidelines should be followed when serving food (see *Exhibit 9g*):

- **Glassware and dishes should be handled properly.** The food-contact area of plates, bowls, glasses, or cups should not be touched. Dishes should be held by the bottom or the edge. Cups should be held by their handles, and glassware should be held by the middle, bottom, or stem.

- **Glassware and dishes should not be stacked when serving.** The rim or surface of one item can be contaminated by the one above it. Glasses should be carried in a rack or on a tray.

- **Flatware and utensils should be held at the handle.** Store flatware so servers grasp handles, not food-contact surfaces.

- **Minimize bare-hand contact with food that is ready to eat.**

- **Use ice scoops or tongs to get ice.** Servers should never scoop ice with their bare hands or use a glass since it may chip or break. Ice scoops should always be stored in a sanitary location—not in the ice bin.

- **Practice good personal hygiene.**

The Flow of Food

Receiving
Storing
Purchasing
Preparing
Cooking
Serving
Holding
Reheating
Cooling

9g   Right and Wrong Ways to Handle Food, Glassware, Dishes, and Utensils

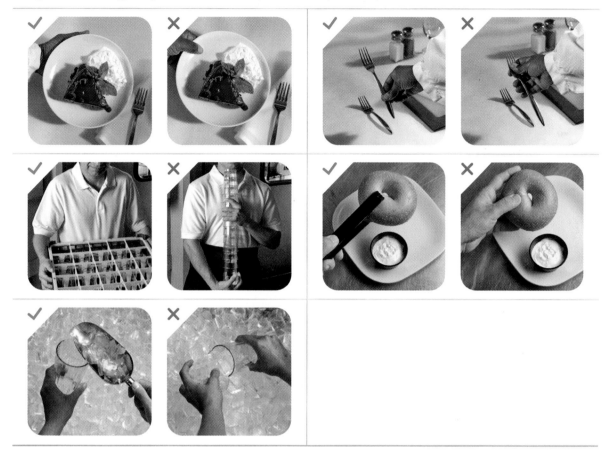

Preset Tableware

If your operation presets tableware on dining tables, you must take steps to prevent it from becoming contaminated. This might include wrapping or covering the items. (See *Exhibit 9h.*)

Table settings do not need to be wrapped or covered if extra settings meet these requirements.

- They are removed when guests are seated.

- If they remain on the table, they are cleaned and sanitized after guests have left.

Division of Labor

To prevent cross-contamination, it is a good idea to schedule staff so they are not assigned to do more than one job during a shift. Serving food, setting tables, and busing dirty dishes are

9h   Wrapped Tableware

Wrapping preset silverware can help prevent it from becoming contaminated.

separate tasks with different responsibilities. Since this division of labor is difficult to manage in most establishments, it is important for servers and busers who do double duty to wash their hands often and handle food safely. After wiping tables or busing dirty dishes, servers must wash their hands before handling food or place settings.

Re-serving Food Safely

Servers and kitchen staff should also know the rules about re-serving food previously served to a customer (see *Exhibit 9i*):

- **Menu items returned by one customer cannot be re-served to another customer.**

- **Never re-serve plate garnishes, such as fruit or pickles.** Served but unused garnishes must be discarded.

- **Never re-serve uncovered condiments.** Do not combine leftovers with fresh food. Opened portions of salsa, mayonnaise, mustard, butter, and other condiments should be thrown away after being served to customers.

- **Do not re-serve uneaten bread or rolls.** Linens used to line bread baskets must be changed after each customer.

In general, only unopened, prepackaged food, such as condiment packets, wrapped crackers, or wrapped breadsticks, can be re-served. You may also re-serve bottles of ketchup, mustard, and other condiments.

Self-Service Areas

Customers choosing food from self-service areas, or food bars, often unknowingly serve themselves in ways that can put them and other customers in danger. A customer may eat from his plate or nibble from the food bar while moving through the line. Another might pick up carrot sticks, pickles, and olives with her fingers, or dip a finger into salad dressing to taste it. Another might return unwanted food items, use a soiled plate for a second helping, or put his head under the sneeze guard to reach items in the back of the display.

To prevent contamination, self-service areas should be monitored closely by employees trained in food safety. Assign a staff member to replenish food-bar items and to hand out fresh plates for return visits. (See *Exhibit 9j*.) Post signs with

9i   Re-serving Food

Never re-serve plate garnishes, uncovered condiments, or uneaten bread.

9j   Self-Service Areas

Assign a trained staff member to monitor food bars and buffets.

Receiving · Storing · Preparing · Cooking · Holding · Cooling · Reheating · Serving · Purchasing

The Flow of Food

9k   Sneeze Guards

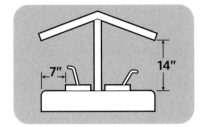

Sneeze guards should be fourteen inches (thirty-six centimeters) above the food counter. The shield should extend seven inches (eighteen centimeters) beyond the food.

9l   Identifying Food Items

Label all items on a food bar.

polite tips about food-bar etiquette. These practices will go a long way toward keeping self-service areas more sanitary.

Here are some additional rules for food bars:

• **Maintain proper food temperatures.** Keep hot food hot—135°F (57°C) or higher, and cold food cold—41°F (5°C) or lower.

• **Keep raw meat, seafood, and poultry separate from ready-to-eat food in self-service areas.**

• **Protect food on display with** sneeze guards **or food shields.** Sneeze guards should be fourteen inches (thirty-six centimeters) above the food counter, and shields should extend seven inches (eighteen centimeters) beyond the food. (See *Exhibit 9k.*)

• **Identify all food items.** Label containers on the food bar. Place names of salad dressings on ladle handles. (See *Exhibit 9l.*)

• **Do not let customers refill soiled plates or use soiled utensils at the food bar.** Encourage customers to take a clean plate for return trips to the food bar. Customers can use glassware for refills as long as beverage-dispensing equipment does not come in contact with the rim or interior of the glass.

• **Ice used to keep food or beverages cold should never be used as an ingredient.**

Off-Site Service

Off-site services, including delivery, mobile/temporary kitchens, and vending machines, all present special challenges. Those operating these services must follow the same food safety rules as permanent establishments. Food must be protected from contamination and time-temperature abuse, and facilities and equipment used to prepare food must be clean and sanitary. Menu items must lend themselves to safe service. Food must be handled safely.

Delivery

Many establishments such as schools, hospitals, caterers, and even restaurants may prepare food at one location and then deliver it to remote sites. The greater the time and distance between the point of preparation and the point of consumption, the greater the risk that food will be exposed to contamination or time-temperature abuse. Equipment used to transport food—both containers and vehicles—must be designed to maintain safe food temperatures and be easy to keep clean.

When transporting food, the following safety procedures should be followed:

- **Use insulated food containers capable of maintaining food at 135°F (57°C) or higher or 41°F (5°C) or lower.** (See *Exhibit 9l.*) Use only food-grade containers designed so that food does not mix, leak, or spill. They must also allow air circulation to keep temperatures even and should be kept clean and sanitized.

- **Clean the inside of delivery vehicles regularly.**

- **Practice good personal hygiene when distributing food.**

- **Check internal food temperatures regularly.** Take corrective action if food is not at the proper temperature. If containers or delivery vehicles are not maintaining proper food temperatures, reevaluate the length of the delivery route or the efficiency of the equipment being used.

- **Label food with a use-by date and time and reheating and service instructions for employees at off-site locations.**

- **Consider providing food safety guidelines for consumers.**

9l   Delivery Containers

When transporting food, use insulated containers capable of maintaining the proper temperature.

Receiving
Storing
Purchasing
Preparing
The Flow of Food
Cooking
Serving
Holding
Reheating
Cooling

Catering

Caterers must follow the same food safety rules as permanent establishments. Food must be protected from contamination and time-temperature abuse. Facilities must be clean and sanitary. Food must be prepared and served safely, and employees must follow good personal hygiene practices.

Caterers must meet the special challenges of off-site foodhandling. They must make sure there is safe drinking water for cooking, dishwashing, and handwashing.

Outdoor catering for barbecues and cookouts may require special arrangements. When power or running water is not available, caterers may have to change their foodhandling procedures:

- **Use insulated containers to hold TCS food.** Raw meat should be wrapped and stored on ice. Deliver milk and dairy products in a refrigerated vehicle or on ice.

- **Serve cold food in containers on ice or in chilled, gel-filled containers.** If that is not desirable, the food may be held without temperature control according to the guidelines specified in this chapter.

- **Store raw and ready-to-eat products separately.** For example, raw chicken should be stored separately from ready-to-eat salads.

- **If leftovers are given to customers, provide instructions on how they should be handled.** Information such as a discard date and the food's storage and reheating instructions should be clearly labeled on the container.

- **Place garbage-disposal containers away from food-preparation and serving areas.**

Key Point

Mobile kitchens serving TCS food must follow the same rules as permanent kitchens.

Mobile Units

Mobile units are portable facilities ranging from concession vans to elaborate field kitchens. Those serving only frozen novelties, candy, packaged snacks, and soft drinks have to meet basic sanitation requirements. Mobile kitchens preparing and serving TCS food, however, must follow the same rules required of permanent foodservice kitchens. Both might be required to apply for a special permit or license from the local regulatory agency.

Like permanent establishments, mobile kitchens must have adequate cooking equipment, cold-storage and hot-holding units, and dishwashing and handwashing sinks with hot and cold potable water under pressure. Mobile kitchens must provide adequate ventilation, garbage storage and disposal facilities, and pest control. Operators should clean and maintain mobile units.

9m   Temporary Unit

It is best to keep the menu simple to limit the amount of on-site food preparation.

Courtesy of the Illinois Restaurant Association

Temporary Units

Temporary units typically operate in one location for less than fourteen days. Foodservice tents or kiosks set up for food fairs, special celebrations, or sporting events may be temporary units. (See *Exhibit 9m.*) In some areas, the definition also extends to units set up for longer periods of time. Temporary units usually serve prepackaged food or food requiring limited preparation, such as hot dogs. It is best to keep the menu simple to limit the amount of on-site food preparation. Check with your local regulatory agency for operating requirements.

Temporary units should be constructed to keep dirt and pests out. If floors are made of dirt or gravel, cover them with mats or platforms to control dust and mud. Construct walls and the ceiling with materials that will protect food from weather and windblown dust.

In addition, the same safe-handling rules previously discussed apply to food preparation in temporary units. If food is prepared on site, the unit must have adequate cooking, cold storage, and hot-holding equipment. If food is prepared off site, it must be transported and held at 135°F (57°C) or higher or 41°F (5°C) or lower.

Safe drinking water must be available for cleaning, sanitizing, and handwashing. Since dishwashing facilities will most likely be limited, it is best to use disposable, single-use items.

Vending Machines

Food prepared and packaged for vending machines must be handled with the same care as any other food served to a customer. Vending operators also have to protect food from contamination and time-temperature abuse during transport, delivery, and service.

To keep vended food safe, it must be held at the proper temperature. Machines that vend TCS food must hold it at an internal temperature of 135°F (57°C) or higher, or 41°F (5°C) or lower.

Check product shelf life daily. If a food item's code date has expired, discard it immediately. If refrigerated TCS food is not used within seven days of preparation, it must be discarded. (See *Exhibit 9n.*) Dispense TCS food, such as milk, in its original container. Fresh fruit with an edible peel should be washed and wrapped before being put into a machine.

Place machines in appropriate locations, away from garbage containers, sewage drains, and overhead pipes. Make sure the vending area is clean and well lighted. Supply safe drinking water for beverage machines.

Clean and service vending machines regularly. Sanitize food-contact surfaces in machines each time food is replenished. Employees must also wash their hands before and after servicing or refilling machines.

9n   Vending Machines

Replace food with expired code dates.

Summary

Safe foodhandling does not stop once food is properly prepared and cooked. You must continue to protect it from time-temperature abuse and contamination until it is eaten. When holding TCS food for service, keep hot food hot—at 135°F (57°C) or higher, and cold food cold—at 41°F (5°C) or lower. Check the internal temperature of food being held at least every four hours and discard it if it is not at the proper temperature. Protect food from contaminants with covers and lids, and establish policies to ensure that food being held for service will be discarded after a predetermined amount of time. If food can be held without temperature control in your jurisdiction, follow requirements closely.

Use clean, sanitized utensils to serve food and minimize bare-hand contact with ready-to-eat food.

Make sure all employees practice good personal hygiene. Train them to avoid cross-contamination when handling service items and tableware. Teach them about the potential hazards posed by re-serving food such as plate garnishes, breads, or open dishes of condiments.

Customers can unknowingly contaminate food in self-service areas. Post signs to communicate self-service rules, and station employees in these areas to ensure compliance. Protect food in food bars and buffets with sneeze guards and make sure equipment can hold food at the proper temperature.

Take special precautions when preparing, delivering, or serving food off site. Catering, mobile kitchens, temporary units, and vending machines pose unique challenges to food safety. Learn and follow all regulations in your jurisdiction.

Apply Your Knowledge

① What did Jill do wrong?

② What should she have done?

A Case in Point 1

Jill, a line cook on the morning shift at Memorial Hospital, was busy helping the kitchen staff put food on display for lunch in the hospital cafeteria. Ann, the kitchen manager who usually supervised lunch in the cafeteria, was at an all-day seminar on food safety. Jill was responsible for making sure meals were trayed and put into food carts for transport to the patients' rooms. The staff also packed two-dozen meals each day for a neighborhood group that delivered them to homebound elderly people.

After Jill helped the kitchen staff, she looked for insulated food containers for the delivery meals. When she could not find them, she loaded the meals into cardboard boxes she found near the back door, knowing the driver would arrive soon to pick them up. To help the cafeteria staff, Jill filled a baine with soup by dipping a two-quart measuring cup into the stockpot and pouring it into the baine. She carried the baine out to the cafeteria, put it into the steam table, and turned it on low.

The lunch hour was hectic. The cafeteria was busy, and the staff had many patient meals to tray and deliver. Halfway through lunch, a cashier came back to the kitchen to tell Jill that the salad bar needed replenishing. Since she was busy, Jill asked a kitchen employee to take pans of prepared ingredients out of the refrigerator and put them on the salad bar. When she looked up a few moments later, she saw the kitchen employee send away two children who were eating carrot sticks from the salad bar.

With lunch almost over, Jill breathed a sigh of relief. She moved down the cafeteria serving line, checking food temperatures. One of the casseroles was about 130°F (54°C). Jill checked the water level in the steam table and turned up the thermostat, and then went to clean up the kitchen and finish her shift.

For answers, please turn to the Answer Key.

Apply Your Knowledge

A Case in Point 2

① What errors did Megan make?

② What should she have done?

Megan, a new server at The Fish House, reported for work ten minutes early on Thursday. Excited about her new job, she made sure to shower and wash her hair before going to work. When she arrived, she changed into a clean uniform, pulled her hair back tightly into a ponytail, and checked her appearance. She had used makeup sparingly and wore only a watch and a few rings.

Her shift started off well. One of her customers ordered a menu item that Megan had not tried yet. When the order came up, Megan dipped her finger into the sauce at the edge of the plate for a taste. As the shift progressed, Megan's station got busier. When the hostess came to ask how soon one of Megan's tables could be cleared, Megan decided to do it herself. She took the dirty dishes to a bus station and then wiped down the table with a serving cloth she kept in her apron.

The buser, John, finished another task and came to help her set the table. While he put out silverware and linens, Megan filled water glasses with ice by scooping the glasses into the ice bin in the bus station. Only one slice of bread and one pat of butter were missing from the basket that had been on a previous customer's table, so she put that on a tray with the water glasses and brought it to the table.

The table was reset in record time, and Megan soon had more guests. While taking their orders, Megan reached up to scratch a sore on her neck. Then she went to the kitchen to turn in the order and pick up a dessert order for another table.

For answers, please turn to the Answer Key.

Apply Your Knowledge

Discussion Questions

Use these questions to review the concepts presented in this chapter.

① What can be done to minimize contamination in self-service areas?

② What hazards are associated with the transportation of food and how can they be prevented?

③ What are the requirements for using time rather than temperature as the only method of control when holding ready-to-eat TCS food?

④ What practices should be followed to serve food safely off site?

For answers, please turn to the Answer Key.

Study Questions

Circle the best answer to each question.

① When serving, it is important to avoid touching the
_____ of a plate.

  A top

  B edges

  C side

  D bottom

② Serving utensils should be used to serve a maximum of
_____ food item(s) at a time.

  A 1   C 3

  B 2   D 4

③ At what maximum internal temperature should cold TCS
food be held?

  A 0°F (–17°C)

  B 32°F (0°C)

  C 41°F (5°C)

  D 60°F (16°C)

④ When returning to self-service lines for more food,
customers should not _____ their dirty plates.

  A carry

  B overload

  C refill

  D stack

⑤ At what minimum internal temperature should hot TCS
food be held?

  A 115°F (46°C)

  B 125°F (52°C)

  C 135°F (57°C)

  D 145°F (63°C)

⑥ Where allowed, hot TCS food can be held without
temperature control for a maximum of _____ hours
before being sold, served, or discarded.

  A 2   C 6

  B 4   D 8

For answers, please turn to the Answer Key.

Additional Resources

Articles and Texts

Angelotti, R., M. J. Foster, and K. L. Lewis. 1961. Time-temperature effects on *Salmonellae and Staphylococci* in foods, II. Behavior in warm holding temperatures. *American Journal of Public Health.* 51:76.

Blankenship, L.C., S.C Craven, R.G. Leffler, and C. Custer. 1988. Growth of Clostridium perfringens in cooked chili during cooling. *Applied and Environmental Microbiology.* 54 (5): 1104.

Chen, Y., W. H. Ross, V. N. Scott, and D. E. Gombas. 2003. *Listeria monocytogenes:* Low levels equal low risk. *Journal of Food Protection.* 66 (4): 570.

Makukutu, C. A., and R. K. Guthrie. 1986. Survival of *Escherichia coli* in food at hot-holding temperatures. *Journal of Food Protection.* 49 (7): 496.

Web Sites

FDA Food Safety
www.fda.gov/Food/FoodSafety/default.htm

Gateway to Government Food Safety Information
foodsafety.gov

National Automatic Merchandising Association
vending.org/index.php

USDA Food Safety and Inspection Service
www.fsis.usda.gov/

Documents and Other Resources

2009 FDA Food Code
www.fda.gov/Food/FoodSafety/RetailFoodProtection/FoodCode/FoodCode2009/default.htm

Risk Assessment for Listeria monocytogenes *in Deli Meats*
www.fsis.usda.gov/OPPDE/rdad/FRPubs/97-013F/ListeriaReport.pdf

Notes

10 Food Safety Management Systems

Inside this chapter:

- Prerequisite Food Safety Programs
- Active Managerial Control
- Hazard Analysis Critical Control Point (HACCP)
- Crisis Management

After completing this chapter, you should be able to:

- Identify how active managerial control can impact food safety.
- Identify HACCP principles for preventing foodborne illness.
- Implement HACCP principles when applicable.
- Identify when a HACCP plan is required.
- Implement a crisis-management program.
- Cooperate with regulatory agencies in the event of a foodborne-illness investigation.

Key Terms

- Food safety management system
- Active managerial control
- HACCP
- HACCP plan
- Critical control point (CCP)

Apply Your Knowledge

Check to see how much you know about the concepts in this chapter. Use the page references provided with each question to explore the topic.

Test Your Food Safety Knowledge

① **True or False:** Active managerial control focuses on controlling the most common foodborne-illness risk factors identified by the Centers for Disease Control and Prevention (CDC). *(See page 10-3.)*

② **True or False:** Purchasing fish directly from a local fisher would be considered a risk in an active managerial control system. *(See page 10-3.)*

③ **True or False:** A critical control point (CCP) is a point in the flow of food where a hazard can be prevented, eliminated, or reduced to safe levels. *(See page 10-8.)*

④ **True or False:** If cooking is a CCP for ground beef patties in a particular establishment, then ensuring the internal temperature reaches 155°F (68°C) for fifteen seconds would be an appropriate critical limit. *(See page 10-9.)*

⑤ **True or False:** An establishment that cures food must have a HACCP plan. *(See page 10-13.)*

For answers, please turn to the Answer Key.

Introduction

In Chapters 5 through 9, you learned how to handle food safely throughout the flow of food. This accumulated knowledge will help you take the next step in preventing foodborne illness—the development of a food safety management system.

A **food safety management system** is a group of procedures and practices intended to prevent foodborne illness. It does this by actively controlling risks and hazards throughout the flow of food. Active managerial control and Hazard Analysis Critical Control Point (HACCP) are two ways to build a system.

Receiving · Storing · Preparing · Purchasing · Cooking · Serving · Reheating · Cooling · Holding

The Flow of Food

Prerequisite Food Safety Programs

For your food safety management system to be effective, you must first have the necessary food safety programs in place. (See *Exhibit 10a.*) The principles presented in the ServSafe program are the basis of these programs. They address the basic operational and sanitation conditions within your establishment and can include processes, policies, and procedures.

10a Prerequisite Food Safety Programs

 Personal hygiene program

 Facility design and equipment-maintenance program

 Supplier selection and specification program

 Food safety training program

 Sanitation and pest control programs

Active Managerial Control

One way to manage food safety risks in your establishment is to implement **active managerial control.** This approach focuses on controlling the five most common risk factors that cause foodborne illness as identified by the Centers for Disease Control and Prevention (CDC). They are:

1 Purchasing food from unsafe sources

2 Failing to cook food adequately

3 Holding food at incorrect temperatures

4 Using contaminated equipment

5 Practicing poor personal hygiene

The *FDA Food Code* has identified five ways to control these risks. It has created the following public-health interventions to protect consumer health.

- **Demonstration of knowledge.** As a manager, you must be able to show that you know what to do to keep food safe. One example is knowing the illnesses that foodborne pathogens can cause.

- **Staff health control.** Staff health controls are policies and procedures that you put into place to make sure your employees are practicing personal hygiene. One example is the exclusion and restriction criteria you learned in Chapter 4.

- **Controlling hands as a vehicle of contamination.** These controls help prevent cross-contamination from hands to food. Using tongs for ready-to-eat food is one example.

- **Time and temperature parameters for controlling pathogens.** You must keep food out of the temperature danger zone. One example is following correct cooling procedures.

- **Consumer advisory.** These are notices that you must provide to your customers about the risks of raw or undercooked food. One example is the notification you must place on your menu if it includes TCS items that are raw or undercooked.

Active Managerial Control Approach

There are specific steps that should be taken when using active managerial control to manage food safety risks in your establishment.

❶ **Consider the five risk factors throughout the flow of food in your establishment, and identify any issues that could impact food safety.**

❷ **Create policies and procedures that address the issues that were identified.** Consider asking your staff for suggestions as you create them. It may be necessary to provide training on these policies and procedures.

10b Active Managerial Control

Managers must monitor policies and procedures to ensure they are being followed.

❸ **Regularly monitor the policies and procedures that have been developed.** This step, which is critical to the success of an active managerial control system, can help you determine if the policies and procedures are being followed. (See *Exhibit 10b.*) If not, it may be necessary to revise them, create new ones, or retrain employees.

❹ **Verify that the policies and procedures you have established are actually controlling the risk factors.** Use feedback from internal sources (records, temperature logs, and self-inspections) and external sources (health-inspection reports, customer comments, and quality assurance audits) to adjust the policies and procedures to continuously improve the system.

Example of Active Managerial Control

Here is an example of how one seafood restaurant chain used active managerial control.

❶ **Considering the risk factors.** The chain identified the purchasing of seafood from unsafe sources as a risk in their operations.

❷ **Creating policies and procedures.** The managers developed a list of approved seafood suppliers. They based the list on criteria that made sure the seafood they received would meet their safety and quality standards. Next, they created a policy that seafood could be purchased only from suppliers on this list.

❸ **Monitoring the policies and procedures.** The managers decided that all seafood invoices and deliveries would be monitored.

❹ **Verifying the system.** On a regular basis, the managers checked the standards they had created for choosing seafood suppliers. They wanted to make sure the standards were still able to control the risk. They also decided to review their policy regularly and change it as needed.

Something to Think About...

Get a Handle on It!

A local health department was inspecting a unit in a large quick-service chain. The inspector noticed that the grill operator handling raw chicken fillets also put cooked fillets in a holding drawer. A sandwich maker touched the handle of the drawer each time she retrieved a cooked fillet.

The health inspector saw that the grill operator was contaminating the handle of the holding drawer each time he put a cooked fillet inside—because his hands had touched raw chicken. When the sandwich maker touched the contaminated handle, there was a chance of cross-contamination.

Working with the unit manager, the inspector recommended adding an extra handle to the holding drawer. The grill operator and sandwich maker were assigned their own handle.

In dealing with the risk of contamination, the chain followed the procedure outlined by its active managerial control system. This included modifying their standard operating procedures (SOPs) to control the risk and retraining staff. They also incorporated the new SOPs in the chain's monitoring program.

Hazard Analysis Critical Control Point (HACCP)

A HACCP system can also be used to control risks and hazards throughout the flow of food. **HACCP** (pronounced *HASS-ip*) is based on identifying significant biological, chemical, or physical hazards at specific points within a product's flow through an operation. Once identified, the hazards can be prevented, eliminated, or reduced to safe levels.

To be effective, a HACCP system must be based on a written plan that is specific to each facility's menu, customers, equipment, processes, and operations. Since each **HACCP plan** is unique, a plan that works for one establishment may not work for another.

10c   The Seven HACCP Principles

❶ Conduct a hazard analysis.

❷ Determine critical control points (CCPs).

❸ Establish critical limits.

❹ Establish monitoring procedures.

❺ Identify corrective actions.

❻ Verify that the system works.

❼ Establish procedures for record keeping and documentation.

The HACCP Approach

A HACCP plan is based on the seven basic principles outlined by the National Advisory Committee on Microbiological Criteria for Foods. (See *Exhibit 10c.*) These principles are seven sequential steps that outline how to create a HACCP plan. Because each principle builds on the information gained from the previous principle, you must consider all seven principles in order when developing your plan.

In general terms:

- Principles 1 and 2 help you identify and evaluate your hazards.

- Principles 3, 4, and 5 help you establish ways for controlling those hazards.

- Principles 6 and 7 help you maintain the HACCP plan and system and verify its effectiveness.

The Seven HACCP Principles

The information covered in the next several pages is designed to provide you with an introduction to the seven HACCP principles and an overview of the process for developing a HACCP program. A real-world example, has also been included for each principle. It documents the efforts of Enrico's, an Italian restaurant, as it implements a HACCP program. The example appears next to the explanation of each principle.

Introduction to the Seven HACCP Principles

Principle 1:
Conduct a Hazard Analysis

To identify and assess potential hazards in the food you serve, start by taking a look at how it is processed in your establishment. Many types of food are processed similarly. The most common processes include:

- Preparing and serving without cooking (salads, cold sandwiches, etc.)
- Preparing and cooking for same-day service (grilled chicken sandwiches, hamburgers, etc.)
- Preparing, cooking, holding, cooling, reheating, and serving (chili, soup, pasta sauce with meat, etc.)

Look at your menu to identify items that are processed similarly. Next, identify the TCS food. Determine where food safety hazards are likely to occur for each TCS food. There are many types of hazards to look for:

- Biological
- Chemical
- Physical

The management team at Enrico's decided to implement a HACCP program. They began by conducting a hazard analysis.

When they reviewed their menu, they noted that many of their dishes were received, stored, prepared, cooked, and served the same day. The most popular of these items was the spicy charbroiled chicken breast.

The team determined that bacteria were the most likely hazard to food prepared by this process.

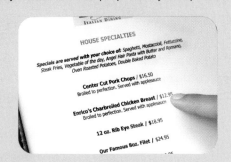

Principle 2:
Determine Critical Control Points (CCPs)

Find the points in the process where the identified hazard(s) can be prevented, eliminated, or reduced to safe levels. These are the **critical control points (CCPs).** Depending on the process, there may be more than one CCP.

Enrico's management identified cooking as the CCP for the chicken breasts and for other products prepared and cooked for immediate service.

These food items must be handled safely throughout the flow of food. However, proper cooking is the only step that will eliminate or reduce bacteria to safe levels.

Because the chicken breasts were prepared for immediate service, cooking was the only CCP identified.

Principle 3:
Establish Critical Limits

For each CCP, establish minimum or maximum limits that must be met to prevent or eliminate the hazard or to reduce it to a safe level.

With cooking identified as the CCP for Enrico's chicken breasts, a critical limit was needed. Management determined that the critical limit would be cooking the chicken to a minimum internal temperature of 165°F (74°C) for fifteen seconds.

They decided that the critical limit could be met by cooking the chicken breasts in the broiler for sixteen minutes.

Principle 4:
Establish Monitoring Procedures

Once critical limits have been established, determine the best way for your operation to check them to make sure they are consistently met. Identify who will monitor them and how often.

At Enrico's, each charbroiled chicken breast is cooked to order. The team decided to check the critical limit by inserting a clean and sanitized thermocouple probe into the thickest part of each chicken breast.

The grill cook is required to check the temperature of each chicken breast after cooking to ensure that it has reached the minimum internal temperature of 165°F (74°C) for fifteen seconds.

Continued on next page ▶

▶ *Continued from previous page*

Principle 5:
Identify Corrective Actions

Identify steps that must be taken when a critical limit is *not* met. These steps should be determined in advance.

If the chicken breast has not reached its critical limit within the sixteen-minute cook time, the grill cook at Enrico's must keep cooking the breast until it has reached it.

This and all other corrective actions are noted in the temperature log.

Principle 6:
Verify That the System Works

Determine if the plan is working as intended. Evaluate it on a regular basis. Use your monitoring charts, records, how you performed your hazard analysis, etc., and determine if your plan adequately prevents, reduces, or eliminates identified hazards.

Enrico's management team performs HACCP checks once per shift to ensure that critical limits were met and appropriate corrective actions were taken when necessary.

Additionally, they check the temperature logs on a weekly basis to identify patterns or to determine if processes or procedures need to be changed. For example, over several weeks they noticed that toward the end of each week, the chicken breast often failed to meet its critical limit. The appropriate corrective action was being taken; however, management discovered that Enrico's received chicken shipments from a different supplier on Thursdays. This supplier provided a six-ounce chicken breast instead of the four-ounce chicken breast listed in Enrico's chicken specifications. Management worked with the supplier to ensure they received four-ounce breasts and changed their receiving procedure to include a weight check.

Principle 7:
Establish Procedures for Record Keeping and Documentation

Maintain your HACCP plan and keep all documentation created when developing it. In addition, keep records for the following actions:

- Monitoring activities
- Taking corrective action
- Validating equipment (checking for good working condition)
- Working with suppliers (i.e., shelf-life studies, invoices, specifications, challenge studies, etc.)

Enrico's management team determined that time-temperature logs should be kept for three months and receiving invoices should be kept for sixty days.

The team used this documentation to support and revise their HACCP plan.

Another HACCP Example

The Enrico's example shows one type of HACCP plan. Another plan may look very different when it deals with food that is processed more simply. For example, food that is prepared and served without cooking needs a different approach.

Here is an example of the HACCP plan developed by The Fruit Basket. This fruit-only restaurant is known for its signature item—the Melon Medley salad.

1. **Analyzing hazards.** The HACCP team at The Fruit Basket decided to look at hazards for the Melon Medley. The salad has fresh watermelon, honeydew, and cantaloupe. The team determined that bacteria pose a risk to the fresh-cut melons.

2. **Determining CCPs.** The melons are prepared, held, and served without cooking. The team determined that preparation and holding are CCPs for the salad. They decided that cleaning and drying the melons' surfaces during preparation would reduce bacteria. Holding the melon at the right temperature could prevent the bacteria's growth. Receiving was ruled out as a CCP, because the operation purchases melons only from approved suppliers.

Continued on next page ▶

► *Continued from previous page*

❸ **Establishing critical limits.** For the preparation CCP, the team decided the critical limit would be met by washing, scrubbing, and drying whole melons. They created an SOP with techniques for washing the melons. For the holding CCP, they decided that the salad must be held at 41°F (5°C) or lower, because it has cut melons.

❹ **Establishing monitoring procedures.** The team decided that the operation's team leader should monitor the salad's critical limits. The team leader must observe foodhandlers to make sure they are preparing the melons correctly. Foodhandlers must remove all surface dirt and debris from the washed melons. Then they must cut, mix, and portion the salad into containers. The finished salads are put in the display cooler.

The team leader must then monitor the temperature of the held salads to make sure the holding critical limit is met. The internal temperature of the salads must be 41°F (5°C) or lower. It must be checked three times per day. A clean, sanitized, and calibrated probe must be inserted into the salad.

❺ **Identifying corrective actions.** Sometimes after preparation, the melons still have surface dirt. The team had to determine a corrective action for this. They decided that the action would be to rewash the melons. Then the team leader must approve the melons before they are sliced.

To correct a holding temperature that is higher than 41°F (5°C), the team leader must check the temperature of every Melon Medley in the cooler. Any salad that is above 41°F (5°C) must be thrown away. The team leader must also record all corrective actions in the Manager Daily HACCP Check Sheet.

❻ **Verifying that the system works.** To make sure the system is working right, the team decided that the operation team leader must review the Manager Daily HACCP Check Sheet at the end of each shift. The team leader makes sure that each item was checked and initialed. The team leader also confirms that all corrective actions have been taken and recorded. The Fruit Basket also evaluates the HACCP system quarterly to see if it is working.

❼ **Establishing procedures for record keeping.** Because a foodborne illness associated with fresh produce can take as long as sixteen weeks to emerge, the team determined that all HACCP records must be maintained for sixteen weeks and kept on file. They also decided that produce suppliers must maintain their records for at least one year.

When a HACCP Plan Is Required

A HACCP plan is required when preparing food in the ways listed below. Always check with your local regulatory authority to see if a variance is also required.

- Smoking food as a method to preserve it (but not to enhance flavor).

- Using food additives or adding components such as vinegar to preserve or alter it so it no longer requires time and temperature control for safety.

- Curing food.

- Custom-processing animals. For example, this may include dressing deer in the operation for personal use.

- Packaging food using reduced-oxygen packaging (ROP) methods. This includes MAP, vacuum-packed, and *sous vide* food. *Clostridium botulinum* and *Listeria monocytogenes* are risks to food packaged in these ways.

- Treating (e.g., pasteurizing) and packaging juice on site for later sale.

- Sprouting seeds or beans.

- Offering live, molluscan shellfish from a display tank.

10d Crisis-Management Plan

A successful crisis-management program will have a written plan that focuses on preparation, response, and recovery.

Crisis Management

Putting the food safety principles you have learned into action can help keep food safe in your operation. However, despite your best efforts, a foodborne-illness outbreak or another type of crisis affecting food safety may occur. How you respond can make a difference in the outcome.

To handle these crises you will need a crisis-management program. To be successful, the program must have a written plan (see *Exhibit 10d*) that focuses on three parts: preparation, response, and recovery. For each of these parts, the plan must identify the resources needed and the procedures to be followed.

The time to prepare for a crisis, is before one happens. There is no "off-the-shelf" disaster plan that works for every establishment. Each plan must be tailored to meet the establishment's individual needs. A good way to make sure your plan meets your needs is to test the plan once it is complete. The results will help you identify potential gaps or problems. Testing the plan will also ensure that it works as intended. You can do this yourself or hire a consulting firm with crisis-management experience. In either case, the test should be designed to simulate a crisis that will be as close as possible to what could happen.

Creating a Crisis-Management Team

10e Develop a Crisis-Management Team

The size of the team will vary depending on the size of the establishment.

To begin, create a crisis-management team. The size of the team will depend on the size of the establishment. (See *Exhibit 10e.*) If your operation is large, the team may include representatives from the following departments:

- Senior management (president/CEO, etc.)

- Risk management (quality assurance, legal, etc.)

- Public relations

- Operations

- Finance

- Marketing

- Human resources

Smaller operations may include the chef, the general manager, and the owner/operator. Regardless of size, you should also consider using other resources. External resources include your local regulatory authority and experts from your suppliers and manufacturers.

Preparing for a Crisis

Your crisis-management team should consider doing the following when preparing for a crisis:

- **Assemble an emergency contact list, and post it by phones.** The list should include the names and numbers of all crisis-management team members, the media spokesperson, management or headquarters personnel, and outside resources, such as police, fire, and health departments, testing labs, and subject matter experts.

- **Develop a crisis communication plan and assign and train a spokesperson to handle media relations.** The crisis communication plan should include:

  ○ List of media responses or a question-and-answer sheet suggesting what to say for each crisis.

  ○ Sample press releases that can be tailored quickly to each incident.

  ○ List of media contacts to call for press conferences or news briefings. Include a media-relations plan with "do's and don'ts" for dealing with the media.

  ○ Plan for communicating with employees during the crisis. Possibilities include shift meetings, email, a telephone tree, etc. There are several guides available to help you develop a crisis communication plan. (See *Exhibit 10f.*)

10f Crisis-Communication Plan

There are several guides available to help you develop your communication plan.

Appoint a single spokesperson to handle all media queries and communications. Designating a point person usually results in more consistent messages and allows you to control media access to your staff. The spokesperson should be familiar with interview skills so that he or she knows what to expect and how to respond. Crisis situations can be very stressful, and training will enable your spokesperson to handle it better. Make sure all of your staff know who the spokesperson is, and instruct them to direct questions to that person.

- **Assemble a crisis kit for the establishment.** The kit can take the form of a three-ring notebook or binder enclosing the plan's materials. Keep the kit in an accessible place, such as the manager's or chef's office.

Preparing for a Foodborne-Illness Outbreak

The greatest threat to your customers is foodborne illness. One of the most important things you can do to prevent an outbreak is to create a food safety program and train your staff on polices and procedures that will keep food safe in your operation. In the event of an outbreak, it will be critical to gather accurate information. To prepare for this, you should develop a foodborne-illness incident report form and train staff to complete it.

Create the form with legal guidance and include all critical information. The form may include:

- When and what the customer ate at the establishment

- When the customer first became ill, what the symptoms where, and how long the customer experienced them

- When and where the customer sought medical attention, what the diagnosis was, and the treatment received

- What other food was eaten by the customer

Crisis Response

A crisis-management plan should include response procedures to help manage a crisis more effectively. When a crisis occurs, call your crisis-management team together to implement your plan. Direct the team to gather information, plan courses of action, and manage events as they unfold.

Good communication is critical when handling a crisis. Consider the following to keep the situation under control:

- **Work with the media.** Make sure your spokesperson is fully informed before arranging a press conference. Contacting the media before they contact you helps you control what they report. Stick to the facts, and be honest. If you do not have all the facts, say so, and let the media know that you will communicate with them as soon as you do know. Keep a cool head, and do not be defensive. The easiest way to magnify or prolong a crisis is to deny, lie, give wrong information, or change your story.

- **Communicate information directly to all of your key audiences.** Do not depend on the media to relay all the facts. Tell your side of the story to employees, customers, stockholders, and the community. Use newsletters, a Web site, flyers, and newspaper or radio advertising.

- **Fix the problem, and communicate to both the media and to your customers what you have done.** Each time you take a step to resolve the problem, let the media know. Hold briefings when you have news, and go into each briefing or press conference with an agenda. Take control rather than simply responding to questions.

Responding to a Foodborne-Illness Outbreak

In the event of a foodborne-illness outbreak, you may be able to avert a crisis by responding quickly. *Exhibit 10g* shows some things to consider.

10g Foodborne-Illness Outbreak Responses

If	Then
A customer calls to report a foodborne illness.	• Take the complaint seriously and express concern. Do not admit responsibility or accept liability. • Complete a foodborne-illness incident report form. • Evaluate the complaint to determine if there are similar complaints.
There are similar customer complaints of foodborne illness.	• Contact the crisis-management team. • Identify common food items to determine the potential source of the complaint. • Contact the local health department to assist with the investigation.
The suspected food is still in the operation.	• Isolate the suspected food and identify it to prevent further sale. • If possible, obtain samples of the suspect food from the customer.
The suspected outbreak is caused by an ill staff member.	• Exclude the suspect staff member from the operation.
The regulatory authority confirms your operation is the source of the outbreak.	• Cooperate with the regulatory authority to resolve the crisis.
The media contacts your operation.	• Follow your crisis communication plan. Let your spokesperson handle all communication.

Crisis Recovery and Assessment

The final step in a crisis-management plan is developing procedures for recovering from a crisis. Determine what you must do to ensure that the operation and the food are safe. This is critical for getting your operation running again.

Recovering from a Foodborne-Illness Outbreak

You must take several steps to recover from a foodborne-illness outbreak. These steps should be planned in advance and include the following:

- Working with the regulatory authority to resolve issues. (See *Exhibit 10h.*)

- Cleaning and sanitizing all areas of the operation.

- Throwing out all suspect food.

- Investigating to find the cause of the outbreak.

- Establishing new procedures or revising existing ones based on the investigation results. This can help prevent the incident from reoccurring.

- Developing a plan to reassure customers that the food served in your establishment is safe.

10h Work with Regulatory Authorities

Cooperate with health officials.

Other Crises

In addition to foodborne-illness outbreaks, other crises can affect the safety of the food you serve. Among these are power outages, water interruption (including water contamination), fire, and flood. These crises require immediate action to prevent endangering people's health and therefore should be addressed in your crisis-management plan. Planning should focus on preparation, recovery, and response.

Power Outage

Consider the following when planning for a power outage:

- Arrange access to an electrical generator and a refrigerated truck to use in the event of an emergency.

- Prepare a menu with items that do not require cooking to be used in the event of an emergency.

- Develop a policy that addresses when refrigerator doors should be opened.

- Make a list of electrical equipment that could be negatively affected when the power is restored.

- Have emergency-contact information for the utility company, garbage service, ice supplier, etc.

To manage your response to a power outage, consider the steps identified in *Exhibit 10i.*

10i | **Power Outage Responses**

If	Then
Refrigeration equipment stops working.	• Write down the time of the power outage. • Check and record food temperatures periodically. • Keep refrigerator and freezer doors closed. • Pack TCS food in ice bought from an approved, reputable supplier.
Ventilation hoods or fans stop working.	• Stop all cooking.
Hot-holding equipment stops working.	• Write down the time of the power outage. • Throw out all TCS food held below 135°F (57°C) for more than four hours. ◦ Food can be reheated if the power outage was less than four hours.

You must also plan for the recovery from a power outage. For example, refrigeration units will need to be checked frequently after the power has been restored to ensure the equipment can maintain product temperatures. TCS food will also have to be discarded if it has been in the temperature danger zone for more than four hours.

Water Service Interruption

Consider the following when planning for a water service interruption:

- Prepare a menu with items that require little or no water to be used in the event of an emergency.

- Keep a supply of single-use items.

- Keep a supply of bottled water, and have a supplier who can provide bottled water in an emergency.

- Have a supplier who can provide ice in an emergency.

- Have emergency-contact information for the local regulatory authority, plumber, and water department.

- Develop procedures that minimize water use during the emergency (i.e., use single-use items for service).

- Work with your local regulatory authority to develop an emergency handwashing procedure that can be used during water service interruptions.

To manage your response to a water service interruption, consider the steps identified in *Exhibit 10j.*

10j   Water Service Interruption Responses

If	Then
Hands cannot be washed.	• Implement an emergency handwashing procedure. • Do not touch ready-to-eat food with bare hands.
Toilets do not flush.	• Find other toilet facilities for employee use during operating hours. • Stop operations if toilet facilities are not available.

Drinking water is not available or it is contaminated.	• Use bottled water. • Use water from an approved, reputable supplier. • Keep water in a covered, sanitized container during hauling or storage.
Food items that require water during preparation cannot be made.	• Throw out any ready-to-eat food made with water before the contamination was discovered. • Use bottled or boiled water for ready-to-eat food.
Water is not available for food preparation and cooking.	• Use water from an approved, reputable supplier. • Use the emergency menu. • Use prewashed, packaged produce or frozen or canned fruit and vegetables. • Thaw food only in the refrigerator, microwave, or as a part of the cooking process.
Ice cannot be made.	• Stop making ice. • Throw out existing ice. • Use ice from an approved, reputable supplier.
Equipment, utensils, and facility cannot be cleaned or sanitized.	• Use single-use items. • Use bottled water or water from an approved source to clean and sanitize.
Beverages made with water cannot be prepared.	• Stop using the drink machines that require water, such as the auto-fill coffee maker, instant hot-water heater, etc.

When water is restored or the local regulatory authority has lifted any boiled-water advisory, you should plan on taking the following actions:

- Clean and sanitize equipment with water-line connections such as spray misters, coffee or tea urns, ice machines, and others. Follow manufacturers' instructions.

- Flush water lines as required by the local regulatory authority.

- Work with your local regulatory authority to resume normal operations.

Fire

Consider the following when planning for a fire:

- Have emergency-contact information for the fire and police departments, local regulatory authority, and management or headquarters personnel.

- Post the fire department phone number by each phone so it is easy to see.

To manage your response to a fire, consider the steps identified in *Exhibit 10k.*

10k   Fire Responses

If	Then
A fire occurs.	• Stop operations if food can no longer be safely prepared. • Block off areas, equipment, utensils, and other items affected by the fire.

Consider the following when planning a recovery from a fire:

- Throw out all food affected by the fire.

- Throw out all damaged utensils, linens, or items that cannot be cleaned and sanitized.

- Clean and sanitize the establishment.

- If necessary, hire a janitorial service specializing in areas exposed to fires.

- Check water lines. The use of fire hoses may have lowered water pressure in the area and could cause backflow and water contamination.

Flood

Consider the following when planning for a flood:

- Have a plan to monitor and maintain flood-control equipment: plumbing, storm drains, sump pumps, etc.

- Have emergency-contact information for the local regulatory authority, plumber, utility companies, etc.

- Keep a supply of bottled water.

To manage your response to a flood, consider the steps identified in *Exhibit 10l.*

10l   Flood Responses

If	Then
A water line leaks or water builds up on the floor, but food, utensils, etc., are not affected.	<ul><li>Keep people away from the wet floor.</li><li>Repair the leak.</li><li>Block off areas, equipment, utensils, and other items affected by the flood.</li></ul>
A flood affects or damages food, utensils, etc.	<ul><li>Stop all operations.</li></ul>
The flood is the result of a sewage backup in the food-preparation area.	<ul><li>Close the affected area immediately.</li><li>Correct the problem</li><li>Clean the area thoroughly.</li></ul>

Consider the following when planning the recovery from
a flood:

- Throw out all damaged utensils, linens, or items that cannot
  be cleaned and sanitized.

- Throw out any food or food packaging that made contact
  with the water.

- Clean and sanitize the facility, utensils, equipment surfaces,
  floors, or other affected areas.

- If needed, hire a janitorial service specializing in cleaning
  areas exposed to floods.

Summary

A food safety management system is a group of programs,
procedures, and measures for preventing foodborne illness
by actively controlling risks and hazards throughout the flow
of food. HACCP and active managerial control offer two
approaches. In order for the food safety system to be effective,
you must first have the necessary food safety programs in place.
These include programs for personal hygiene, facility design,
supplier selection and specifications, sanitation and pest
control, equipment maintenance, and food safety training.

One way to control risks associated with foodborne illness is
to implement active managerial control. This approach focuses
on controlling the five most common risk factors that cause
foodborne illness as identified by the CDC. These include
purchasing food from unsafe sources, failing to cook food
adequately, holding food at improper temperatures, using
contaminated equipment, and practicing poor personal hygiene.
There are specific steps that should be taken when using active
managerial control to manage these risks in your establishment.
First, you must consider the five risk factors as they apply
throughout the flow of food and then identify any issues that
could impact food safety. Next, you will need to develop policies
and procedures that address the issues that were identified. These
will require regular monitoring to determine if they are being
followed. Finally, you must verify that the policies and procedures
you have established are actually controlling the risk factors.

A HACCP system focuses on identifying specific points within a product's flow through the operation that are essential to prevent, eliminate, or reduce biological, chemical, or physical hazards to safe levels. To be effective, a HACCP system must be based on a plan specific to a facility's menu, customers, equipment, processes, and operation. The HACCP plan is developed following seven sequential principles—essential steps for building a food safety system.

First, the establishment must identify and assess potential hazards in the food they serve by taking a look at how it is processed. Once common processes have been identified, they can determine where food safety hazards are likely to occur for each one. The establishment must then identify points where they can be prevented, eliminated, or reduced to safe levels. These are the CCPs. Next, the establishment must determine minimum or maximum limits that must be met for each CCP to prevent, eliminate, or reduce the hazard. The establishment must determine how they will monitor the CCPs they have identified and what actions will be taken when critical limits have not been met. Finally, the establishment must find ways to verify that the HACCP system is working, and establish procedures for record keeping and documentation.

A food safety management system can help ensure that the food you serve is safe. Despite your best efforts, however, a foodborne-illness outbreak—and other crises—can occur in your establishment. The time to prepare for a crisis is before one occurs. The key is to start with a written plan that focuses on preparation, response, and recovery. For each of these parts, the plan must identify the resources needed and the procedures to be followed.

There is no "off-the-shelf" disaster plan that works for every operation. Each plan must be tailored to meet the operation's individual needs. A good way to make sure your plan meets your needs is to test the plan once it's complete. The results of the test will help you identify potential gaps and problems.

Apply Your Knowledge

Use these questions to review the concepts presented in this chapter.

Discussion Questions

① What food safety programs must be in place for a food safety management system to be effective?

② What are the five most common risk factors that cause foodborne illness as identified by the CDC?

③ List the specific steps that should be taken when using active managerial control to manage food safety risks.

④ List the seven HACCP principles in order.

⑤ When is an establishment required to have a HACCP plan?

For answers, please turn to the Answer Key.

Study Questions

Circle the best answer to each question.

① **The temperature of a roast is checked to see if it has met its critical limit of 145°F (63°C) for four minutes. This is an example of which HACCP principle?**

A Verification

B Monitoring

C Record keeping

D Hazard analysis

② **The temperature of a pot of beef stew is checked during holding. The stew has not met the critical limit and is thrown out according to house policy. Throwing out the stew is an example of which HACCP principle?**

A Corrective action

B Hazard analysis

C Verification

D Monitoring

③ **The CDC has determined five common risk factors for foodborne illness. They are: purchasing food from unsafe sources, failing to cook food adequately, holding food at incorrect temperatures, practicing poor personal hygiene, and using**

A   imported supplies.

B   incorrect shellstock tags.

C   unapproved chemicals.

D   contaminated equipment.

④ **What is the first step in developing a HACCP plan?**

A   Identify corrective actions.

B   Conduct a hazard analysis.

C   Establish monitoring procedures.

D   Determine critical control points.

⑤ **A food safety management system is a group of_____ preventing foodborne illness.**

A   managers and customers

B   measurements and graphs

C   procedures and practices

D   detergents and sanitizers

⑥ **What is the purpose of a food safety management system?**

A   To keep all areas of the facility clean and pest free

B   To identify, tag, and repair faulty equipment within the facility

C   To identify, document, and use the correct methods for receiving food

D   To identify and control possible hazards

Continued on next page ▶

► *Continued from previous page*

⑦ **An operation that wants to smoke food as a method of preservation must have a(n)**

A current organization chart.

B crisis-management plan.

C HACCP plan.

D MSDS.

⑧ **A chef sanitized a thermometer probe and then checked the temperature of minestrone soup being held in a hot-holding unit. The temperature was 120°F (49°C), which did not meet the operation's critical limit of 135°F (57°C). The chef recorded the temperature in the log and reheated the soup to 165°F (74°C) for 15 seconds within two hours. Which was the corrective action?**

A Reheating the soup

B Checking the critical limit

C Sanitizing the thermometer probe

D Recording the temperature in the log

⑨ **What is the third step in active managerial control?**

A File the documentation in case of a crisis.

B Monitor the policies and procedures.

C Revise the policies and procedures.

D Determine staffing needs.

⑩ **Which is an example of when a HACCP plan is required?**

A Serving smoked meat on a metal platter

B Serving chili made from a family recipe

C Serving wild game with cream sauce

D Serving raw oysters from a display tank

For answers, please turn to the Answer Key.

Additional Resources

Articles and Texts

Food Products Association. *HACCP Manual 4th Edition: A Systematic Approach to Food Safety.* 2006.

Bryan, Frank L. 2000. Conducting Effective Foodborne-Illness Investigations. *Journal of Environmental Health.* 63 (1): 9.

McFee, Kathryn and Liz Guthridge. *Leading People Through Disasters: An Action Guide.* Berrett-Koehler Publishers, 2006.

Web Sites

Association of Food and Drug Officials
afdo.org

Center for Infectious Disease Research & Policy
www.cidrap.umn.edu

Conference for Food Protection
foodprotect.org

FDA Food Safety
www.fda.gov/Food/FoodSafety/default.htm

Gateway to Government Food Safety Information
foodsafety.gov

International HACCP Alliance
haccpalliance.org

Risk and Insurance Management Society, Inc.
rims.org

Society for Risk Analysis
sra.org

USDA Food Safety and Inspection Service
www.fsis.usda.gov/

Documents and Other Resources

Conference for Food Protection: Emergency Guidance for Retail Food Establishments
www.foodprotect.org/media/guide/EmergencyActionPlanforRetailFoodEstablishments2008.pdf

Crisis Management: Imminent Health Hazards
michigan.gov/mda/0,1607,7-125—105442—,00.html

FEMA Emergency Management Guide for Business and Industry
fema.gov/business/guide/index.shtm

Continued on next page ▶

► *Continued from previous page*

Additional Resources

FDA Enforcement Report Index
fda.gov/opacom/Enforce.html

2009 FDA Food Code
www.fda.gov/Food/FoodSafety/RetailFoodProtection/FoodCode/
FoodCode2009/default.htm

FDA Food Establishment Plan Review Guide
www.fda.gov/Food/FoodSafety/RetailFoodProtection/
ComplianceEnforcement/ucm101639.htm

FDA Foodborne Illness Resource Page
www.fda.gov/Food/FoodSafety/FoodborneIllness/default.htm

FDA Hazard Analysis Critical Control Point Info Page
www.fda.gov/Food/FoodSafety/HazardAnalysisCriticalControlPoints
HACCP/default.htm

*Hazard Analysis and Critical Control Point Principles and Application
Guidelines*
www.fsis.usda.gov/OPHS/NACMCF/past/JFP0998.pdf

Institute for Business and Home Safety Small Business Protection
ibhs.org/business_protection

IRS Business Casualty, Disaster, and Theft Loss Workbook
www.irs.gov/publications/p584b/index.html

*Managing Food Safety: A Manual for the Voluntary Use of HACCP Principles
for Operators of Foodservice and Retail Establishments*
www.fda.gov/Food/FoodSafety/RetailFoodProtection/ManagingFood
SafetyHACCPPrinciples/Operators/default.htm

Notes

III Sanitary Facilities and Pest Management

Chapters in This Unit

11 Sanitary Facilities and Equipment

Inside this chapter:

- Designing a Sanitary Establishment
- Considerations for Other Areas of the Facility
- Sanitation Standards for Equipment
- Installing and Maintaining Kitchen Equipment
- Utilities

After completing this chapter, you should be able to:

- Identify when a plan review is required.
- Identify organizations that certify equipment that meets sanitation standards.
- Identify characteristics of an appropriate food-contact and nonfood-contact surface.
- Identify the requirements for installing stationary and mobile equipment.
- Recognize the importance of maintaining equipment.
- Identify and prevent cross-connection and backflow.
- Identify requirements for handwashing facilities including appropriate locations and numbers.
- Identify the proper response to a wastewater overflow.
- Recognize the importance of properly installing and maintaining grease traps.
- Identify lighting-intensity requirements for different areas of the establishment.
- Identify potable water sources and testing requirements.
- Identify methods for preventing lighting sources from contaminating food.
- Identify methods for preventing ventilation systems from contaminating food and food-contact surfaces.
- Identify requirements for storing indoor and outdoor waste.
- Identify proper methods for cleaning waste receptacles.
- Recognize the need for frequent waste removal to prevent odor and pest problems.
- Identify characteristics of appropriate flooring.
- Recognize the importance of keeping physical facilities in proper repair.
- Identify requirements for dishwashing facilities.

Key Terms

- Porosity
- Resiliency
- Coving
- NSF International
- Underwriters Laboratories (UL)
- Potable water
- Booster heater
- Cross-connection
- Backflow
- Air gap

Apply Your Knowledge

Check to see how much you know about the concepts in this chapter. Use the page reference provided with each question to explore the topic.

Test Your Food Safety Knowledge

1. **True or False:** A hose attached to a utility-sink faucet and left sitting in a bucket of dirty water could contaminate the water supply. *(See page 11-20.)*

2. **True or False:** There must be a minimum of twenty foot-candles of light (215 lux) in a food-preparation area. *(See page 11-23.)*

3. **True or False:** Handwashing stations are required in dishwashing and service areas. *(See page 11-10.)*

4. **True or False:** When mounted on legs, tabletop equipment must be at least two inches (five centimeters) off the floor. *(See page 11-17.)*

5. **True or False:** Grease on an establishment's ceiling can be a sign of inadequate ventilation. *(See page 11-23.)*

For answers, please turn to the Answer Key.

Introduction

Many breakdowns in sanitation are caused by facilities and equipment that are simply too difficult to keep clean. Sanitary facilities and equipment are basic parts of a well-designed food safety system. In this chapter, you will find a wide range of information on various equipment and facility-related issues that are key to keeping an establishment safe.

Designing a Sanitary Establishment

When designing or remodeling a facility, consider how the building and the equipment in each area will be kept clean. Poorly designed areas are generally harder to clean and can become a breeding ground for microorganisms. As a result, food passing through these areas runs a much higher risk of contamination. Facilities should be arranged so contact with contaminated sources such as garbage or dirty tableware, utensils, and equipment is unlikely to occur.

This chapter focuses on four topics related to the sanitary layout and design of equipment and facilities:

- Design and arrangement of equipment and fixtures to comply with sanitation standards

- Material selection for walls, floors, and ceilings that will make cleaning these surfaces easier

- Design of utilities to prevent contamination and to make cleaning easier

- Proper waste management to avoid contaminating food and attracting pests

Layout

Your kitchen should be designed so that it can be cleaned quickly and effectively. A well-designed kitchen will address the following factors:

- **Work flow.** A work flow must be established that will minimize the amount of time food spends in the temperature danger zone. It must also minimize the number of times food is handled. For example, storage areas should be located near the receiving area to prevent delays in storing food. Prep tables should be located near refrigerators and freezers for the same reason. (See *Exhibit 11a.*)

11a **A Well-Designed Kitchen**

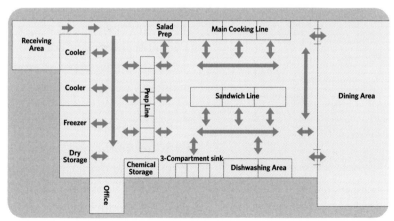

Locating storage areas near receiving areas and prep tables near refrigerators and freezers can minimize time-temperature abuse.

- **Contamination.** A good layout will minimize the risk of cross-contamination. Place equipment to prevent splashing or spilling from one piece of equipment onto another. For example, it is not a good practice to place the soiled-utensil table next to the salad-preparation sink.

- **Equipment accessibility.** Since hard-to-reach areas are less likely to be cleaned, a well-planned layout will ensure that equipment is accessible for cleaning.

The Plan Review

Before starting any new construction or a large remodeling project, check with your local regulatory authority. You may need approval for your design plan. Even if you do not need approval, you should ask your regulatory authority to review the plan. A review can have several benefits:

- It ensures that the design meets regulatory requirements.

- It ensures a safe flow of food.

- It may save time and money.

Additionally, these authorities provide information on what is necessary for good sanitation.

Materials for Interior Construction

Materials used during construction must be selected with several factors in mind. Sound-absorbent surfaces that resist absorption of grease and moisture and reflect light will probably create an environment acceptable to your regulatory agency. The most important consideration when selecting construction materials is how easy the establishment will be to clean and maintain. (See *Exhibit 11b*.)

Flooring

Each area of the establishment has specific flooring needs. While cost and appearance are important considerations, the selection of flooring materials must also be based upon health and safety requirements. Flooring should be smooth, durable, nonabsorbent, and easy to clean. It should also resist wear and help prevent slips. Once installed, flooring should be kept in good condition and be replaced if damaged or worn.

Key Point

Even if local laws do not require it, design plans should be reviewed by the local regulatory agency.

11b Construction Materials

The most important consideration when selecting construction materials is how easy the establishment will be to clean and maintain.

The porosity of flooring material is an especially important consideration. **Porosity** is the extent to which a material will absorb liquids. You should avoid high-porosity flooring for a number of reasons. Its absorbency often makes it an ideal place for microorganisms to grow. High-porosity flooring can also cause people to slip or fall, and it often deteriorates more quickly.

To prevent such problems, nonabsorbent flooring is recommended for specific areas of the establishment, including:

- Walk-in refrigerators
- Food-preparation areas
- Food storage
- Dishwashing areas
- Restrooms
- Dressing and locker rooms

Nonporous, Resilient Flooring

In most areas of the establishment, nonporous, resilient flooring is the best choice. **Resiliency** means a material has the ability to react to a shock without breaking or cracking.

Nonporous, resilient materials such as vinyl or rubber tiles are relatively inexpensive and are easy to clean and maintain. If individual tiles break, they can be easily replaced. (See *Exhibit 11c.*) They are capable of handling heavy traffic and are resistant to grease and alkalis.

However, this type of flooring does have its disadvantages. Cigarette burns or sharp objects can easily damage it. It also tends to be slippery when wet. It is usually a poor choice for dining rooms or public areas. However, it is practical for employee dressing rooms, break rooms, and foodservice offices. See *Exhibit 11d* on the next page for characteristics and recommended uses of nonporous, resilient flooring.

11c   Vinyl Tile

Vinyl tile is nonabsorbent and is easy to clean and maintain.

11d   Characteristics of Nonporous, Resilient Flooring

	Where to Use	Durability	Advantages	Disadvantages
Rubber tile	Kitchens; restrooms	Less durable and less resistant to grease and alkalis	Nonslip; resilient; easy to clean	Can only be used in moderate traffic areas
Vinyl sheet	Offices; kitchens; corridors	Less resistant to grease and alkalis	Very resilient; easy to clean	Can only be used in light or moderate traffic areas
Vinyl tile	Offices; employee restrooms	Wears out quickly with high traffic	Very resilient; easy to clean	Requires waxing and machine buffing

Key Point

Hard-surface flooring is also commonly used in establishments since it is non-absorbent and very durable.

Hard-Surface Flooring

Hard-surface flooring is also commonly used since it is nonabsorbent and very durable. These types of flooring are an excellent choice for public restrooms or high-soil areas, especially quarry and ceramic tile.

Still, there are several disadvantages to these flooring materials. They may crack or chip if heavy objects are dropped on them. They may also break objects dropped on them. In addition, hard-surface flooring does not absorb sound. They are more expensive to install and maintain and are somewhat difficult to clean.

While most hard-surface floors, especially marble, can be slippery, unglazed tiles can provide a hard, slip-resistant surface. See *Exhibit 11e* for characteristics and recommended uses of hard-surface flooring.

11e Characteristics of Hard-Surface Flooring

	Where to Use	Durability	Advantages	Disadvantages
Marble; terrazzo	Public corridors; dining rooms; public restrooms	Wear resistant	Nonporous; good appearance	Nonresilient; heavy; expensive; requires special care; difficult to install
Quarry tile	Kitchen; service, dishwashing, and receiving areas; offices; restrooms; dining rooms	Wear resistant	Nonporous	Nonresilient; heavy; expensive; slippery when wet unless an abrasive is added
Wood	Offices; dining rooms	Durable in lower traffic areas	Good appearance and sound absorption	Requires frequent polishing and periodic refinishing to maintain surface qualities

Carpeting

Carpeting is a popular choice for some areas of the establishment, such as dining rooms, because it absorbs sound. However, it is not recommended in high-soil areas, such as waitstaff service areas, tray and dish drop-off areas, beverage stations, and major traffic aisles. Carpet can be maintained by simple vacuuming. Areas prone to heavy traffic and moisture will require routine cleaning. Special carpet can be purchased for areas where sanitation, soiling, moisture, and fire safety are concerns.

Special Flooring Needs

Nonslip surfaces should be used in traffic areas. In fact, nonslip surfaces are best for the entire kitchen, since slips and falls are a potential hazard. Rubber mats are allowed for safety reasons in areas where standing water may occur, such as the dish room. Rubber mats should be picked up and cleaned separately when scrubbing floors.

11f   Coving

Coving is a curved, sealed edge placed between the floor and the wall to eliminate sharp corners or gaps.

Coving is required in establishments using resilient or hard-surface flooring materials. Coving is a curved, sealed edge placed between the floor and the wall to eliminate sharp corners or gaps that would be impossible to clean. (See *Exhibit 11f*.) The coving tile or strip must adhere tightly to the wall to eliminate hiding places for insects. This will also prevent moisture from deteriorating the wall.

Finishes for Interior Walls and Ceilings

Interior finishes are the materials used on the surface of walls, ceilings, and doors of an establishment. As with flooring, these finishes must be smooth, nonabsorbent, durable, and easy to clean.

When selecting finishes for walls and ceilings, consider location. A material that might be suitable in one area may be a poor choice for another. Walls and ceilings in food-preparation areas must be light in color to distribute light and to make it easier to spot soil when cleaning. They should be kept in good repair, free of cracks, holes, or peeling paint. The best wall finish in cooking areas is ceramic tile; however, it must be monitored for grout loss and regrouted whenever necessary. Stainless steel is used occasionally because of its durability and resistance to moisture. The most common ceiling materials are acoustic tile, painted drywall, painted plaster, or exposed concrete.

The support structures for walls and ceilings (studs, joists, and rafters) and pipes should not be exposed unless they are finished and sealed for cleaning. Flexible materials such as paper, vinyl, and thin wood veneers are often used for walls and ceilings. Vinyl wall coverings are used in many areas of an establishment because they are attractive, relatively inexpensive, easy to clean, and durable. Vinyl wall coverings are rated for flammability by testing agencies. Plaster or cinder-block walls that have been sealed and painted with oil-resistant, easy-to-wash, glossy paints are appropriate for dry areas of the facility.

Considerations for Other Areas of the Facility

11g   Acceptable Dry-Storage Facility

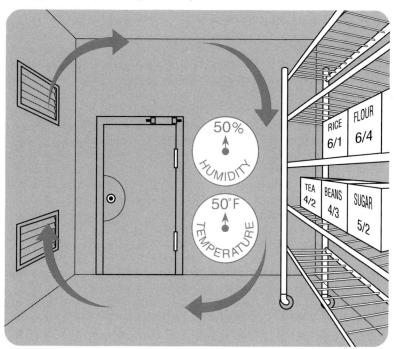

Dry storerooms should be constructed of easy-to-clean materials that allow good air circulation.

Dry Storage

Dry storerooms should be constructed of easy-to-clean materials that allow good air circulation. (See *Exhibit 11g.*) Shelving, table tops, and bins for dry ingredients should be made of corrosion-resistant metal or food-grade plastic.

Any windows in the storeroom should have frosted glass or shades. Direct sunlight can increase the temperature of the room and affect food quality.

Steam pipes, water lines, and other conduits have no place in a well-designed storeroom. Dripping condensation or leaks in overhead pipes can promote microbial growth in such normally stable items as crackers, flour, and baking powder. Leaking overhead sewer lines can be a source of contamination for any food. Hot water heaters or steam pipes can increase the temperature of the storeroom to levels that will allow foodborne pathogens to grow.

Dry food is especially susceptible to attack by insects and rodents, therefore, cracks and crevices in floors or walls should be filled. Doors leading to the exterior of the building should be self-closing. Screens for windows and doors should be sixteen mesh to the inch, without holes or tears.

Restrooms

Local building and health codes usually specify how many sinks, stalls, toilets, and urinals are required in an establishment. It is best if separate restrooms are provided for employees and customers. If this is not possible, the establishment must be designed so patrons do not pass through food-preparation areas to reach the restroom, since they could contaminate food or food-contact surfaces.

Restrooms should be convenient, sanitary, fully equipped with a handwashing station, and have self-closing doors. They must be adequately stocked with toilet paper and trash receptacles must be provided if disposable paper towels are used. Covered waste containers must be provided in women's restrooms for the disposal of sanitary supplies.

Handwashing Stations

Key Point

Handwashing stations must be conveniently located in food-preparation areas, service areas, dishwashing areas, and restrooms.

Handwashing stations must be conveniently located so employees will be encouraged to wash their hands often. They are required in restrooms and areas used for food preparation, service, and dishwashing. These stations must be operable, stocked, and maintained. A handwashing station must be equipped with the following items (see *Exhibit 11h*):

- **Hot and cold running water.** Hot and cold water should be supplied through a mixing valve or combination faucet at a temperature of at least 100°F (38°C).

- **Soap.** The soap can be liquid, bar, or powder.

- **A means to dry hands.** Most local codes require establishments to supply disposable paper towels in handwashing stations. Installing at least one hand dryer in a handwashing station will provide an alternate method for drying hands if paper towels run out. Hand dryers that use warm air or room-temperature air delivered at high velocity can be used. Continuous-cloth towel systems, if allowed, should be used only if the unit is working properly and the towel rolls are checked and changed regularly. The use of common cloth towels is not permitted because they can transmit contaminants from one person's hands to another.

- **Waste container.** Waste containers are required if disposable paper towels are provided.

- **Signage indicating employees are required to wash hands before returning to work.** The sign should reflect all languages used in the establishment.

11h   Acceptable Handwashing Station

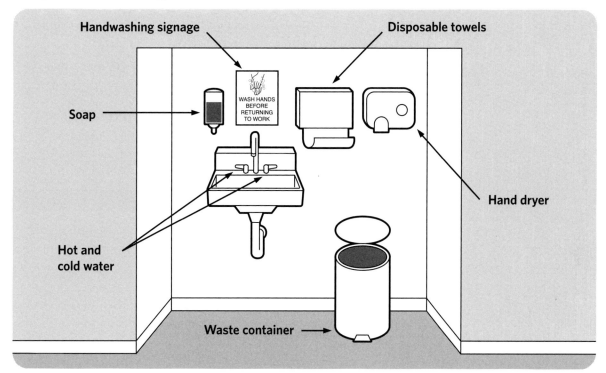

A handwashing station must be equipped with hot and cold running water, soap, a means to dry hands, a waste container (if disposable towels are used), and signage reminding employees to wash hands.

11i   Sink Use

To prevent cross-contamination, employees must use each sink in an establishment for its intended purpose.

Sinks

To prevent cross-contamination, employees must use each sink in an establishment for its intended purpose. (See *Exhibit 11i.*) Handwashing sinks are used for handwashing. Food-preparation sinks are used for food preparation. Service sinks are used for cleaning mops and disposing of wastewater. At least one service sink or curbed drain area is required in an establishment to dispose of soiled water.

Dressing Rooms and Lockers

Dressing rooms are not required. If available, they must not be used for food preparation, storage, or utensil washing. Lockers should be located in a separate room or a room where contamination of food, equipment, utensils, linens, and single-service items will not occur.

Premises

The parking lot and walkways should be kept free of litter and graded so that standing pools of water do not form. In addition, they must be surfaced to minimize dirt and blowing dust. It is recommended that concrete and asphalt be used for walkways and parking lots. Gravel, while acceptable, is not recommended.

Patron traffic through food-preparation areas is prohibited, although guided tours are allowed. The premises may not be used for living or sleeping quarters.

Sanitation Standards for Equipment

It is important to purchase equipment that has been designed with sanitation in mind. Food contact surfaces must be:

- Safe

- Durable

- Corrosion resistant

- Nonabsorbent

- Sufficient in weight and thickness to withstand repeated cleaning

- Smooth and easy to clean

- Resistant to pitting, chipping, crazing (spider cracks), scratching, scoring, distortion, and decomposition

Equipment surfaces that are not designed to come in contact with food but are exposed to splash, spillage, or other food soiling or require frequent cleaning must be:

- Constructed of smooth, nonabsorbent, corrosion-resistant material

- Free of unnecessary ledges, projections, and crevices

- Designed and constructed to allow easy cleaning and maintenance

11j NSF and UL EPH Marks

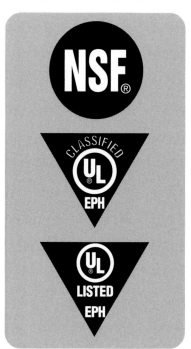

Look for the NSF International mark or UL EPH product marks on equipment acceptable for use in a restaurant or foodservice establishment.

Key Point

The size and type of machine you choose depends on the nature and volume of the items to be cleaned.

The task of choosing equipment designed for sanitation has been simplified by organizations such as NSF International and Underwriters Laboratories (UL). NSF International develops and publishes standards for sanitary equipment design. The presence of the NSF mark on foodservice equipment means it has been evaluated, tested, and certified by NSF International as meeting international commercial food equipment standards. UL similarly provides sanitation classification listings for equipment found in compliance with NSF International standards. UL also lists products complying with their own published environmental and public health (EPH) standards. Equipment that meets these standards is acceptable for use in a foodservice establishment. Restaurant and foodservice managers should look for the NSF International mark or the UL EPH product mark on foodservice equipment. *Exhibit 11j* shows examples of the NSF International mark and the UL EPH product marks.

Only commercial foodservice equipment should be used in establishments, because household equipment is not built to withstand heavy use.

Although all equipment used in an establishment must meet sanitation standards, certain equipment requires particular attention.

Dishwashing Machines

Dishwashing machines vary widely by size, style, and method of sanitizing. High-temperature machines sanitize with extremely hot water while chemical-sanitizing machines use a chemical solution.

The size and type of machine you choose depends upon the nature and volume of the items to be cleaned and the required turnaround time for clean tableware and utensils. Because a dishwashing machine is a big investment, the manager must carefully match the machine to the establishment's needs.

The following types of dishwashing machines are common in restaurant and foodservice establishments:

- **Single-tank, stationary-rack machine, with doors.** This machine holds a stationary rack of tableware and utensils.

Items are washed by detergent and water from below and, sometimes, from above the rack. The wash cycle is followed by a hot-water or chemical-sanitizer final rinse.

- **Conveyor machine.** With this machine, a conveyor moves racks of items through the various cycles of washing, rinsing, and sanitizing. The machine may have a single tank or multiple tanks.

- **Carousel or circular conveyor machine.** This multiple-tank machine moves tableware and utensils on a peg-type conveyor or in racks. Some models have an automatic stop after items go through the final rinse cycle. In other models, items must be removed after the final rinse, or they will continue to travel through the machine.

- **Flight-type.** This is a high-capacity, multiple-tank machine with a peg-type conveyor. It may also have a built-in dryer. It is commonly used in institutions and very large establishments.

- **Batch-type, dump.** This stationary-rack machine combines the wash and rinse cycles in a single tank. Each cycle is timed, and the machine automatically dispenses both the detergent and the sanitizing chemical or hot water. Wash and rinse water are drained after each cycle.

- **Recirculating, door-type, nondump machine.** This stationary-rack machine is not completely drained of water between cycles. The wash water is diluted with fresh water and reused from cycle to cycle.

Consider these general guidelines regarding the installation and use of dishwashing machines:

- Water pipes to the dishwashing machine should be as short as possible to prevent the loss of heat.

- The machine must be raised at least six inches (fifteen centimeters) off the floor to permit easy cleaning underneath.

- Materials used in dishwashing machines should be able to withstand wear, including the action of detergents and sanitizers.

11k Dishwashing Machine Setting

Post setting information on the machine where it is easily readable.

- Information should be posted on the machine regarding proper water temperature, conveyor speed, and water pressure. (See *Exhibit 11k*.)

- The machine's thermometer should be located so it is readable, with a scale in increments no greater than 2°F (1°C).

Clean-in-Place Equipment

Some equipment is designed to be cleaned and sanitized by having detergent solution, a hot-water rinse, and sanitizing solution pass through it. Certain soft-serve ice cream and frozen yogurt dispensers are cleaned and sanitized this way. This process should be performed daily unless otherwise indicated by the manufacturer. Instructions should be followed carefully.

Food-contact cleaning and sanitizing solutions must remain within the tubes and pipes for a predetermined amount of time, reach all food-contact surfaces, and must be completely drained after use.

Refrigerators and Freezers

There are several types of refrigerator and freezer units. The two most common are walk-in and reach-in refrigerators and freezers. These units should be made of stainless steel or a combination of stainless steel and aluminum. The doors should be constructed to withstand heavy use and should close with a slight nudge. Door gaskets can be fixed in place or removable for easy cleaning. A drain must be provided and maintained for disposal of condensation and defrost water. A properly plumbed, indirect drain can be used in the walk-in refrigerator. Excess condensation can be minimized by maintaining a flush-fitting floor sweep (gasket) under the door.

Walk-in refrigerators and freezers with windows in the door may reduce unnecessary opening. Forced-air circulating fans are essential to help provide a quick recovery time so refrigerators and freezers maintain the appropriate temperature.

In addition to the sanitation standards mentioned earlier in this chapter, consider these factors when purchasing a refrigerator or freezer unit:

- **Choose a unit with adequate storage space.** An uncrowded unit can maintain required holding temperatures, is easier to

11l Commercial-Type Walk-In Refrigerator

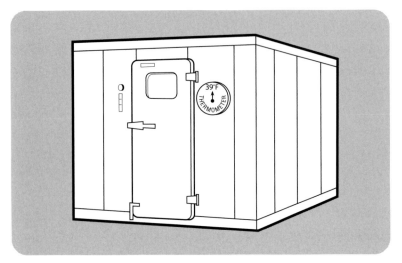

Make sure walk-in units can be sealed to the floor and wall.

11m Commercial-Type Reach-In Freezer

Note the caster wheels, which make it easier to move the unit for cleaning.

Courtesy of Hobart Corporation

clean, will prevent moisture buildup, and can minimize breakdowns.

- **Make sure walk-in units can be sealed to the floor and wall.** (See *Exhibit 11l.*) They should offer no access to moisture or rodents. Flooring materials must be able to withstand heavy impact.

- **Purchase reach-in refrigerator or freezer units with legs that elevate them six inches (fifteen centimeters) off the floor.** Otherwise, mount and seal them on a masonry base. Casters, which make it easier to move the unit for cleaning, are often preferred or required by local regulatory agencies. (See *Exhibit 11m.*)

- **Make sure the unit meets the temperature requirements of the food you store.** Built-in thermometers should be easy to locate and read and be accurate to within ±3°F (2°C).

Blast Chillers and Tumble Chillers

Blast chillers are designed to cool food quickly. (See *Exhibit 11n.*) Many are able to cool food from 135°F to 37°F (57°C to 3°C) within ninety minutes. Most units allow the operator to set target chill temperatures and monitor the temperature of food throughout the chill cycle. Once chilled to safe temperatures, the food then can be stored in conventional refrigerators or freezers.

Tumble chillers are also designed to cool food quickly. Prepackaged, hot food is placed into a drum, which rotates inside a reservoir of chilled water. The tumbling action increases the effectiveness of the chilled water in cooling the food.

11n Blast Chiller

Many blast chillers can cool food from 135°F to 37°F (57°C to 3°C) within ninety minutes.

Courtesy of Hobart Corporation

Cook-Chill Equipment

Some operations prepare food using a cook-chill system. By this method, food is partially cooked, rapidly chilled, and then held in refrigerated storage. When needed, the food simply is reheated. A cook-chill unit is an integrated piece of equipment capable of cooking, cooling, and reheating food.

Cutting Boards

Many jurisdictions allow the use of either wooden or synthetic cutting boards. However, some experts prefer synthetic boards, which can be cleaned and sanitized in a dishwashing machine or by immersion in a three-compartment sink.

If wooden cutting boards and baker's tables are allowed by local codes, they must be made from a nonabsorbent hardwood, such as maple or oak. They must also be free of seams and cracks, nontoxic, and must not transfer any odor or taste to food.

Separate cutting boards should be used for raw and ready-to-eat food to prevent cross-contamination. Cutting boards must be washed, rinsed, and sanitized between uses. Due to the high risk of cross-contamination, procedures for cleaning and sanitizing cutting boards should be included in your standard operating procedures.

Installing and Maintaining Kitchen Equipment

When installing equipment, keep in mind that it should be easy for employees to clean the equipment and the surrounding floors, walls, and tabletops. Portable equipment makes it much simpler to do this.

Installing Kitchen Equipment

Follow the manufacturer's directions when installing equipment, and check with your local regularity authority for requirements. In general, floor-mounted equipment must be mounted on legs at least six inches (fifteen centimeters) off the floor or sealed to a masonry base. (See *Exhibit 11o* on the next page.)

Tabletop equipment should be mounted on legs, providing a minimum clearance of four inches (ten centimeters)

11o Installing Stationary Equipment

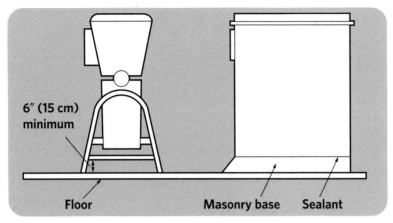

6" (15 cm) minimum

Floor   Masonry base   Sealant

Stationary equipment must be mounted on legs at least six inches (fifteen centimeters) off the floor or sealed to a masonry base.

between the base of the equipment and the tabletop. Alternatively, the equipment can be sealed to the countertop.

All cracks or seams must be filled with a sealant to prevent food buildup or pests. However, sealant should not be used to cover wide gaps resulting from faulty construction or repairs. Instead, gaps should be properly repaired before equipment is installed.

Maintaining Equipment

Once equipment has been properly installed, it must receive regular maintenance from qualified personnel. Follow the manufacturers' recommended maintenance schedule.

Key Point

Equipment must receive regular maintenance from qualified personnel.

Utilities

An establishment uses many utilities and building systems. Utilities include water, electricity, gas, sewage, and garbage disposal. Building systems include plumbing, lighting, and ventilation. There must be enough utilities to meet the needs of the establishment. In addition, the utilities and systems must work properly. If they do not, the risk of contamination is greater.

Water Supply

In a foodservice operation, water is used for dishwashing, cleaning, cooking, and drinking. Having safe water is critical, because contaminated water can carry foodborne pathogens. Water that is safe to drink is called potable water. Sources of potable water include approved public water mains and private water sources that are regularly maintained and tested. Other sources include closed, portable water containers filled with potable water and properly maintained water-transport vehicles.

If your establishment uses a private water supply, such as a well, rather than an approved public source, you should check with your local regulatory agency for information on inspections, testing, and other requirements. Generally, nonpublic water systems should be tested at least annually and the report kept on file in the establishment.

The use of nonpotable water is extremely limited. If nonpotable water is allowed by local codes, the uses are generally limited to air conditioning, cooling equipment (nonfood), fire protection, and irrigation.

Hot Water

Providing a continuous supply of hot water can be a problem for many establishments serving the public. They must have enough hot water to meet peak demand. Water heaters should be evaluated regularly to make sure they can meet this demand. Consider how quickly the heater produces hot water, the size of the holding tanks, and the location of the heater in relation to sinks or dishwashing machines.

Since most general-purpose water heaters will not heat water to temperatures required for hot-water sanitizing, a **booster heater** may be needed to maintain water temperature. Many dishwashing machines now come with booster heaters.

Plumbing

Key Point

Only licensed plumbers should install and maintain plumbing systems in an establishment.

In almost every community in the United States, plumbing design is regulated by law, and with good reason. Improper plumbing design can have serious consequences. Improperly installed or poorly maintained plumbing that allows the mixing of potable and nonpotable water has been implicated in outbreaks of typhoid fever, dysentery, hepatitis A, Norovirus, and other gastrointestinal illnesses. Improperly installed water pipes can also lead to contamination from metals, such as toxic-metal poisoning from beverage dispensers or contamination from chemicals used in the system, such as detergents, sanitizers, or drain cleaners.

Local plumbing codes vary widely regarding the types of connections permitted and the kind of protection required. If in doubt about the plumbing regulations governing your establishment, contact your local regulatory agency. Only licensed plumbers should install and maintain plumbing systems in an establishment.

Cross-Connections

The greatest challenge to water safety comes from cross-connections. A **cross-connection** is a physical link through which contaminants from drains, sewers, or other wastewater sources can enter a potable water supply. A cross-connection is dangerous because it allows the possibility of **backflow.** Backflow is the unwanted, reverse flow of contaminants through a cross-connection into a potable water system. It can occur whenever the pressure in the potable water supply drops below the pressure of the contaminated supply. A running faucet located below the flood rim of a sink or a running hose in a mop bucket are examples of cross-connections that can lead to backflow.

Exhibit 11p illustrates a situation in which a hose has been attached to the faucet of a utility sink to add hot water to a partially-filled mop bucket. The nozzle of the hose is left submerged in the bucket of dirty water, accidentally creating a cross-connection. Because of heavy water usage somewhere else in the facility, the water pressure could drop low enough that contaminated water from the mop bucket would be drawn back through the hose and into the potable water supply.

11p   Common Cross-Connection

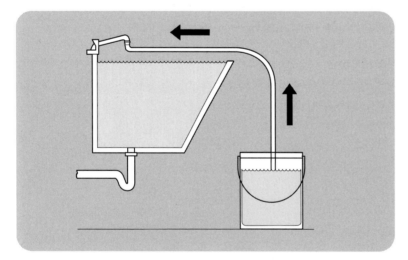

A hose connected to a faucet and left submerged in a mop bucket creates a dangerous cross-connection.

11q   Vacuum Breaker

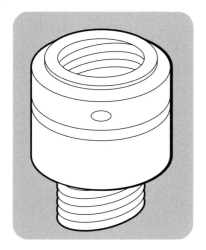

A vacuum breaker should be installed on threaded faucets to prevent backflow.

Backflow Prevention

To prevent cross-connections like this, do not attach a hose to a faucet unless a backflow-prevention device, such as a vacuum breaker, is attached. (See *Exhibit 11q*.) Threaded faucets and connections between two piping systems must have a vacuum breaker or other approved backflow-prevention device. However, even if these devices are installed, never create a cross-connection. This way, if the device breaks, your water supply will not be endangered.

The only completely reliable method for preventing backflow is creating an **air gap.** An air gap is an air space used to separate a water supply outlet from any potentially contaminated source. A properly designed and installed sink typically has two air gaps to prevent backflow. One is the air space between the faucet and the flood rim of the sink. The other is located between the drain pipe of the sink and the floor drain of the establishment. (See *Exhibit 11r*.) Typically, the size of the air gap should be twice the diameter of the water supply outlet.

For example, if a faucet has an opening with a diameter of one inch (2.5 centimeters), the air gap between the faucet and the flood rim of the sink must be at least two inches (five centimeters).

11r   Air Gaps to Prevent Backflow in a Sink

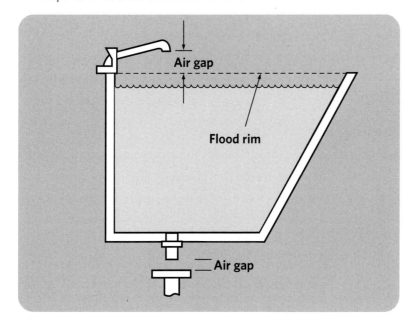

Air gaps between the faucet and the flood rim and between the drainpipe and floor drain of a sink prevent backflow.

Grease Condensation and Leaking Pipes

Grease condensation in pipes is another common problem in plumbing systems. Grease traps are often installed to prevent buildup from creating a drain blockage. If used, grease traps must be easily accessible, installed by a licensed plumber, and cleaned periodically according to manufacturers' recommendations. If the traps are not cleaned or are not cleaned properly, a backup of wastewater could lead to odor and contamination.

Overhead wastewater pipes or fire-safety sprinkler systems can leak and become a source of contamination. Even overhead lines carrying potable water can be a problem, since water can condense on the pipes and drip onto food. Check all pipes regularly to ensure they are in good condition and not leaking. They should be serviced immediately when leaks occur.

Sewage

Sewage and wastewater are reservoirs of pathogens, soils, and chemicals. It is absolutely essential to prevent them from contaminating food or food-contact surfaces.

If there is a backup of raw sewage, the affected area must be closed immediately. The problem must be corrected, and the area must be thoroughly cleaned. Other backups might not be as serious, but they still require an immediate correction of the problem, followed by a thorough clean up.

The facility must have adequate drainage to handle all wastewater. Any area subjected to heavy water exposure should have its own floor drain. Wastewater from equipment and from the potable supply should be channeled into an open, accessible waste sink or floor drain. The drainage system should be designed to prevent floors from flooding.

Lighting

Good lighting generally results in improved employee work habits, easier and more effective cleaning, and a safer work environment. Lighting intensity requirements are typically based on a unit of measurement called a foot-candle or lux. The lighting required in various areas of the establishment are highlighted in *Exhibit 11s*. Use shatter-resistant lightbulbs and protective covers made of metal mesh or plastic to prevent broken glass from contaminating food or food-contact surfaces. Shields should also be provided for heat lamps.

Key Point

A backup of raw sewage on the floor is cause for immediate closure of the establishment, correction of the problem, and thorough cleaning.

11s   Minimum Lighting Intensity Requirements for Different Areas of the Establishment

Minimum Lighting Intensity	Area
50 foot-candles (540 lux)	• Food-preparation areas
20 foot-candles (215 lux)	• Handwashing or dishwashing areas • Buffets and salad bars • Displays for produce or packaged food • Utensil-storage areas • Wait stations • Restrooms • Inside some pieces of equipment (e.g., reach-in refrigerators)
10 foot-candles (108 lux)	• Inside walk-in refrigerators and freezer units • Dry-storage areas • Dining rooms (for cleaning)

11t   Hood Filters

Hood filters should be cleaned on a regular basis.

Ventilation

Proper ventilation helps maintain an establishment's indoor air quality by removing steam, smoke, grease, and heat from the establishment. Adequate ventilation is particularly important in the food-preparation area because it reduces the level of odors, gases, dirt, mold, humidity, grease, and fumes present in the air, all of which can contribute to contamination. Excess humidity can cause condensation on walls and ceilings, which may drip onto food. An accumulation of grease can cause fires. If ventilation is adequate, there will be little or no buildup of grease and condensation on walls and ceilings.

Mechanical ventilation must be used in areas for cooking, frying, and grilling. Ventilation must be designed so hoods, fans, guards, and ductwork do not drip onto food or equipment. Hood filters or grease extractors must be tight fitting and easy to remove, and they should be cleaned on a regular basis. (See *Exhibit 11t*.) Thorough cleaning of the hood and ductwork should also be done periodically by professionals.

Since so much air is moved through exhaust hoods, clean air must be taken in to replace it. This replacement air is called make-up air, which must be replaced without creating drafts. All outside air intakes must be screened to keep pests out.

In many areas of the United States, clean-air ordinances restrict the use of exhaust fans. Exhaust air containing food odors, smoke, and grease might have to be purified by filters or other devices. It is the establishment's responsibility to see that the ventilation system meets local regulations.

Solid Waste Management

Waste management is an important issue in every establishment. There are many things foodservice managers can do to improve their waste management practices. The Environmental Protection Agency (EPA) has recommended three approaches to managing waste:

❶ **Reduce the amount of waste produced.** Eliminate unnecessary packaging.

❷ **Reuse when possible.** Before using containers again, they must be cleaned and sanitized. Never reuse chemical containers as food containers.

❸ **Recycle materials.** Store recyclables so they cannot contaminate food or equipment or attract pests.

When these practices are followed, the amount of waste can be greatly reduced.

Garbage Disposal

Garbage can attract pests and contaminate food, equipment, and utensils if handled improperly.

Garbage containers must be leak proof, waterproof, pest proof, easy to clean, and durable. Plastic bags and wet-strength paper bags may be used to line these containers.

Garbage should be removed from food-preparation areas as soon as possible. Frequent disposal prevents odor and pest problems. Garbage-storage areas, inside or outside, should be large enough to contain all garbage and must be located away from food-preparation and storage areas.

All garbage containers should be cleaned frequently and thoroughly. Both the inside and outside of containers must be cleaned. A cleaning area equipped with hot and cold water and a floor drain is recommended for indoor cleaning. It must be located so food being prepared or in storage will not be contaminated when garbage containers are being cleaned.

Food waste can also be disposed of through the use of in-drain garbage disposals, which reduce the amount of waste that goes into garbage containers. However, local regulations often limit

11u Outdoor Trash Receptacles

Receptacles and compactor systems should be located on or above a smooth surface of nonabsorbent material, such as concrete or machine-laid asphalt.

their use in establishments, since these disposals create large amounts of food and water waste that might overload local wastewater systems.

Pulpers, or grinders, are another garbage-disposal alternative. Pulpers grind food and some other types of waste (such as paper) into small parts that are flushed with water. The water is then removed so the processed solid waste weighs less and is more compact for easier disposal.

Outdoor trash receptacles should be kept covered with their drain plugs in place at all times except during cleaning. Receptacles and compactor systems should be located on or above a smooth surface of nonabsorbent material such as sealed concrete or machine-laid asphalt. The area must be kept clean. (See *Exhibit 11u*.)

Summary

An establishment that is difficult to clean will not be cleaned well. Sanitation efforts will be more effective if the establishment is designed and equipped with ease of cleaning in mind. In most communities, plans for new construction or extensive remodeling are subject to review and approval by local regulatory agencies. Sanitation can be built into the facility through the design and construction of floors, walls, ceilings, and doors. The selection of materials should be based on ease of cleaning and durability, as well as appearance.

Separate restrooms should be provided for employees and customers. If this is not possible, restrooms should be positioned so that customers do not pass through food-preparation areas to reach them. Restrooms should be cleaned regularly and have a fully-equipped handwashing station and self-closing doors. They should also be stocked adequately with toilet paper and have trash receptacles.

Handwashing stations must be conveniently located, operable, and fully stocked and maintained. They are required in food-preparation areas, service areas, dishwashing areas, and restrooms. They must be equipped with hot and cold running water, soap, a means to dry hands, a waste container, and signage reminding employees to wash hands.

Purchase equipment that has been designed with sanitation in mind. Food-contact surfaces must be corrosion resistant, nonabsorbent, and smooth, and they must resist pitting and scratching. Equipment should be installed so both the equipment and the area surrounding it can be cleaned easily. Floor-mounted equipment must be mounted on legs at least six inches (fifteen centimeters) off the floor, or it must be sealed to a masonry base. Tabletop equipment should be mounted on legs with a clearance of four inches (ten centimeters) between the equipment and the tabletop, or it should be sealed to the tabletop. Gaps should be filled with sealant to prevent food buildup and pests.

Utilities and building systems must be designed to meet the establishment's cleaning needs, and they must not contribute to contamination. Potable water is vital in an establishment. Sources include public water mains and private water sources that are regularly maintained and tested.

Improperly installed or maintained plumbing can have serious consequences. Only licensed plumbers should install and maintain plumbing systems. The greatest challenge to water safety comes from cross-connections—a physical link through which contaminants from drains, sewers, and other wastewater sources can flow back into the potable-water supply. Vacuum breakers and air gaps can be used to prevent backflow. It is essential to prevent wastewater from contaminating food and food-contact surfaces. A backup of raw sewage is cause for immediate closure of the area, correction of the problem, and thorough cleaning.

Good lighting in an establishment generally results in improved employee work habits, easier and more effective cleaning, and a safer work environment. Follow the lighting intensity requirements for each area of the establishment. Use shatter-resistant lightbulbs and protective covers to prevent broken glass from contaminating food or food-contact surfaces. Proper ventilation improves the indoor air quality of the establishment by removing smoke, grease, steam, and heat. If ventilation is adequate, there will be little or no buildup of grease and condensation on walls and ceilings. Ventilation must be designed so hoods, fans, guards, and ductwork do not drip onto food or equipment. Hood filters and grease extractors must be cleaned regularly.

Garbage containers must be leak proof, waterproof, pest proof, easy to clean, and durable. All garbage containers should be cleaned frequently and thoroughly both inside and out. Garbage should be removed from food-preparation areas as soon as possible.

Apply Your Knowledge

A Case in Point

① Why did the people become ill?

② What should Carlos do to correct the problem?

Several people became ill shortly after drinking beverages at the bar in a local restaurant. They all complained that their iced drinks had an odd taste. At the time of the incident, the glasswasher in the bar had been out of service.

When interviewed, Carlos, the manager, explained that the glasswasher was functional but that the unit could not be used because the large volume of water discharged after each wash load was worsening a recent drain-blockage problem. Carlos also mentioned there had been intermittent backups in the plumbing during the previous week and a large pool of water had been found under the glasswasher. Drain cleaners had been used repeatedly with no change in the blockage.

The icemaker shared piping with the glasswasher in the bar and the grease trap on the sink in the restaurant. Carlos revealed he had installed the plumbing himself.

When ice cubes were removed from the icemaker, congealed grease and food debris were found on them. Grease and debris also covered the bottom of the ice bin.

For answers, please turn to the Answer Key.

Apply Your Knowledge

Use these questions to review the concepts presented in this chapter.

Discussion Questions

1. What is one of the most important considerations when choosing flooring for food-preparation areas?

2. What action must be taken in the event of a backup of raw sewage in an establishment?

3. What can be done to prevent backflow in an establishment?

4. What are some potable-water sources for an establishment? What are the testing requirements for nonpublic water systems?

5. What are the requirements of a handwashing station? In what areas of an establishment are handwashing stations required?

6. What are the requirements for installing stationary equipment?

For answers, please turn to the Answer Key.

Study Questions

Circle the best answer to each question.

1. **Generally, operations that use a private water source, such as a well, must have it tested at least**

   A once a year.
   B every 2 years.
   C every 3 years.
   D every 5 years.

2. **What is the only completely reliable method for preventing backflow?**

   A Air gap
   B Ball valve
   C Vacuum breaker
   D Cross-connection

③ **When installing tabletop equipment on legs, the space between the base of the equipment and the tabletop must be at least**

A 1 inch (3 centimeters).

B 2 inches (5 centimeters).

C 4 inches (10 centimeters).

D 6 inches (15 centimeters).

④ **How hot should the hot water at a handwashing station get?**

A At least 70°F (21°C)

B At least 100°F (38°C)

C At least 130°F (54°C)

D At least 160°F (71°C)

⑤ **Foodservice equipment that has been certified as meeting certain standards may be stamped with the _____ mark.**

A FDA

B NSF

C USDA

D USPS

⑥ **What information should be posted on or near a dishwasher?**

A Water temperature, conveyor speed, and water pressure

B Load start time, estimated load completion time, and initials of person who started the load

C Water temperature in 4°F (2°C) increments and clearance space between the machine and the floor

D Maintenance records including service dates, work done, and name of the company that did the work

Continued on next page ▶

▶ *Continued from previous page*

⑦ **To keep food from being contaminated by lighting, use**

A   shields on heat lamps.

B   signage next to lights in food-contact areas.

C   fluorescent and other energy-efficient lightbulbs.

D   lighting that meets the minimum intensity requirements.

⑧ **Which is a source of potable water?**

A   Collected rain water

B   Gray water-collection tanks

C   Untested private water sources

D   Water transport vehicles

⑨ **Outdoor garbage containers should be**

A   labeled with collection times.

B   kept covered with tight-fitting lids.

C   kept away from customer parking areas.

D   lined with plastic or wet-strength paper.

⑩ **What is a cross-connection?**

A   Threaded faucet

B   Device that prevents a vacuum

C   Valve that mixes hot and cold water

D   Link between sources of safe and dirty water

⑪ **Backflow is when water**

A   flows in pipes behind a wall.

B   backs up in a drain because of grease condensation.

C   goes down the toilet in a counter-clockwise direction.

D   flows opposite its normal direction because of water pressure.

For answers, please turn to the Answer Key.

Additional Resources

Articles and Texts

Barbaran, Regina S. and Joseph F. Durocher. *Successful Restaurant Design.* Hoboken, NJ: John Wiley & Sons, Inc. 2001.

Birchfield, John C. *Design and Layout of Foodservice Facilities.* Hoboken, NJ: John Wiley & Sons, Inc. 2007.

Katsigris, Costas and Chris Thomas. *Design and Equipment for Restaurants and Foodservice: A Management View.* Hoboken, NJ: John Wiley & Sons, Inc. 2005.

Web Sites

American Society of Heating, Refrigeration, and Air-Conditioning Engineers
ashrae.org

Environmental Protection Agency
epa.gov

FDA Food Safety
www.fda.gov/Food/FoodSafety/default.htm

Foodservice Consultants Society International
fcsi.org

International Association of Plumbing and Mechanical Officials
iapmo.org

International Code Council
iccsafe.org

North American Association of Food Equipment Manufacturers
nafem.org

NSF International
nsf.org

Underwriters Laboratories, Inc.
ul.com

Documents and Other Resources

2009 FDA Food Code
www.fda.gov/Food/FoodSafety/RetailFoodProtection/FoodCode/FoodCode2009/default.htm

Environmental Protection Agency Cross-Connection Control Manual
epa.gov/safewater/crossconnection.html

FDA Food Establishment Plan Review Guide
www.fda.gov/Food/FoodSafety/RetailFoodProtection/ComplianceEnforcement/ucm101639.htm

12 Cleaning and Sanitizing

Inside this chapter:

- Cleaning vs. Sanitizing
- Cleaning
- Sanitizing
- Machine Dishwashing
- Manual Dishwashing
- Cleaning the Premises
- Tools for Cleaning
- Storing Utensils, Tableware, and Equipment
- Using Foodservice Chemicals
- Developing a Cleaning Program

After completing this chapter, you should be able to:

- Explain the difference between cleaning and sanitizing.
- Identify appropriate cleaners for specific tasks.
- Identify approved sanitizers.
- Identify factors affecting the efficiency of sanitizers (i.e., time, temperature, concentration, water hardness, and pH).
- Follow the requirements for frequency of cleaning and sanitizing food-contact surfaces.
- Follow the legal requirements for the use of poisonous or toxic material in a food establishment.
- Properly clean and sanitize items in a three-compartment sink.
- Properly clean and sanitize food-contact surfaces.
- Properly clean nonfood-contact surfaces.
- Identify proper machine-dishwashing techniques.
- Identify storage requirements for poisonous or toxic materials.
- Dispose of poisonous or toxic materials according to legal requirements.
- Properly store tools, equipment, and utensils that have been sanitized.
- Use the appropriate test kit for each sanitizer.

Key Terms

- Cleaning
- Sanitizing
- Detergents
- Degreasers
- Delimers

- Abrasive cleaners
- Heat sanitizing
- Chemical sanitizing
- Sanitizers
- Master cleaning schedule

Apply Your Knowledge

Check to see how much you know about the concepts in this chapter. Use the page references provided with each question to explore the topic.

Test Your Food Safety Knowledge

① **True or False:** Chemicals can be stored in food-preparation areas if they are properly labeled. *(See page 12-15.)*

② **True or False:** The temperature of the final sanitizing rinse in a high-temperature dishwashing machine should be 140°F (60°C). *(See page 12-9.)*

③ **True or False:** Cleaning reduces the number of microorganisms on a surface to safe levels. *(See page 12-3.)*

④ **True or False:** Utensils cleaned and sanitized in a three-compartment sink should be dried with a clean towel. *(See page 12-11.)*

⑤ **True or False:** Tableware and utensils that have been cleaned and sanitized should be stored at least two inches off of the floor. *(See page 12-14.)*

For answers, please turn to the Answer Key.

Introduction

In Chapter 10, you learned that a good food safety management system depends on food safety programs. A cleaning and sanitation program is one of the most important of these.

If you do not keep your facility and equipment clean and sanitary, food can easily become contaminated. No matter how carefully you prepare and cook food, without a clean and sanitary environment, bacteria and viruses—such as those that cause salmonellosis and hepatitis A—can quickly spread to both cooked and uncooked food. Cleaning and sanitizing must be done carefully and correctly. If not used properly, cleaning and sanitizing chemicals can be just as harmful to customers and employees as the illnesses they help prevent.

Cleaning & Sanitizing

Surfaces must *first* be cleaned and rinsed *before* being sanitized.

Cleaning vs. Sanitizing

It is important to understand the difference between cleaning and sanitizing. Cleaning is the process of removing food and other types of soil from a surface, such as a countertop or plate. Sanitizing is the process of reducing the number of microorganisms on that surface to safe levels.

There are four steps for cleaning and sanitizing a surface:

1 Clean the surface.

2 Rinse the surface.

3 Sanitize the surface.

4 Allow the surface to air-dry.

All surfaces must be cleaned and rinsed. This includes walls, storage shelves, and garbage containers. However, any surface that touches food, such as knives, stockpots, and cutting boards, must be cleaned *and* sanitized.

All food-contact surfaces must be washed, rinsed, and sanitized:

- After each use

- Any time you begin working with a different type of food

- Any time you are interrupted during a task and the tools or items you have been working with may have been contaminated

- At four-hour intervals, if the items are in constant use

Cleaning

Several factors affect the cleaning process. These include:

- **Type of soil.** Certain types of soil require special cleaning methods.

- **Condition of the soil.** The condition of the soil or stain affects how easily it can be removed. Dried or baked-on stains will be more difficult to remove than soft, fresh stains.

- **Water hardness.** Cleaning is more difficult in hard water because minerals react with the detergent, decreasing its effectiveness. Hard water can cause scale or lime deposits to build up on equipment, requiring the use of lime-removal cleaners.

- **Water temperature.** In general, the higher the water temperature, the better a detergent will dissolve and the more effective it will be in loosening dirt.

- **Surface being cleaned.** Different surfaces require different cleaners. Some cleaners work well in one situation but might not work well or might even damage equipment when used in another.

- **Agitation or pressure.** Scouring or scrubbing a surface helps remove the outer layer of soil, allowing a cleaning agent to penetrate deeper.

- **Length of treatment.** The longer soil on a surface is exposed to a cleaning agent, the easier it is to remove.

Cleaners

Cleaners are chemicals that remove food, soil, rust, stains, minerals, or other deposits. They must be stable, noncorrosive, and safe for employee use. Since cleaners have different cleaning properties, ask your supplier to help you select those that will best meet your needs.

For best results, use cleaners as directed. They can be ineffective and even dangerous if misused. Follow manufacturers' instructions carefully. Employees should never combine compounds or attempt to make up their own cleaners. Also, do not substitute one type of cleaner for another unless the intended use is stated clearly on the label. Detergents used for dishwashing machines, for example, can cause severe burns to the skin if used for manual dishwashing.

Cleaners are divided into four categories: detergents, degreasers, delimers, and abrasive cleaners. Some categories may overlap. For example, most abrasive cleaners and some delimers contain detergents. Some detergents also may contain degreasers.

Detergents

There are different types of detergents for different cleaning tasks. All detergents, however, contain surfactants (surface-acting agents) that reduce surface tension between the soil and the surface being cleaned. These allow the detergent to quickly penetrate and soften the soil. General-purpose detergents are mildly alkaline cleaners that remove fresh soil from floors, walls, ceilings, prep surfaces, and most equipment and utensils. Heavy-duty detergents are highly alkaline cleaners that remove wax, aged or dried soil, and baked-on grease. Dishwashing detergents, for example, are highly alkaline.

Degreasers

Degreasers are detergents that contain a grease-dissolving agent. These cleaners work well in areas where grease has been burned on, such as grill backsplashes, oven doors, and range hoods.

Delimers

12a Delimers

Delimers are often used to remove scale in dishwashing machines.

Delimers are used on mineral deposits and other soils that other types of cleaners cannot remove. These cleaners are often used to remove scale in dishwashing machines and steam tables, as well as rust stains and tarnish on copper and brass. (See *Exhibit 12a*.) The type and strength of the delimer varies with the cleaner's purpose. Follow the instructions carefully and use delimers with caution.

Abrasive Cleaners

Abrasive cleaners contain a scouring agent that helps scrub hard-to-remove soil. These cleaners are often used to remove baked-on food in pots and pans. Use abrasives with caution since they can scratch surfaces.

Sanitizing

There are two methods used to sanitize surfaces: heat sanitizing and chemical sanitizing.

Heat Sanitizing

12b Temperature-Sensitive Label

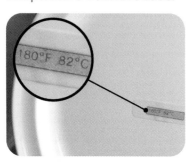

Check the water temperature in high-temperature machines by attaching a temperature-sensitive label to an item.

One way to heat-sanitize tableware, utensils, or equipment is to immerse them in hot water. To be effective, the water must be at least 171°F (77°C) and the items must be immersed for thirty seconds. It may be necessary to install a heating device to maintain this temperature. Use a thermometer to check water temperature when heat-sanitizing by immersion.

High-temperature dishwashing machines use hot water to sanitize tableware, utensils, and other items. To check the water temperature in these machines, you can attach temperature-sensitive labels or tape to items and run them through the machine. (See *Exhibit 12b.*) You can also place a high-temperature thermometer in a dish rack and run it through the machine.

Chemical Sanitizing

Chemical sanitizers are regulated by state and federal environmental protection agencies (EPAs). The three most common types are chlorine, iodine, and quaternary ammonium compounds (quats). Refer to your local regulatory agency for recommendations on selecting a sanitizer. For a list of approved sanitizers, check the Code of Federal Regulations 40CFR180.940—"Food-Contact Surface Sanitizing Solutions."

Chemical sanitizing is done in two ways: either by immersing a clean object in a specific concentration of sanitizing solution for a specific amount of time or by rinsing, swabbing, or spraying the object with a specific concentration of sanitizing solution.

In some instances, detergent-sanitizer blends may be used to sanitize surfaces. Operations that have two-compartment sinks often use these. If you use a detergent-sanitizer blend, use it once to clean. Then use it a second time to sanitize.

Factors Influencing the Effectiveness of Sanitizers

Several factors influence the effectiveness of chemical sanitizers. The most critical include contact time, temperature, water hardness, pH, and concentration.

- **Contact time.** In order for a sanitizing solution to kill microorganisms, it must make contact with the object for a specific amount of time. Since minimum times may differ for each sanitizer, check with your supplier.

- **Temperature.** The water in sanitizing solutions must be the correct temperature. Follow manufacturers' recommendations.

- **Water hardness.** This can affect how well a sanitizer works. Water hardness is the amount of minerals in your water. Find out what your water hardness is from your municipality. Then work with your supplier to identify the right amount of sanitizer to use for your water.

- **pH.** Water pH can also affect a sanitizer. Find out what the pH of your water is from your municipality. Then work with your supplier to find out the right amount of sanitizer to use for your water.

- **Concentration.** Chemical sanitizers are mixed with water until the proper concentration, or ratio of sanitizer to water, is reached. Mixing the sanitizer to the proper concentration is critical, since concentrations below those required in your jurisdiction or recommended by the manufacturer could fail to sanitize objects. Concentrations higher than recommended can be unsafe, leave an odor or bad taste on objects, and corrode metals.

Concentration is measured using a sanitizer test kit and is expressed as ppm—parts per million. (See *Exhibit 12c.*) The test kit should be designed for the sanitizer you are using and is usually available from the manufacturer or your supplier. The concentration of a sanitizing solution must be checked

12c Sanitizer Test Kit

Use a test kit to check the concentration of a sanitizing solution.

frequently since the sanitizer is depleted during use. Hard water, food particles, and detergent inadequately rinsed from a surface can quickly reduce the sanitizer's effectiveness. A sanitizing solution must be changed when it is visibly dirty or when its concentration has dropped below the required level. *Exhibit 12d* provides some general guidelines for using chlorine, iodine, and quats effectively.

12d   General Guidelines for the Effective Use of Chlorine, Iodine, and Quats

	Chlorine		Iodine	Quats
Water temperature	≥100°F (38°C)	≥75°F (24°C)	68°F (20°C)	75°F (24°C)
Water pH	≤10	≤8	≤5 or as per manufacturer's recommendation	As per manufacturer's recommendation
Water hardness	As per manufacturer's recommendation		As per manufacturer's recommendation	≤500 ppm or as per manufacturer's recommendation
Sanitizer concentration	50-99 ppm	50-99 ppm	12.5–25 ppm	As per manufacturer's recommendation
Sanitizer contact time	≥7 sec	≥7 sec	≥30 sec	≥30 sec

Machine Dishwashing

Tableware and utensils are often cleaned and sanitized in a dishwashing machine. These sanitize by using either hot water or a chemical-sanitizing solution.

High-Temperature Machines

High-temperature machines rely on hot water to clean and sanitize. Water temperature is critical. If the water is *not* hot enough, items will not be properly sanitized. If the water is too hot, it may vaporize before tableware and utensils have been sanitized. Extremely hot water can also bake food onto these items.

The temperature of the final sanitizing rinse must be at least 180°F (82°C). For stationary rack single-temperature machines, it must be at least 165°F (74°C). The dishwasher must be equipped with a built-in thermometer that measures water temperature at the manifold—the point where the water sprays into the tank. Establishments that clean and sanitize high volumes of tableware may need to install a heating device to keep up with the demand for hot water.

Chemical-Sanitizing Machines

Chemical-sanitizing machines can clean and sanitize at much lower temperatures. Since different sanitizers require different temperatures, it is important to follow the dishwashing temperature guidelines provided by the manufacturer. Items washed and rinsed at these lower temperatures may take longer to air-dry, so you may need more room at the clean end of the machine and more tableware during peak periods.

The effectiveness of your dishwashing program will depend on a number of factors:

* A well-planned layout in the dishwashing area, with a scraping and soaking area and adequate space for both soiled and clean items

* Sufficient water supply, especially hot water

* Separate area for cleaning pots and pans

* Devices that indicate water pressure and temperature of the wash and rinse cycles

* Protected storage areas for clean tableware and utensils

* Employees who are trained to operate and maintain the equipment and use the proper chemicals

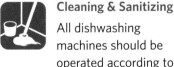

Cleaning & Sanitizing

All dishwashing machines should be operated according to manufacturers' instructions.

All dishwashing machines should be operated according to manufacturers' instructions. These instructions will typically be located on the machine.

Never overload dish racks, and make sure all surfaces are exposed to the spray action of the dishwasher.

Dishwashing Machine Operation

There are general procedures to follow to clean and sanitize tableware, utensils, and related items in a dishwashing machine:

- **Check the machine for cleanliness at least once a day, cleaning it as often as needed.** Fill tanks with clean water. Clear spray nozzles of food and foreign objects. Use a delimer on the machine whenever necessary to remove mineral deposits caused by hard water. Make sure detergent and sanitizer dispensers are properly filled.

- **Scrape, rinse, or soak items before washing.** Presoak items with dried-on food.

- **Load dish racks correctly.** Make sure all surfaces are exposed to the spray action. Use racks designed for the items being washed, and never overload them. (See *Exhibit 12e*.)

- **Check temperatures and pressure.** Follow manufacturer's recommendations.

- **Check each rack for soiled items as it comes out of the machine.** Run dirty items through again until they are clean. Most items will need only one pass if the water temperature is correct and proper procedures are followed.

- **Air-dry all items.** Towels can recontaminate items.

- **Keep your dishwashing machine in good repair.**

Manual Dishwashing

Establishments that do not have a dishwashing machine may use a three-compartment sink to wash items. These sinks are often used to wash larger items. A properly set-up station includes:

- Area for rinsing away food or for scraping food into garbage containers

- Drain boards to hold both soiled and clean items

- Thermometer to measure water temperature

- Clock with a second hand, allowing employees to time how long items have been immersed in the sanitizing solution

Cleaning and Sanitizing in a Three-Compartment Sink

Before cleaning and sanitizing tableware, utensils, and equipment in a three-compartment sink, each sink and all work surfaces must be cleaned and sanitized. Follow the steps below and as shown in *Exhibit 12f* on the next page when manually cleaning and sanitizing tableware, utensils, and equipment.

❶ **Rinse, scrape, or soak all items before washing.**

❷ **Clean items in the first sink.** Wash them in a detergent solution at least 110°F (43°C). Use a brush, cloth, or nylon scrub pad to loosen the remaining soil. Replace the detergent solution when the suds are gone or the water is dirty.

❸ **Rinse items in the second sink.** Immerse them in the rinse water or spray-rinse them. Remove all traces of food and detergent. If using the immersion method, replace the rinse water when it becomes cloudy or dirty.

❹ **Sanitize items in the third sink following the guidelines on pages 12-6 and 12-7.** Never rinse items after sanitizing them. This could contaminate their surfaces. The only exception to this rule is when you are washing items in a dishwasher that can safely rinse items after they have been sanitized. The dishwasher must meet these requirements.

   ○ The cycle sanitizes items before they are rinsed.

   ○ The sanitizer is used according to the guidelines provided by the Environmental Protection Agency (EPA).

❺ **Air-dry all items.** Place them upside down so they will drain.

Wood surfaces, such as cutting boards, handles, and bakers' tables, need special care. After each use, scour them in a detergent solution with a stiff-bristle nylon brush, rinse them in clean water, and sanitize them. Do not soak wood surfaces in detergent or sanitizing solutions.

Key Point

After washing and rinsing, immerse items in hot water or a chemical-sanitizing solution.

12f Steps for Cleaning and Sanitizing Items in a Three-Compartment Sink

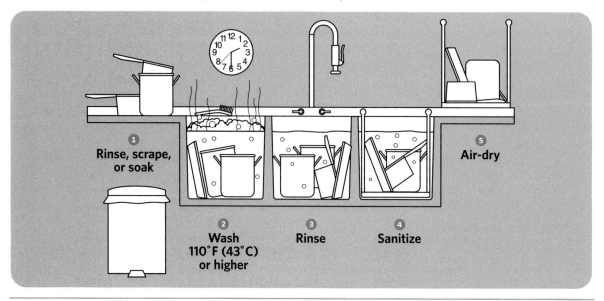

1 Rinse, scrape, or soak
2 Wash 110°F (43°C) or higher
3 Rinse
4 Sanitize
5 Air-dry

Cleaning the Premises

Nonfood-contact surfaces must be cleaned regularly. Examples include floors, ceilings, equipment exteriors, restrooms, and walls. Regular cleaning prevents dust, dirt, food residue and other debris from building up.

Tools for Cleaning

Key Point

Color-coding can help ensure that the right tools are used for the right tasks.

Cleaning is easier when you have the right cleaning tools. For example, worn-out tools will not give you the pressure or friction needed for cleaning, and tools that are the wrong size will be ineffective. However, even the correct tools can contaminate surfaces if they are not handled carefully. Cleaning all tools before putting them away can help prevent this, as does designating tools for specific tasks. For example, some establishments designate one set of tools to clean food-contact surfaces and another set for nonfood-contact surfaces. Similarly, one set of tools can be designated for cleaning and another for sanitizing.

Color-coding each set of tools often helps reinforce these different uses. Whatever you do, always use a separate set of tools for the restroom.

Something to Think About...

The Contamination Culprit

A local health department noted that a routine sample of soft-serve ice cream from an establishment tested extremely high for *E. coli*. The health inspector and manager examined all aspects of the ice-cream mix, the soft-serve machine, and the maintenance and cleaning of the machine. Everything appeared to be in order. The mix was fine, the machine was in perfect working order, and the employees cleaned and sanitized the machine every night according to the manufacturer's specifications.

The source of the *E. coli* was found, eventually, in the utility closet. A new employee responsible for cleaning and sanitizing the machine had been using a brush that was also used for heavy cleaning of the restaurant itself, including the restrooms. Each night as he cleaned the machine with the dirty brush, the employee was unknowingly contaminating the machine with *E. coli*.

What could have been done to prevent this situation?

Brushes

Brushes apply more effective pressure than wiping cloths, and the bristles loosen soil more easily. Worn brushes will not clean effectively and can be a source of contamination. They should be discarded.

Brushes come in different shapes and sizes for each task. Lacquered wood or plastic brushes with synthetic bristles are preferred. They do not absorb moisture, are nonabrasive, and last longer. Use the right brush for the job.

Scouring Pads

Steel wool and other abrasives are sometimes used to clean heavily soiled pots and pans, equipment, or floors. However, metal scouring pads can break apart and leave residue on surfaces, which can later contaminate food. Nylon scouring pads provide an alternative.

Mops and Brooms

Keep both light- and heavy-duty mops and brooms on hand. Mop heads can be all-cotton or synthetic blends. It makes sense to have a bucket and wringer for both the front and back of the house. Both vertical and push-type brooms will also be useful.

Towels

Never use towels meant for cleaning food spills for any other purpose. Store towels in a sanitizer solution between uses. Keep towels that come in contact with raw meat, fish, or poultry separate from other cleaning towels.

Storing Utensils, Tableware, and Equipment

Once tableware, utensils, and equipment have been cleaned and sanitized, store them so they stay that way. It is equally important to ensure that cleaning tools and supplies are stored properly.

Tableware and Equipment

- Store tableware and utensils at least six inches (fifteen centimeters) off the floor. Keep them covered or otherwise protected from dirt and condensation.

- Clean and sanitize drawers and shelves before clean items are stored.

- Clean and sanitize trays and carts used to carry clean tableware and utensils. Do this daily or as often as necessary.

- Store glasses and cups upside down on a cleaned and sanitized shelf or rack. Store flatware and utensils with handles up so employees can pick them up without touching food-contact surfaces.

- Keep the food-contact surfaces of stationary equipment covered until ready for use.

Key Point

Store flatware and utensils with handles up so employees can pick them up without touching food-contact surfaces.

Cleaning Tools and Supplies

Cleaning tools and chemicals should be placed in a storage area away from food and food-preparation sites. The area should be well lighted so employees can identify chemicals easily. It should also be equipped with hooks for hanging mops, brooms, and other cleaning tools. A utility sink should be provided for filling buckets and cleaning tools, as well as a floor drain for dumping dirty water. (See *Exhibit 12g*.) To prevent contamination, never clean mops, brushes, or other tools in sinks used for handwashing, food preparation, or dishwashing. Additionally, never dump mop water or other liquid waste into toilets or urinals.

When storing tools and supplies, consider the following:

* Air-dry wiping cloths overnight.

* Hang mops, brooms, and brushes on hooks to air-dry. Do not leave brooms or brushes standing on their bristles.

* Clean and rinse buckets. Let them air-dry, and store them with other tools.

12g Storage Area for Cleaning Tools and Supplies

Tools and chemicals should be placed in a storage area away from food and food-preparation sites.

Using Foodservice Chemicals

Chemicals pose little threat to employees if used properly. Used improperly, they can become a health hazard that can cause injury. To reduce this risk, you should only purchase chemicals that are approved for use in a restaurant or foodservice establishment.

Because of the potential dangers of chemicals used in the workplace, the Occupational Safety and Health Administration (OSHA) requires employers to comply with its Hazard Communication Standard (HCS). This standard, also known as Right-to-Know or HAZCOM, requires employers to tell their employees about chemical hazards to which they might be exposed at the establishment. It also requires employers to train employees on how to safely use the chemicals they work with. Employers must comply with OSHA's HCS by developing a hazard communication program for their establishment.

A hazard communication program must include the following components:

- Inventory of hazardous chemicals used at the establishment

- Chemical labeling procedures

- Material Safety Data Sheets (MSDS)

- Employee training

- Written plan addressing the HCS

Inventory of Hazardous Chemicals

A hazardous chemical is any chemical that poses a physical or health hazard to humans. Chemicals known to have acute or chronic health effects or that are explosive, flammable, or unstable are considered hazardous. Virtually any chemical with toxic properties should be included in an establishment's HAZCOM program.

Take an inventory of the hazardous chemicals stored in your establishment. List the name of the chemical and where it is stored. Update the list when chemicals are added or no longer used.

Key Point

OSHA requires employers to tell employees about the chemical hazards they might be exposed to and to train employees to safely use the chemicals they work with.

Key Point

If chemicals are transferred to a new container, it must be labeled with the common name of the chemical.

Labeling Procedures

OSHA requires chemical manufacturers to clearly label the outside of containers with the chemical name, manufacturer's name and address, and possible hazards. When receiving chemicals, only accept containers with proper labels, and make sure they remain readable and attached to the container.

If chemicals are transferred to a new container, the label on that container must list the common name of the chemical.

Material Safety Data Sheets (MSDS)

OSHA requires chemical suppliers and manufacturers to provide Material Safety Data Sheets (MSDS) (see *Exhibit 12h* on the next page) for each hazardous chemical at your establishment. These sheets are sent periodically with shipments of the chemical or can be requested by the establishment. MSDS are part of employees' right to know about the hazardous chemicals they work with and, therefore, must be kept in a location accessible to all employees while on the job. MSDS contain the following information about the chemical:

- Information about safe use and handling

- Physical, health, fire, and reactivity hazards

- Precautions

- Appropriate personal protective equipment (PPE) to wear when using the chemical

- First-aid information and steps to take in an emergency

- Manufacturer's name, address, and phone number

- Preparation date of MSDS

- Hazardous ingredients and identity information

12h Sample Material Safety Data Sheet

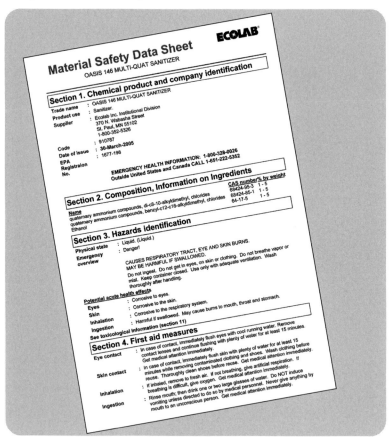

Courtesy of Ecolab, Inc®, St. Paul, MN

Training

OSHA requires that every employee who might be exposed to hazardous chemicals during normal or regular working conditions be informed of the hazards and trained to use the chemicals properly. Employees should receive this training annually, and new employees must receive it when first assigned to a department or area. The following topics should be covered during training:

- Existence and requirements of the HCS

- How the HCS is implemented in the workplace

- Operations and processes in which hazardous chemicals are used

- Inventory of chemicals in your establishment

- Location of MSDS

- How to read MSDS and product labels

- Physical and health hazards of all chemicals used

- Specific procedures adopted to provide protection, such as work practices

- Use of PPE and steps to prevent or reduce exposure to chemicals

- Safety and emergency procedures

- Information on the normal use of chemicals

Written Plan

Key Point

OSHA requires employers to develop a written plan that describes how they will meet the requirements of the Hazard Communication Standard (HCS) in their establishment.

OSHA requires employers to develop a written plan describing how they will meet the requirements of the HCS in their establishment. The following items should be included in your written plan:

- List of hazardous chemicals stored on the premises and their amounts

- Purchasing specifications for chemicals

- Procedures for receiving and storing chemicals

- Labeling requirements in your establishment

- Procedures for accessing MSDS

- List of PPE

- Employee training procedures

- Reporting and record-keeping procedures

- How the employer will inform employees of the hazards of nonroutine tasks

Disposing of Hazardous Materials

Many chemicals used in the establishment pose a hazard to people and the environment if not disposed of properly. When disposing of chemicals, follow the instructions on the label and any local regulations that may apply.

Cleaning & Sanitizing
An effective cleaning program takes commitment from management and the involvement of employees.

Developing a Cleaning Program

A clean and sanitary establishment is a prerequisite for a successful food safety management system. Keeping the establishment in this condition requires an effective cleaning program. To develop this program, the needs of the establishment must first be identified and a master cleaning schedule created. Employees must receive training so they know how to properly clean equipment and surfaces. Finally, you need to monitor the program to ensure it is effective.

Identifying Cleaning Needs

- **Identify all surfaces, tools, and equipment in the facility that need cleaning.** Walk through every area of the facility.

- **Look at the way cleaning is done currently.** Get input from employees. Ask them how and why they clean a certain way. Find out which procedures can be improved.

- **Estimate the time and skills needed for each task.** Some jobs may be done more efficiently by two or more people. Others might require an outside contractor. Determine how often things need to be cleaned.

Creating a Master Cleaning Schedule

Use information gathered while identifying your cleaning needs to develop a master cleaning schedule. The schedule should include the following:

- **What should be cleaned.** Arrange the schedule in a logical way so nothing is left out. List all cleaning jobs in one area, or list jobs in the order they should be performed. Keep the schedule flexible enough so you can make changes if needed.

- **Who should clean it.** Assign each task to a specific individual. In general, employees should clean their own areas. Rotate other cleaning tasks to distribute them fairly.

- **When it should be cleaned.** Employees should clean and sanitize as needed. Schedule major cleaning when food will not be contaminated or service interrupted—usually after closing. Schedule work shifts to allow enough time. Employees rushing to clean before their shifts end may cut corners.

- **How it should be cleaned.** Provide clearly written procedures for cleaning. Lead employees through the process step by step. Always follow manufacturers' instructions when cleaning equipment. Specify cleaning tools and chemicals by name. Post cleaning instructions near the item to be cleaned. A sample master cleaning schedule is provided in *Exhibit 12i*.

12i   Sample Master Cleaning Schedule for a Food-Preparation Area

	Who should clean it?	What should be cleaned?	When it should be cleaned?	How it should be cleaned?
Floor	Busers	Wipe up spills	Immediately	Cloth mop and bucket, broom, and dustpan
		Damp mop	Once per shift, between rushes	Mop, bucket, safety signs
		Scrub	Daily, at closing	Brushes, squeegee, bucket, detergent, safety signs
Walls and ceilings	Dishwashing staff	Wipe up splashes	As soon as possible	Clean using cloths and detergents
		Wash walls	Food-prep and cooking areas: daily All other areas: first of month	Clean using cloths and detergents
Worktables	Prep cooks	Clean and sanitize tops	Between uses and at the end of the day	See cleaning procedure for each table
		Empty, clean, and sanitize drawers	Weekly	See cleaning procedure for each table

Choosing Cleaning Materials

When selecting cleaning tools for your establishment, consider the following:

- **Select tools and cleaners according to the needs identified on the master cleaning schedule.** Talk to suppliers for suggestions on which tools and supplies are appropriate for your operation. Make sure your supplies match the needs listed on the master schedule.

- **Replace worn tools.** Equipment that is worn or soiled may not clean or sanitize surfaces properly.

- **Provide employees with the right protective gear.** Make sure there is an adequate supply of rubber gloves, aprons, goggles, and other supplies.

Implementing the Cleaning Program

Training is critical to the success of the cleaning program. Employees must understand the tasks you want them to perform and the level of quality expected. To ensure the success of the program, follow these guidelines:

- **Schedule a kickoff meeting to introduce the program to employees.** Explain the reason behind it. Stress how important cleanliness is to food safety. If people understand why they are supposed to do something, they are more likely to do it.

- **Schedule enough time for training.** Work with small groups, or conduct training by area. Show employees how to clean equipment and surfaces in each area. (See *Exhibit 12j.*)

- **Provide plenty of motivation.** Reward employees for any job well done. Create small incentives for individuals or teams, such as "Clean Team of the Month" awards. Tie performance to specific measurements or goals, such as achieving high marks during health department inspections.

12j Employee Training

Employees should be shown how to clean equipment and surfaces in each area.

Monitoring the Program

Once you have implemented the cleaning program, you must monitor it to make sure it is working. This includes:

- **Supervising daily cleaning routines.**

- **Checking the daily completion of all cleaning tasks against the master cleaning schedule.**

- **Modifying the master schedule to reflect any changes in menu, procedures, or equipment.**

- **Requesting employee input on the program during staff meetings.** Ask employees if they need additional equipment, supplies, staff, time, or training to get cleaning jobs done. Find out if they have suggestions for improving the program.

Summary

Cleaning is the process of removing food and other types of soil from a surface. Sanitizing is the process of reducing the number of harmful microorganisms on a clean surface to safe levels. You must clean and rinse a surface before it can be sanitized. Then the surface must be allowed to air-dry. Surfaces can be sanitized with hot water or with a chemical-sanitizing solution.

All surfaces should be cleaned and rinsed on a regular basis. Food-contact surfaces must be cleaned and sanitized after every use, whenever you begin working with a different type of food, any time a task is interrupted, and after four-hours if items are in constant use.

Dishwashing machines can be used to clean, rinse, and sanitize most tableware and utensils. Follow manufacturers' instructions, and make sure your machine is clean and in good working condition. Check the temperature and pressure of wash and rinse cycles daily.

Items cleaned in a three-compartment sink should be presoaked or scraped clean, washed in a detergent solution, rinsed in clean water, and sanitized in either hot water or in a chemical sanitizing solution for a predetermined amount of time. All items should then be air-dried.

Clean all nonfood-contact surfaces, such as kitchen floors, walls, shelves, and ceilings regularly.

Cleaning tools and chemicals should be placed in a storage area away from food and food-preparation areas. Make sure chemicals are clearly labeled. Keep MSDS for each chemical in a location accessible to all employees while on the job.

Develop and implement a cleaning program. Identify cleaning needs by walking through the operation and talking to employees. Create a master cleaning schedule listing all cleaning tasks, as well as when and how tasks should be completed. Assign responsibility for each task to specific employees. Enlist employees' support by including their input in the program's design and rewarding good performance. Explain to employees the important relationship between cleaning and sanitizing and food safety.

Monitor the cleaning program to keep it effective. Supervise cleaning procedures. Check completion of each job against the master schedule. Adjust cleaning and sanitizing procedures when there is a change in menu, equipment, or procedures.

Apply Your Knowledge

① What do you think went wrong?

② How can Tim prevent this from happening again?

③ How should any cleaning policy changes be introduced?

A Case in Point 1

It was only 9:05 a.m., but Tim, the day shift manager, already could tell it was going to be a bad day. While the executives from American Widget munched unenthusiastically on complimentary doughnuts, they threw annoyed looks at Tim and the buser, who were cleaning the banquet room American Widget had reserved for 9:00 a.m. Tim had opened the room at 8:50 a.m. and found, to his dismay, the remains of the annual banquet of the Pine Valley Martial Arts Club still strewn about the room.

Later, Tim sat down with his cleaning schedule and tried to figure out what had gone wrong. The banquet had been scheduled to end at 11:30 p.m. the previous night. The buser was scheduled to clean the room at midnight. But a note from Norman, the night shift manager, told Tim the banquet had been a wild one and the last guest had left long after the 1:00 a.m. closing time. The buser had punched out at 12:30 a.m., as he always did. Tim sighed.

For answers, please turn to the Answer Key.

Apply Your Knowledge

① What alternative methods can be used to clean and sanitize the tableware, since the machine is not functioning properly?

A Case in Point 2

The kitchen employees in the university cafeteria had scraped and rinsed every piece of tableware, placed them in racks, and fed them into the high-temperature dishwashing machine. When the wash and rinse cycles were complete, one of the employees noticed that the items were spotted. The thermometer registering the final rinse temperature for the sanitizing cycle had a reading of 140°F (60°C), rather than the required 180°F (82°C) indicated on the manufacturer's label. The employee went to inform the manager, who called for service.

For answers, please turn to the Answer Key.

Apply Your Knowledge

Use these questions to review the concepts presented in this chapter.

Discussion Questions

1. When should food-contact surfaces be cleaned and sanitized?

2. What is the difference between cleaning and sanitizing?

3. What are the steps that should be taken (in order) when cleaning and sanitizing items in a three-compartment sink?

4. How should clean and sanitized tableware, utensils, and equipment be stored?

5. What factors affect the efficiency of a sanitizer?

6. What are the requirements for storing cleaning materials?

For answers, please turn to the Answer Key.

Study Questions

Circle the best answer to each question.

1. **What is sanitizing?**
   A Reducing dirt from a surface
   B Reducing the pH of a surface
   C Reducing the hardness of water
   D Reducing pathogens to safe levels

2. **If food-contact surfaces are in constant use, how often must they be cleaned and sanitized?**
   A Every four hours
   B Every five hours
   C Every six hours
   D Every seven hours

③ **An employee wants to make a sanitizer solution to spray onto food-contact surfaces. What must be done to ensure that it has been made correctly?**

A   Test the solution with a sanitizer test kit.

B   Use very hot water when making the solution.

C   Try out the solution on a food-contact surface.

D   Compare the color to another solution of the right strength.

④ **How can foodservice managers find out which chemical sanitizers are appropriate for their operations?**

A   Check with the FDA.

B   Check with the CDC.

C   Check with the local regulatory authority.

D   Check the label on the sanitizer container.

⑤ **What should be done when throwing away chemicals?**

A   Pour leftover chemicals into a drain and throw the container away.

B   Seal the container in a bag and put it next to the garbage container.

C   Follow label instructions and any regulatory requirements that apply.

D   Take the lid off the container and put it into a garbage container.

⑥ **Material Safety Data Sheets (MSDS) should be**

A   kept so employees can access them.

B   kept with paperwork from the supplier.

C   sent to the local regulatory authority.

D   memorized in case of an emergency.

Continued on next page ▶

► *Continued from previous page*

⑦ **Flatware and utensils that have been cleaned and sanitized should be stored**

A with the handles facing up.

B at a temperature of 41°F (5°C) or lower.

C above cleaning supplies.

D within six inches (fifteen centimeters) of the floor.

⑧ **What is the correct way to clean and sanitize a prep table?**

A Wash, rinse, sanitize, air-dry

B Rinse, wash, sanitize, air-dry

C Sanitize, wash, rinse, air-dry

D Air-dry, rinse, sanitize, wash

For answers, please turn to the Answer Key.

Additional Resources

Articles and Texts

Marriott, Norman G. and Robert B. Gravani. *Principles of Food Sanitation.* New York: Kluwer Academic/Plenum, 2005.

Scott, Elizabeth and Sally F. Bloomfield. 1990. The Survival and Transfer of Microbial Contamination via Cloths, Hands, and Utensils. *Journal of Applied Bacteriology.* 68: 271.

Web Sites

American Chemistry Council
americanchemistry.com/s_acc/index.asp

Environmental Protection Agency
epa.gov

FDA Food Safety
www.fda.gov/Food/FoodSafety/default.htm

National Institute for Occupational Safety and Health
cdc.gov/niosh/homepage.html

Occupational Safety and Health Administration
osha.gov

Documents and Other Resources

2009 FDA Food Code
www.fda.gov/Food/FoodSafety/RetailFoodProtection/FoodCode/FoodCode2009/default.htm

OSHA. Hazard Communication
www.osha.gov/dsg/hazcom/index.html

Tolerance Exemptions for Active and Inert Ingredients for Use in Antimicrobial Formulations (Food-Contact Surface Sanitizing Solutions). Title 40 Code of Federal Regulations, Pt. 180.940. 2007 ed.
edocket.access.gpo.gov/cfr_2007/julqtr/pdf/40cfr180.940.pdf

13 Integrated Pest Management

Inside this chapter:

- The Integrated Pest Management (IPM) Program
- Identifying Pests
- Working with a Pest Control Operator (PCO)
- Treatment
- Control Measures
- Using and Storing Pesticides

After completing this chapter, you should be able to:

- Implement appropriate procedures for an integrated pest management program.
- Follow requirements for applying approved pesticides.
- Identify the signs of pest infestation and/or activity.
- Differentiate between pest prevention and pest control.
- Identify appropriate means for protecting outside openings in a food establishment.

Key Terms

- Infestation
- Integrated pest management
- Pest control operator
- Air curtains
- Pesticide
- Residual sprays
- Contact sprays
- Glue boards

Apply Your Knowledge

Check to see how much you know about the concepts in this chapter. Use the page references provided with each question to explore the topic.

Test Your Food Safety Knowledge

① **True or False:** A strong oily odor may indicate the presence of roaches. *(See page 13-7.)*

② **True or False:** The main purpose of an integrated pest management (IPM) program is to control pests once they have entered the establishment. *(See page 13-3.)*

③ **True or False:** Stationary equipment should not be covered before applying pesticides since it gives pests a place to hide. *(See page 13-17.)*

④ **True or False:** Glue traps are used to prevent roaches from entering the establishment. *(See page 13-7.)*

⑤ **True or False:** Pesticides can be stored in food-storage areas if they are labeled properly and closed tightly. *(See page 13-17.)*

For answers, please turn to the Answer Key.

Introduction

Pests such as insects and rodents can pose serious problems for restaurants and foodservice establishments. Not only are they unsightly to customers, they also damage food, supplies, and facilities. The greatest danger from pests comes from their ability to spread diseases, including foodborne illnesses.

The Integrated Pest Management (IPM) Program

Once pests have come into the facility in large numbers—an infestation—they can be very difficult to eliminate. Developing and implementing an integrated pest management program is the key. An IPM program uses *prevention* measures to keep pests from entering the establishment and *control* measures to eliminate any pests that do get inside.

For your IPM program to be successful, it is best to work closely with a licensed pest control operator. These professionals use safe, up-to-date methods to prevent and control pests.

Prevention is critical in pest control. If you wait until there is evidence of pests in your establishment, they may already be there in large numbers.

An IPM program has three basic rules:

❶ Deny pests access to the establishment.

❷ Deny pests food, water, and a hiding or nesting place.

❸ Work with a licensed PCO to eliminate pests that do enter.

Deny Pests Access to the Establishment

Pests can enter an establishment in one of two ways. They either are brought inside with deliveries, or they enter through openings in the building itself.

Deliveries

To prevent pests from entering the establishment with deliveries:

Key Point

Check all deliveries before they enter the establishment, and refuse any shipment in which you find pests or signs of pests.

- Use approved, reputable suppliers

- Check all deliveries before they enter your establishment.

- Refuse shipments that have pests or signs of pests, such as egg cases and body parts (legs, wings, etc.).

Doors, Windows, and Vents

To prevent pests from entering the establishment through doors, windows and vents:

- **Screen all windows and vents with at least sixteen mesh per square inch screening.** Anything larger might let in mosquitoes or flies. Check screens regularly, and clean, patch, or replace them as needed.

- **Install self-closing devices and door sweeps on all doors.** Repair gaps and cracks in door frames and thresholds. Use weather stripping on the bottoms of doors with no threshold.

- **Install air curtains (also called air doors or fly fans) above or alongside doors.** These devices blow a steady stream of air across the entryway, creating an air shield around doors left open.

- **Keep all exterior openings closed tightly.** Drive-through windows should be closed when not in use.

Denying Entry to Pests

Concrete

Sheet Metal

Fill openings or holes around pipes with concrete or cover them with sheet metal.

Pipes

Mice, rats, and insects such as cockroaches use pipes as highways through a facility. To prevent this:

- **Use concrete to fill holes or sheet metal to cover openings around pipes.** (See *Exhibit 13a.*)

- **Install screens over ventilation pipes and ducts on the roof.**

- **Cover floor drains with hinged grates to keep rodents out.** Rats are very good swimmers and can enter buildings through drainpipes.

Floors and Walls

Rodents often burrow into buildings through decaying masonry or cracks in building foundations. They move through floors and walls the same way. To prevent this:

- **Seal all cracks in floors and walls.** Use a permanent sealant recommended by your PCO or local health department.

- **Properly seal spaces or cracks where stationary equipment is fitted to the floor.** Use an approved sealant or concrete, depending on the size of the spaces.

Deny Food and Shelter

Pests are usually attracted to damp, dark, and dirty places. A clean establishment offers them little in the way of food and shelter. The stray pest that might get in cannot thrive or multiply in a clean kitchen. Besides adhering to your master cleaning schedule, follow these additional guidelines:

- **Dispose of garbage quickly and correctly.** Garbage attracts pests and provides them with a breeding ground. Keep garbage containers clean, and in good condition. Keep outdoor containers tightly covered. Clean up spills around garbage containers immediately. Wash and rinse containers regularly.

- **Store recyclables in clean, pest-proof containers as far away from your building as local regulations allow.** Bottles, cans, paper, and packaging material provide shelter and food for pests.

- **Store all food and supplies properly and as quickly as possible.**

    ◦ Keep all food and supplies away from walls and at least six inches (fifteen centimeters) off the floor.

    ◦ When possible, keep humidity at 50 percent or lower. Low humidity helps prevent roach eggs from hatching.

    ◦ Refrigerate food such as powdered milk, cocoa, and nuts after opening. Most insects that might be attracted to this food become inactive at temperatures below 41°F (5°C).

    ◦ Rotate products so pests do not have time to settle into them and breed.

- **Clean the establishment thoroughly.** Careful cleaning eliminates the pests' food supply, destroys insect eggs, and reduces the number of places pests can safely take shelter. (See *Exhibit 13b*.)

    ◦ Clean up food and beverage spills immediately, including crumbs and scraps.

    ◦ Clean toilets and restrooms as often as necessary.

    ◦ Train employees to keep lockers and break areas clean. Food and dirty clothes should *not* be kept in or around lockers. Break rooms should be cleaned properly after use.

    ◦ Keep cleaning tools and supplies clean and dry. Store wet mops on hooks rather than on the floor, since roaches can hide in them.

    ◦ Empty water from buckets to keep from attracting rodents.

Grounds and Outdoor Dining Areas

The popularity of outdoor dining offers a different set of pest concerns. Birds, flies, bees, and wasps can be annoying and dangerous to the health of your customers. As with indoor pests, the key to controlling them lies in denying food and shelter. (See *Exhibit 13c* on the next page.)

- Mow the grass, pull weeds, get rid of standing water, and pick up litter.

13b Thorough Cleaning

Cleaning eliminates pests' food supply, destroys insect eggs, and reduces the number of places pests can take shelter.

13c Minimize Pests in Outdoor Dining Areas

Cover garbage containers, remove dirty dishes, and clean up spills to deny food to pests.

- Cover all outdoor garbage containers.

- Remove dirty dishes and uneaten food from tables, cleaning them as quickly as possible.

- Do not allow employees or customers to feed birds or wildlife on the grounds.

- Locate electronic insect eliminators, or "zappers," away from food, customers, employees, and serving areas.

- Call your PCO to remove hives and nests.

Identifying Pests

Pests may still get into your establishment even if you take measures to prevent them. Pests are good hitchhikers, hiding in delivery boxes and even coming in on employees' clothing or personal belongings. It is important to be able to spot signs when pests are present and to determine the type you are dealing with. Record the time, date, and location when you spot signs of pests, and report this to your PCO. Early detection allows the PCO to start treatment as soon as possible.

Cockroaches

Roaches often carry disease-causing microorganisms such as *Salmonella* spp., fungi, parasite eggs, and viruses. Research shows that many people are allergic to residue left by roaches on food and surfaces. Roaches reproduce quickly and can adapt to some pesticides, making it difficult to control them.

13d   Common Roaches Found in Restaurants and Foodservice Establishments

American

German

Brown-banded

Oriental

Courtesy of Orkin Commercial Services

There are several different types of roaches. (See *Exhibit 13d.*) Most live and breed in dark, warm, moist, hard-to-clean places. You will typically find them in the following areas:

- Behind refrigerators, freezers, and stoves
- In sink and floor drains
- In spaces around hot-water pipes
- Inside equipment, often near motors and other electrical devices
- Under shelf liners and wallpaper
- Underneath rubber mats
- In delivery bags and boxes
- Behind unsealed coving (especially rubber-based)

Roaches generally feed in the dark. If you see a cockroach in daylight, you may have a major infestation, since only the weakest roaches come out in daylight. If you suspect you have a roach problem, check for these signs:

- Strong oily odor
- Droppings (feces) that look like grains of black pepper
- Capsule-shaped egg cases that are brown, dark red, or black and may appear leathery, smooth, or shiny

You may have problems with more than one type of roach. Glue traps—containers with sticky glue on the bottom—should be used to find out what type of roaches might be present. Work with your PCO to place the traps where roaches typically can be found. If possible, place them on the floor in the corner where two walls meet. Check the traps after twenty-four hours, and show them to your PCO. The type of roach present and its stage of development (nymph or adult) will determine the type of treatment needed.

Key Point

Flies can spread pathogens such as *Shigella* spp. which causes dysentery, and *Salmonella* Typhi, which causes the illness typhoid fever.

Flies

The common housefly is also a great threat to human health. Because they feed on garbage and animal waste, flies can spread pathogens such as *Shigella* spp., which causes dysentery, and *Salmonella* Typhi, which causes the illness typhoid fever.

In general, houseflies have the following characteristics:

- They prefer calm air and the edges of objects, such as rims of garbage cans.

- To find food and lay their eggs, they are drawn to odors of decay, garbage, and animal waste.

- In warm weather, they reproduce rapidly—eggs can hatch in as few as thirty hours. For their eggs to hatch, they need warm, moist, decayed material located out of the sun. Eggs hatch into maggots, which can grow into adult flies in six days.

Other types of flies can be just as bothersome. Fruit flies are somewhat less harmful because they are primarily attracted to spoiled fruit, not animal waste. They can still transmit diseases, however. "Biting" flies, such as deer flies and horse flies, can be an additional nuisance to outdoor diners.

Other Insects

- **Beetles, weevils, and moths.** Flour-moth larvae and beetles are usually found in dry-storage areas. Look for insect bodies, wings, or webs, as well as clumped-together food and holes in food and packaging. To prevent these pests, cover food tightly, keep storage areas clean and sanitary, and practice the first in, first out (FIFO) rule.

- **Ants.** Ants often nest in walls and floors near stoves and hot-water pipes. They are drawn to grease and sweet food. Clean up all food scraps and spills to keep them out.

- **Termites and carpenter ants.** These insects can cause great structural damage, boring into wood and weakening walls, floors, and ceilings. They are rarely visible. Carpenter ants nest in wood but forage for food elsewhere. Look for signs of sawdust that has fallen from the ceiling. Call your PCO immediately if you see signs of these insects.

- **Spiders.** Look for webs in corners and around fixtures. Spiders can be controlled by checking for and removing webs daily. The bites of some spiders, such as the black widow and brown recluse, are poisonous and can cause illness but are rarely fatal. If you see either type, call your PCO.

- **Bees, wasps, and hornets.** Bees, wasps, and hornets can sting outdoor diners. Some people are allergic to their venom and can go into shock or even die from just one or two stings. In general, these insects are drawn to sweet food. Here are some suggestions for handling them:

  ○ Bees make hives in hollow trees, under eaves, or in other protected places. They usually will not bother people unless their hives are threatened. If you find a hive, call your PCO to remove it.

  ○ Wasps and hornets often build nests under eaves. Call your PCO to remove them.

  ○ Yellow jackets usually nest in the ground and are drawn to proteins in early summer and sweets in late summer. They aggressively defend their nests, so call a PCO to remove them.

- **Mosquitoes and gnats.** Mosquitoes carry diseases such as malaria, typhoid, yellow fever, and encephalitis. These members of the fly family feed on the blood of animals and humans. Mosquitoes are drawn to heat and are most active at dawn and dusk. Gnats are annoying to outdoor diners. To minimize their presence, keep all outdoor areas free of stagnant water and move lights away from the building.

- **Deer ticks.** Ticks can carry Lyme disease and cause other serious illnesses. Minimize risk by keeping the grass short around dining areas.

Rodents

Rodents are a serious health hazard. They eat and ruin food, damage property, and can spread disease. Most rodents have a simple digestive system. They urinate and defecate as they move around a facility. Their waste can fall into food and can contaminate surfaces.

13e Common Types of Rodents

Roof rat

Common house mouse

Norway rat

Courtesy of Orkin Commercial Services

Rats and mice are the most common types of rodent. (See *Exhibit 13e*.) They hide during the day and search for food at night. Like other pests, they reproduce often. Typically, they do not travel far from their nests—rats travel only 100 to 150 feet, while mice travel only ten to thirty feet. Mice can squeeze through a hole the size of a nickel to enter a facility, while rats can fit through holes the size of a half dollar. Rats can stretch to reach an item as high as eighteen inches (forty-six centimeters), can jump three feet (one meter) in the air, and can even climb straight up brick walls. Rats and mice have very good senses of hearing, touch, and smell and are smart enough to avoid poison bait and poorly laid traps. Effective control of these rodents requires the knowledge and experience of professionals.

A building can be infested with both rats and mice at the same time. Look for these signs:

- **Signs of gnawing.** Rats and mice gnaw to reach food and to wear down their teeth, which grow continuously. Rats' teeth are so strong they can gnaw through pipes, concrete, and wood.

- **Droppings and urine stains.** Fresh droppings are shiny and black. Older droppings are gray. Rodent urine will "glow" when exposed to a black (ultraviolet) light.

- **Tracks.** Rodents tend to use the same pathways through your establishment. If rodents are a problem in your establishment, you may see dirt tracks along light-colored walls.

- **Nesting materials.** Rats and mice use soft materials such as scraps of paper, cloth, hair, feathers, and grass to build their nests.

- **Holes.** Rats usually nest in holes in quiet places. Nests are often found near food and water and may be found next to buildings.

Birds

Bird droppings carry fungi and bacteria that can make people sick. They also may carry mites and microorganisms that can cause encephalitis and other diseases. Birds can be drawn to crumbs and food scraps in outdoor dining areas. Keep these areas clean, and remove food from tables quickly. Post signs asking customers not to feed birds. If birds become a problem, call a PCO specializing in bird-control measures.

Other Animals

Though less common, other animals such as bats, raccoons, and squirrels can infest your building too. Building damage, bites, and the possible spread of rabies are the biggest concerns. Prevent these types of animals from getting inside the establishment. If there is evidence any of these pests have entered your establishment, work with a PCO or your local animal-control department to remove them.

- **Bats.** Bats will nest in high places that are warm, dark, and dry, often in eaves or attics. Bats are beneficial since they eat insects. In many places, it is against the law to kill them. However, they will bite if cornered and can spread rabies. Established bat colonies can be hard to eliminate. At dusk, after bats have left to feed, block all crevices and entrances. Light the area for several days to keep them away until they find a new place to roost.

- **Raccoons.** Raccoons have adapted to humans and urban growth. They feed at night, but it is not unusual to see them during the day. They prefer wooded areas, but females will nest in dark places, such as attics and chimneys, to give birth. Raccoons can contract rabies, and they will bite if cornered.

- **Squirrels.** Like raccoons, squirrels will nest in attics if given the chance. Clear branches away from buildings, and fill any holes or cracks around eaves and gutters.

Working with a Pest Control Operator (PCO)

Few pest problems are solved simply by spraying pesticides—chemical agents used to destroy pests. Although you can take many preventive measures to reduce the risk of infestation, most control measures should be carried out by professionals. Employ a licensed PCO to handle pest control. Working as a team, you and the PCO can prevent and/or eliminate pests and keep them from coming back. You can rely on your PCO to:

- Help you develop an integrated approach to pest management. This may include using a combination of chemical and nonchemical treatments to solve and prevent problems.

- Stay up-to-date on new equipment and products.

- Provide prompt service to address problems as they occur. Contracts should stipulate regular visits plus immediate service when pests are spotted.

- Keep records that document all steps taken to prevent and control pests.

How to Choose a PCO

Hiring a PCO is like choosing any other service provider. You must do your homework. Check references, and make sure that the PCO is licensed, if required by your state. You also might want a PCO who is a member of a pest management association, or who is certified by one.

Service Contract

Always require a written service contract from your PCO. Service contracts outline the work to be performed and what is expected from both you and the PCO. Read your contract carefully and have your lawyer review it, if possible. A contract should include the following:

- Description of services to be provided, including an initial inspection, regular monitoring visits, follow-up visits, and emergency service

- Warranty for work to be done

- Legal liability of the PCO

- Period of service

- Your duties, including preventive measures and facility preparation before and after treatment

- Records to be kept by the PCO, such as:

  ○ Pests sighted and trapped; species, location, and actions taken

  ○ All chemicals used and Material Safety Data Sheets (MSDS) for each (copies should be accessible to employees)

  ○ Building and maintenance problems noted and fixed

  ○ Maps or photos of the facilities noting location of traps, bait, and problem spots

  ○ Schedule for checking and cleaning traps, replacing bait, and reapplying chemicals

  ○ Regular written summary reports from the PCO; copies should be kept on file in the establishment for reference when planning improvements and assessing facility goals

Treatment

Key Point

After the initial inspection, your PCO should outline a treatment plan in writing.

Courtesy of the National Pest Management Association

Effective treatment starts with a thorough inspection of your facility and grounds. Give the PCO complete access to the building and cooperate fully during the inspection.

- Prepare employees to answer the PCO's questions.

- Provide building plans and equipment layouts.

- Point out possible trouble spots.

After the initial inspection, your PCO should provide a treatment plan in writing. In addition to price, the plan should:

- **Specify exactly what treatment will be used for each area or problem and the potential risks involved.**

- **Indicate dates and times of each treatment.** The federal government requires a PCO to give you enough advance warning to prepare the facility properly. Employees must not be on site during the treatment.

- **Provide steps you can take to control pests.**

- **Detail building defects that may cause problems for prevention and control measures.**

- **Determine timing of follow-up visits.** The PCO should review how well treatment is working and suggest alternate treatments if pests reappear.

Control Measures

PCOs use a variety of pest-control methods that are environmentally sound and safe for establishments. They know which techniques will work best to control the types of pests in your area. Since new technologies are developed all the time, the more you know about each of these methods, the better you can evaluate how well your PCO is doing.

Controlling Insects

There are several methods your PCO can use to control insects, depending on the type of insect and degree of infestation.

- **Repellents.** Repellents are liquids, powders, or mists that keep insects away from an area but do not kill them. Repellents are often used in hard-to-reach places, such as the spaces behind wallboards and plaster.

- **Sprays.** Chemical pesticide sprays are used to control insects. They include residual and contact sprays.

  ○ Residual sprays leave a film of insecticide that insects absorb as they crawl across it. Used in cracks and crevices like those along baseboards, these sprays can be liquid or a dust, such as boric acid.

  ○ Contact sprays kill insects on contact. They are usually used on groups of insects, such as clusters of roaches or a nest of ants.

- **Bait.** Chemical bait sometimes is used to control roaches or ants. The bait contains an attractant. When insects eat it, the chemical kills them. The advantage of using baits is that kitchen areas do not need to be prepped and people can remain on site while they are set.

13f Methods for Controlling Rodents

Rodent spring trap

Box trap

Glue board

Several devices can be used to control rodents.

Courtesy of Orkin Commercial Services

- **Traps.** There are several types of traps.

  ○ Light-only units simply entice insects to crawl inside where they find it hard to escape.

  ○ Electronic insect eliminators, or "zappers," use an electrically charged grid to kill insects attracted to the light.

  ○ Other units use both light and chemical attractants to lure insects onto a glue board.

Wasp and hornet traps are designed to hold nectar, which attracts these insects. Once inside, they cannot escape. Most fly traps use a light source—usually UV light—to attract insects to the trap. Tests have shown that different insects respond to different types or ranges of UV light. Make sure your PCO is using the most current technology.

The placement of traps is important. Never place them above or near food-preparation or storage areas or food-contact surfaces.

Controlling Rodents

Rats and mice tend to use the same routes through an establishment. Your PCO will choose the best method to eliminate these pests, which could include the following (see *Exhibit 13f*):

- **Traps.** Traps are a safe, effective way to kill rats and mice. If the infestation is large, however, traps will take time. Work with your PCO to set traps near or in rodent runways. Check traps often, and remove dead rodents carefully. If a trapped rodent is still alive, have your PCO remove it.

- **Glue boards.** Glue boards kill mice. When these devices are placed in runways, the mice stick to the board and die in several hours from exhaustion or lack of water or air. Check boards often, and throw away any with trapped mice. Glue boards are not effective for controlling rats since these rodents are usually strong enough to escape.

- **Bait.** Chemical bait should only be used by a PCO in areas where it cannot contaminate food or food-contact surfaces. It is usually placed in special covered, locked containers near rodent runways and possible entry points. Your PCO may change the baits and their locations often until they work properly. Rats can easily detect chemical bait and often avoid it.

Controlling Birds

Birds can be a serious problem in outdoor dining areas. While there is no way to eliminate birds, your PCO can use several techniques to keep them from nesting and roosting on your building.

• **Repellents.** Chemical pastes are sometimes used on gutters and ledges to repel birds. Paste must be used carefully so it does not fall into food or onto tables.

• **Netting.** Fine-mesh wire netting is used to keep birds from roosting on statues and bas-relief carvings on buildings.

• **Wires.** A PCO might string wires across the roof to prevent birds from roosting. The wires can be electrified to deliver a mild shock.

• **Sound.** In some instances, birds can be frightened away by the sound of other birds in distress. Prerecorded tapes are played through loudspeakers near roosting sites, though birds might eventually ignore the sounds and return to roost.

• **Balloons.** Birds sometimes can be frightened away with helium-filled mylar balloons. Ask your PCO about this technique.

Using and Storing Pesticides

While it may seem more cost effective to purchase and apply pesticides on your own, there are many reasons *not* to do so:

• Applied improperly, they may be ineffective or harmful.

• Pests can develop resistance and immunity to pesticides.

• Each region has its own pest-control problems, and some control measures are more effective than others.

• Pesticides are regulated by federal, state, and local laws; some are not approved for use in restaurants and foodservice establishments.

13g Pesticide Use

Rely on your PCO to decide if and when pesticides should be used in your establishment.

Courtesy of the National Pest Management Association

Rely on your PCO to decide if and when pesticides should be used in your establishment. They are trained to determine the best pesticide for each pest and how and where to apply it. (See *Exhibit 13g.*)

To minimize the hazard to people, have your PCO use pesticides only when you are closed for business and employees are not on site. When pesticides will be applied, prepare the area to be sprayed by removing all food and movable food-contact surfaces. Cover equipment and food-contact surfaces that cannot be moved. Wash, rinse, and sanitize food-contact surfaces after the area has been sprayed.

Any time pesticides are used or stored on the premises, you should have a corresponding MSDS, since they are hazardous materials. Your PCO should store and dispose of all pesticides used in your facility. If they are stored on the premises, follow these guidelines:

- **Keep pesticides in their original containers.**

- **Store pesticides in a secure location away from areas where food, utensils, and food equipment are stored.**

- **Check local regulations before disposing of pesticides.** Many are considered hazardous waste. Dispose of empty containers according to manufacturers' directions and local regulations.

Summary

Pests can carry and spread a variety of diseases. Once they have infested a facility, it can be very difficult to eliminate them. Developing and implementing an integrated pest management (IPM) program is the key. An IPM program uses prevention measures to keep pests from entering the establishment and control measures to eliminate any pests that do get inside. To be successful, establishments must deny pests access to the facility, food, water, and shelter. Finally, you must work with a licensed pest control operator (PCO) to eliminate pests that do enter.

Pests can be brought inside the establishment with deliveries, or they can enter through openings in the building itself. To prevent them from getting inside, check deliveries before they enter your facility and refuse any shipment in which you find pests or signs of infestation. Screen all windows and vents, install self-closing doors and air curtains, and keep exterior openings closed when not in use. Fill or cover holes around pipes, and seal cracks in floors and walls.

Pests are usually attracted to damp, dark, and dirty places. A clean and sanitary establishment offers them little food and shelter. Stick to your master cleaning schedule. Dispose of garbage quickly, and keep containers clean and tightly covered in all areas. Store recyclables as far from your building as allowed. Keep food and supplies away from walls and at least six inches (fifteen centimeters) off the floor. Rotate products so pests do not have time to settle into them and breed. Protect outdoor diners by denying pests food and shelter in these areas as well. Mow grass, remove standing water, and pick up litter. Cover outdoor garbage containers. Remove dirty dishes and uneaten food from tables, and clean them as quickly as possible. Do not allow employees or customers to feed birds or wildlife on the grounds.

Understanding pests is the key to controlling them. Roaches live and breed in dark, warm, and moist places. Check for a strong oily odor; droppings, which look like grains of black pepper; and egg cases. Use glue traps to find out what types of roaches are present. Rodents also are a serious health hazard. A building can be infested with both rats and mice at the same time. Look for droppings, signs of gnawing, tracks, nesting materials, and holes.

Although you can take many prevention measures yourself, most control measures should be carried out by professionals. Employ a licensed PCO to handle pest control, and require him or her to provide a written service contract outlining the work to be performed, as well as what is expected from both of you. Working as a team, you can prevent and/or eliminate pests and keep them from coming back.

There are several methods your PCO can use to control insects, depending on the type of insect and degree of infestation. Control methods include repellents, sprays, chemical bait, and traps. Rodents can be controlled through the use of traps set near runways, glue boards (for mice), and chemical bait.

While it might seem cost effective to apply pesticides yourself, there are many reasons for not doing so. Pesticides can be dangerous to your employees, customers, and food. Some pesticides are not approved for use in a restaurant or foodservice establishment, and pests can develop immunity to them. Rely on your PCO to decide if and when pesticides should be used in your establishment. PCOs are trained to determine the best pesticide for each pest and how and where to apply it.

Pesticides are hazardous materials. Any time they are used or stored on the premises, you should have corresponding Material Safety Data Sheets (MSDS). To minimize the hazard to people, have your PCO use pesticides only when you are closed for business and your employees are not on site. Your PCO should store and dispose of all pesticides used in your facility. If they are stored on the premises, they should be stored in a secure location away from areas where food, utensils, and food equipment are stored.

Apply Your Knowledge   A Case in Point

① What factors might Fred
   have overlooked in his
   recent remodeling that
   could have led to this
   infestation?

② What should Fred do to
   eliminate the roaches?

Now We're Cooking is a restaurant located in the middle of
town on the first floor of a landmark ninety-year-old building.
The building is in a shopping area that includes several other
restaurants. Fred, the manager, recently remodeled the
restaurant. He chose materials that are easy to clean. All of
the new foodservice equipment is designed for ease of
cleaning as well. The cleaning procedures listed on Fred's
master cleaning schedule are written out in detail and
completed by the employees as scheduled, with frequent self
inspections. Spills are cleaned up immediately. FIFO is
followed, and food is stored on metal racks away from walls
and six inches (fifteen centimeters) off the floor.

During a self inspection two weeks after he finished
remodeling, Fred found live cockroaches behind the sinks, in
the vegetable-storage area, in the public restrooms, and near
the garbage-storage area.

For answers, please turn to the Answer Key.

Apply Your Knowledge   Discussion Questions

Use these questions to
review the concepts
presented in this chapter.

① What is the purpose of an integrated pest management
   program?

② How can you prevent pests from entering your
   establishment?

③ How can you tell if your establishment has been infested
   with cockroaches or rodents?

④ What are the storage requirements for pesticides?

⑤ What precautions must be taken both before and after
   pesticides are applied in your establishment?

For answers, please turn to the Answer Key.

Study Questions

Circle the best answer to each question.

① **Who should apply pesticides?**
  A Shift manager
  B Person in charge
  C Pest control operator
  D Designated pest employee

② **Cockroaches typically are found in places that are**
  A cold, dry, and light.
  B warm, dry, and light.
  C cold, moist, and dark.
  D warm, moist, and dark.

③ **What kind of odor is a sign that roaches might be present?**
  A Strong, oily
  B Warm, spicy
  C Sharp, musty
  D Mild, seaweed

④ **The three basic rules of an integrated pest management program are 1) deny pests access to the operation, 2) _____, and 3) work with a licensed PCO to eliminate pests that do enter.**
  A deny pests food, water, and a nesting or hiding place
  B document all infestations with the local regulatory authority
  C prepare a chemical application schedule and post it publicly
  D notify the EPA that pesticides are being used in the establishment

⑤ **After pesticides have been applied, food-contact surfaces should be**
  A used only after a 20-minute wait.
  B checked with a sanitizer test kit.
  C washed, rinsed, and sanitized.
  D replaced with new equipment.

Continued on next page ▶

► *Continued from previous page*

⑥ **If pesticides are stored in the operation, where should they be kept?**

A In a secure location, away from food

B In a glass container, in a walk-in cooler

C In dry storage, on a shelf below the food

D In a plastic container, in any location

For answers, please turn to the Answer Key.

Additional Resources

Articles and Texts

Marriott, Norman G. and Robert B. Gravani. *Principles of Food Sanitation*. New York: Kluwer Academic/Plenum, 2005.

Web Sites

Environmental Protection Agency
epa.gov

FDA Food Safety
www.fda.gov/Food/FoodSafety/default.htm

National Pest Management Association
pestworld.org

Occupational Safety and Health Administration
osha.gov

Documents and Other Resources

2009 FDA Food Code
www.fda.gov/Food/FoodSafety/RetailFoodProtection/FoodCode/FoodCode2009/default.htm

OSHA Hazard Communication
www.osha.gov/dsg/hazcom/index.html

Notes

IV Food Safety Regulation and Employee Training

14   Food Safety Regulation and Standards

Inside this chapter:

- Objectives of a Foodservice Inspection Program
- Government Regulatory System for Food
- The *FDA Food Code*
- The Inspection Process
- Self-Inspections
- Federal Regulatory Agencies
- Voluntary Controls within the Industry

After completing this chapter, you should be able to:

- Identify the importance of regulatory inspections and self-inspections.
- Identify government agencies that regulate food establishments.
- Recognize the key components of an inspection.
- Take corrective action when found to be in violation of a regulation.

Key Terms

- U.S. Department of Agriculture (USDA)
- Food and Drug Administration (FDA)
- Regulations
- Health inspectors
- Centers for Disease Control and Prevention (CDC)
- Environmental Protection Agency (EPA)
- National Marine Fisheries Service (NMFS)

Apply Your Knowledge

Check to see how much you know about the concepts in this chapter. Use the page references provided with each question to explore the topic.

Test Your Food Safety Knowledge

① **True or False:** The Food and Drug Administration (FDA) issues food regulations that must be followed by each establishment. *(See page 14-4.)*

② **True or False:** Health inspectors are employees of the Centers for Disease Control and Prevention (CDC). *(See page 14-3.)*

③ **True or False:** You should accompany the health inspector during the inspection of your establishment. *(See page 14-7.)*

④ **True or False:** An establishment can be closed if it has significant lack of refrigeration. *(See page 14-9.)*

⑤ **True or False:** You should refuse entry to a health inspector if you are not ready for the inspection. *(See page 14-7.)*

For answers, please turn to the Answer Key.

Introduction

There are several reasons why it is important to have a foodservice inspection program. Most important is that failure to ensure food safety can jeopardize the health of your customers and could cost you your business. All establishments, including quick-service and fine-dining restaurants, delicatessens, hospitals, nursing homes, and schools, must follow standard food safety practices critical to the safety and quality of the food served. An inspection system lets the establishment know how well it is following these practices.

Objectives of a Foodservice Inspection Program

All establishments serving the public must provide safe food and are subject to inspection. An inspection evaluates whether the establishment is meeting minimum food safety standards. It also produces a written report that notes deficiencies, a tool that will help bring your establishment into compliance with safe food practices.

Government Regulatory System for Food

Every country has a history of government involvement in the development of health laws. Today, government control of food in the United States is exercised at three levels: federal, state, and local.

At the federal level, the **U.S. Department of Agriculture (USDA)** and the **Food and Drug Administration (FDA)** are directly involved in the inspection process.

The USDA is responsible for inspection and quality grading of meat, meat products, poultry, dairy products, eggs and egg products, and fruit and vegetables shipped across state lines. The USDA provides these services through the Food Safety and Inspection Service (FSIS) agency.

The FDA issues the *FDA Food Code* jointly with the USDA and Centers for Disease Control and Prevention (CDC). In addition, it inspects foodservice operations that cross state borders because they overlap the jurisdictions of two or more states. This includes interstate foodservice establishments such as those on planes and trains, as well as food manufacturers and processors. The FDA shares responsibility with the USDA for inspecting food-processing plants to ensure standards of purity, wholesomeness, and compliance with labeling requirements.

In the United States, most food regulations affecting restaurant and foodservice operations are written at the state level (except regulations for interstate or international establishments, which are determined at the federal level). Each state decides whether to adopt the *FDA Food Code* or some modified form of it.

State regulations may be enforced by state or local (city or county) health departments. In a large city, the city health department will probably be responsible for enforcing health codes. In smaller cities or in rural areas, a county or state health department may be responsible for enforcement. In any case, the manager must be familiar with the local agencies and their enforcement system. City, county, or state health inspectors (also called sanitarians, health officials, or environmental health specialists) conduct restaurant and foodservice inspections in most states. They generally are trained in food safety, sanitation, and public health principles.

Key Point

For restaurant and foodservice operations, recommendations for regulations are issued at the federal level, the regulations are written at the state level, and enforcement is carried out at the local level.

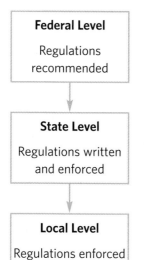

Federal Level

Regulations recommended

↓

State Level

Regulations written and enforced

↓

Local Level

Regulations enforced

The *FDA Food Code*

14a *FDA Food Code*

The *FDA Food Code* lists the government's recommendations for foodservice regulations.

The *FDA Food Code* is issued by the FDA based on input from the Conference for Food Protection (CFP). CFP representatives come from foodservice, government, academic and consumer groups. The *FDA Food Code* lists the government's recommendations for foodservice regulations. Currently, these recommendations are updated every two years to reflect developments in the restaurant and foodservice industry and the field of food safety. (See *Exhibit 14a.*)

The *FDA Food Code* is intended to assist state health departments in developing regulations for a foodservice inspection program. It is not an actual law. Although the FDA recommends adoption by the states, it cannot require it. Rather, the *FDA Food Code* represents the FDA's best advice for a uniform system of regulation to ensure food safety. Some states use the *FDA Food Code* as a basis for their own codes instead of adopting it in its entirety. The *FDA Food Code* covers the following areas:

- **Foodhandling and preparation:** criteria for receiving, storage, display, service, transportation
- **Personnel:** health, personal cleanliness, clothing, hygiene practices
- **Equipment and utensils:** materials, design, installation, storage
- **Cleaning and sanitizing:** facility, equipment
- **Utilities and services:** water, sewage, plumbing, restrooms, waste disposal, integrated pest management (IPM)
- **Construction and maintenance:** floors, walls, ceilings, lighting, ventilation, dressing rooms, locker areas, storage areas
- **Foodservice units:** mobile, temporary
- **Compliance procedures:** restaurant and foodservice inspections, enforcement actions

Adoption and interpretation of food safety standards may vary widely from one state to another or, in some cases, from one locality to another. Therefore, restaurant and foodservice managers must consult with local health departments to find out which specific regulations apply to their operations.

Key Point

Managers must contact local health departments to find out which regulations apply to their operations.

Currently, when a state adopts, develops, or amends its food code, it is required to provide time for public input and comment. This is the time when any interested person or association can comment on how the proposed changes will impact an establishment. If you are interested in participating in this process, make sure you keep in contact with your health department or State Restaurant Association.

The lack of uniformity in local food codes can frustrate efforts by the restaurant industry to establish uniform food safety standards. For example, some jurisdictions require hot holding food temperatures to be 140°F (60°C), while others require 135°F (57°C) or higher. States may also differ in the recommended inspection frequency. Some states require inspections for restaurant and foodservice establishments at least every six months, while others schedule inspections more or less frequently. Some states may even differ as to which establishments should be inspected; for example, some states do not inspect convenience food stores. Some states might have separate regulations or agencies for different types of foodservice operations (such as vending machines or delicatessens in grocery stores).

Although all inspectors focus on food safety practices, the areas emphasized during the inspection can vary among jurisdictions or individual inspectors. For example, some inspectors are more concerned with refrigeration temperatures while others may focus on the physical appearance of the facility. One inspector may examine the flow of food while another may focus primarily on the personal hygiene of employees. It is the responsibility of the manager to keep food safe and wholesome throughout the establishment at all times, regardless of the inspector or the inspection process.

The Inspection Process

All establishments serving the public, including quick-service and fine-dining restaurants, delicatessens, hospitals, nursing homes and schools, are subject to inspection. The inspection lets the establishment know how well it is following practices critical to the safety and quality of the food it serves.

During health department inspections, the local health code serves as the inspector's guide. You should keep a current copy of your local or state sanitation regulations and be familiar with them. Regularly compare the code to procedures at your establishment, but remember that code requirements are only minimum standards to keep food safe.

Regulatory authorities have begun using a more risk-based approach when conducting inspections. Inspections now cover more than just normal compliance issues. Many regulatory authorities look at how the operation is managing risks, using the five CDC risk factors (as you learned about in Chapter 1) and the FDA's public health interventions (as you learned about in Chapter 10) as a guide.

The FDA recommends that regulatory authorities use the following three risk designations when evaluating establishments. These replace the "critical" and "noncritical" risk designations recommended previously.

- **Priority items**

- **Priority foundation items**

- **Core items**

Priority items are the most critical. These are actions and procedures that prevent, eliminate, or reduce hazards associated with foodborne illness to an acceptable level. Proper handwashing would be considered a priority item. Priority foundation items are those that support a priority item. Having soap at a handwashing sink is an example. Core items relate to general sanitation, the facility, equipment design, and general maintenance. Keeping equipment in good repair is an example.

Inspection Frequency

Some health departments are required to conduct inspections at least every six months. However, the frequency will vary depending on the area, type of establishment, or food served. Many health departments use a risk-based approach to inspection frequency. Determining factors can include:

- **Size and complexity of the operation.** Larger operations offering a considerable number of TCS food items might be inspected more frequently.

- **An establishment's inspection history.** Establishments with a history of low sanitation scores or consecutive violations might be inspected more frequently.

- **Clientele's susceptibility to foodborne illness.** Nursing homes, schools, daycare centers, and hospitals might receive more frequent inspections.

- **Workload of the local health department and the number of inspectors available.**

Steps in the Inspection Process

In most cases, inspectors will arrive without warning. They will usually ask for the manager of the operation. Make sure your employees know who is in charge of food safety in your absence. Also, keep in mind any policies your company has on how to handle an inspection.

14b Foodservice Inspection

Ask for identification.

The following guidelines can help you get the most out of food safety inspections:

- **Ask for identification.** (See *Exhibit 14b.*) Do not let anyone enter the back of the operation without the right identification. Many inspectors will volunteer their credentials. Also, make sure you know the reason for the inspection. The visit may be a routine inspection or the result of a customer complaint, or it could be for some other purpose.

  Do not refuse entry to an inspector. In some areas, inspectors may have authority to gain access to the operation. They also may have authority to revoke the operation's permit for refusing entry.

- **Cooperate.** Answer all the inspector's questions to the best of your ability. Tell your employees to do the same. Go with the inspector during the inspection. You will be able to answer any questions and possibly correct problems immediately. If something cannot be fixed immediately, tell the inspector when it can be corrected. Open communication is important for building a good working relationship with the inspector. You will also have the chance to learn from the inspector's comments and get food safety advice.

- **Take notes.** As you walk with the inspector, make note of any problems pointed out. This will help you remember exactly what was said. Make it clear that you are willing to fix any problems. If you believe the inspector is incorrect about something, note what was mentioned. Then contact the regulatory authority.

- **Keep the relationship professional.** Be polite and friendly, and treat inspectors with respect. Be careful about offering food, drink or anything else that could be misunderstood as trying to influence the inspection report.

- **Be prepared to provide records requested by the inspector.** An inspector might ask for the following types of records:

  ◦ Purchasing records to make sure that food has been received from an approved source

  ◦ Pest control treatment

  ◦ List of chemicals used in the operation

  ◦ Proof of food safety knowledge, such as a food protection manager certificate (See *Exhibit 14c.*)

  ◦ HACCP records, in some cases

  You can ask the inspector why these records are needed. If a request seems inappropriate, check with the inspector's supervisor. You can also check with your lawyer about limits on confidential information. Remember, any records you give to the inspector will become part of the public record.

- **Discuss violations and time frames for correction with inspectors.** After the inspection, the inspector will discuss the results and the score, if one is given. Study the inspection

14c Record of Food Safety
        Knowledge

A food protection manager certificate is one way of showing proof of food safety knowledge.

report closely. You must understand the exact nature of a violation. You must also know how a violation affects food safety, how to correct it, and whether or not the inspector will follow up.

You will be asked to sign the inspection report. Signing the report means acknowledging that you have received it. Follow your company's policy regarding this issue. A copy of the report will then be given to you or the person in charge at the time of the inspection. Copies of all reports should be kept on file in the operation. You can refer to these reports when planning improvements and assessing operation goals. Copies of reports are also kept on file at the regulatory authority. They are considered public documents that may be available to anyone upon request.

- **Act on all deficiencies noted in the report.** You must make corrections within the time line given by the inspector. Review your inspection report. Determine why the deficiencies happened by reviewing standard operating procedures. The master cleaning schedule, employee training, and foodhandling practices also should be reviewed. (See *Exhibit 14d.*) Revise current procedures or set up new ones to correct problems permanently. Inform employees of any deficiencies, and retrain them if necessary.

Closure

In some states, if the inspector determines a facility poses an immediate and substantial health hazard to the public, he or she may ask for a voluntary closure or issue an immediate suspension of the permit to operate. Examples of hazards calling for closure include:

- Significant lack of refrigeration
- Backup of sewage into the establishment or its water supply
- Emergency, such as a building fire or flood
- Significant infestation of insects or rodents
- Long interruption of electrical or water service
- Clear evidence of a foodborne-illness outbreak related to the establishment

---

14d   Inspection Follow-Up

Determine why a violation occurred by evaluating procedures, the master cleaning schedule, and employee foodhandling practices. Establish new procedures or revise existing ones.

14e Suspension Order

The suspension order may be posted at a public entrance to the establishment.

 Key Point

Consider health department inspections only a supplement to your self-inspection programs.

A suspension requires the approval of the local health department. If an establishment receives a suspension, it must cease operations immediately. However, the owner can request a hearing if he or she believes the suspension was unjustified. There is often a time limit to request such a hearing (usually within five to ten days of the inspection). Check local regulations to determine these limits.

The suspension order may be posted at a public entrance to the establishment as shown in *Exhibit 14e*; however, this is not required if the establishment closes voluntarily. Regulations vary from one jurisdiction to another, but to reinstate a permit to operate, the establishment must eliminate the hazards causing the suspension and then pass a reinspection.

Self-Inspections

Well-managed operations have frequent self-inspections to keep food safe. These are done in addition to regulatory inspections. In fact, regulatory inspections should be a supplement to self-inspections. They can be conducted in house or by a third-party organization.

A good self-inspection program provides many benefits:

- Safer food
- Improved food quality
- Cleaner environment for employees and customers
- Higher inspection scores

Strive to exceed the standards of the local regulatory authority. This will help you perform well on regulatory inspections. Also, your customers will see your commitment to safe dining experiences.

Consider the following guidelines when conducting a self-inspection:

- Use the same type of checklist that the regulatory authority uses.
- Start the inspection outside the establishment and then proceed inside.
- Identify risks to food safety in your establishment.
- After the inspection, meet with staff to review any problems.

Federal Regulatory Agencies

Several federal government agencies work to protect the sanitary quality of food in an establishment. Earlier in this chapter, the roles of the FDA and the USDA were discussed. A few other agencies concerned with food safety should also be mentioned.

The **Centers for Disease Control and Prevention (CDC),** located in Atlanta, Georgia, are agencies of the U.S. Department of Health and Human Services.

The Centers provide these services:

- Investigate outbreaks of foodborne illness

- Study the causes and control of disease

- Publish statistical data and case studies in the *Morbidity and Mortality Weekly Report* (*MMWR*)

- Provide educational services in the field of sanitation

- Conduct the Vessel Sanitation Program—an inspection program for cruise ships

The **Environmental Protection Agency (EPA)** sets air- and water-quality standards and regulates the use of pesticides (including sanitizers) and the handling of wastes. The **National Marine Fisheries Service (NMFS),** of the U.S. Department of Commerce, implements a voluntary inspection program that includes product standards and sanitary requirements for fish-processing operations.

Something to Think About...   Cool It!

The owner of a small, traditional Italian restaurant in the Midwest had built her business around weekend diners. The specialty of the house was a very thick meat sauce that was served over nearly all of the dishes offered.

To have sufficient quantities of sauce available for the weekend rush, the staff had developed a pattern of preparing a large batch of meat sauce on Sunday night and storing it in five-gallon buckets for the following weekend. Unfortunately, no plan had been established for proper cooling before placing the buckets into the restaurant's small refrigerator. As a result, temperatures at the center of the buckets of sauce were found to be as warm as 70°F (21°C) when the buckets were opened the following weekend—five days after being placed in the refrigerator.

The local health inspector was quick to spot the time-temperature abuse. Because purchasing a blast chiller was not an option, another solution was developed using the existing equipment. Working together, the inspector and restaurant owner established a system that involved adding ice to the cooked sauce to help it cool and filling storage containers only half full. They also determined that the sauce should be cooked in smaller batches—cooking it twice per week rather than in a single batch. As a result, the sauce was cooled properly, preventing a potentially hazardous situation.

Voluntary Controls within the Industry

Few industries have devoted as much effort to regulating themselves as the restaurant and foodservice and food-processing industries. Scientific and trade associations, manufacturing firms, and foodservice corporations have vigorously pursued programs to raise the standards of the industry through research, education, and cooperation with government. Although participation in these programs is voluntary, these organizations have actively promoted professional standards, recommended legislative policy, sponsored uniform enforcement procedures, and provided educational opportunities. The overall results in food safety have included:

- Increased understanding of foodborne illness and its prevention

- Improvements in the sanitary design of equipment and facilities

- Industry-wide efforts to maintain the sanitary quality of food during processing, shipment, storage, and service

- Efforts to make foodservice laws more practical, uniform, and science based

While many organizations have contributed to these endeavors, those having the most relevance for the foodservice operator can be found in the resources section at the end of each chapter.

Summary

Government control regarding food safety in the United States is exercised at three levels: federal, state, and local. Recommendations for restaurant and foodservice regulations are issued at the federal level by the FDA in the form of the *FDA Food Code.* Regulations are written at the state level, and enforcement is usually carried out at the state and local levels. Some agencies at the federal level, such as the FDA and the USDA, are directly involved in the inspection process.

All establishments must follow practices critical to the safety of the food served. The inspection process lets the establishment know how well it is following these practices. During the inspection, cooperate with the health inspector and keep the relationship professional. Accompany him or her during the inspection. When the inspector points out a problem, take notes. If a deficiency can be corrected immediately, do so. Be prepared to provide records that are requested. Discuss violations and time frames, and then follow up.

Well-managed establishments will perform continuous self-inspections to protect food safety, in addition to the regular inspections performed by the health department. Establishments with high standards for sanitation and food safety consider health department inspections only a supplement to their own self-inspection programs.

Apply Your Knowledge

Use these questions to review the concepts presented in this chapter.

Discussion Questions

① What are some hazards that require the closure of an establishment?

② What are the roles of federal, state, and local agencies regarding the regulation of food safety in establishments?

③ What should a manager do during and after an inspection?

④ What are some factors that determine the frequency of health inspections in an establishment?

For answers, please turn to the Answer Key.

Study Questions

Circle the best answer to each question.

① **A backup of raw sewage and significant lack of refrigeration can result in**

A   a delay of an inspection until the situation is corrected.

B   closure of the operation by the regulatory authority.

C   improved inspection scores.

D   being issued a permit to operate.

② **A person shows up at a restaurant claiming to be a health inspector. What should the manager ask for?**

A   Inspection warrant

B   Inspector's identification

C   Hearing to determine if the inspection is necessary

D   One-day postponement to prepare for the inspection

③ **Which agency enforces food safety in a restaurant?**

A   Centers for Disease Control and Prevention

B   Food and Drug Administration

C   State or local regulatory authority

D   U.S. Department of Agriculture

④ **Who is responsible for keeping food safe in an operation?**

A   Food and Drug Administration

B   Health inspectors

C   Manager/operator

D   State health department

For answers, please turn to the Answer Key.

Additional Resources

Articles and Texts

Jacobs, Don. 2003. Food Safety I.Q: The Health Inspection Process is No Longer what it Once was. *Restaurant Hospitality*. 87 (11): 76.

Jacobs, Don. 2004. Food Safety: Establishing Good Communication and a Solid Relationship with Your Local Health Authority is the Smart Thing to Do for the Future of Your Business. *Restaurant Hospitality*. 88 (1): 78.

Continued on next page ▶

▶ *Continued from previous page*

Web Sites

Association of Food and Drug Officials
afdo.org

CDC Vessel Sanitation Program
cdc.gov/nceh/vsp

Conference for Food Protection
foodprotect.org

Environmental Protection Agency
epa.gov

Food and Drug Administration
fda.go

Gateway to Government Food Safety Information
foodsafety.gov

Morbidity and Mortality Weekly Report
cdc.gov/mmwr

National Association of City and County Officials
naccho.org

National Marine Fisheries Service
www.nmfs.noaa.gov/

U.S. Department of Agriculture
usda.gov/wps/portal/usdahome

Documents and Other Resources

2009 FDA Food Code
www.fda.gov/Food/FoodSafety/RetailFoodProtection/
FoodCode/FoodCode2009/default.htm

FDA Food Establishment Plan Review Guide
www.fda.gov/Food/FoodSafety/RetailFoodProtection/
ComplianceEnforcement/ucm101639.htm

FDA Enforcement Report Index
fda.gov/opacom/Enforce.html

FDA Retail Food Program Database of Foodborne Illness Risk Factors
www.fda.gov/Food/FoodSafety/RetailFoodProtection/FoodCode/
FoodCode2001/ucm123544.htm

Hazard Analysis and Critical Control Point (HACCP) Principles and Application Guidelines
www.fsis.usda.gov/OPHS/NACMCF/past/JFP0998.pdf

Managing Food Safety: A Manual for the Voluntary Use of HACCP Principles for Operators of Food Service and Retail Establishments
www.fda.gov/Food/FoodSafety/RetailFoodProtection/
ManagingFoodSafetyHACCPPrinciples/Operators/default.htm

Notes

15 Employee Food Safety Training

Inside this chapter:

- Training Staff
- Training Delivery Methods

After completing this chapter, you should be able to:

- Identify employee duties and specific training needs for each duty.
- Identify training methods specific to employees and their duties.
- Maintain food safety training records.
- Ensure all employees are trained initially and on an ongoing basis.

Key Terms

- Training need

Apply Your Knowledge

Check to see how much you know about the concepts in this chapter. Use the page references provided with each question to explore the topic.

Test Your Food Safety Knowledge

1. **True or False:** Technology-based training is an appropriate training method when staff works in different locations. *(See page 15-10.)*

2. **True or False:** Staff does not require further food safety training if they received initial training when they were hired. *(See page 15-3.)*

3. **True or False:** When using videos as a self-study training method, you should supply staff with print materials as a supplement. *(See page 15-9.)*

4. **True or False:** It is important for legal reasons to keep records of food safety training conducted at the establishment. *(See page 15-3.)*

5. **True or False:** It is the manager's responsibility to provide staff with food safety training. *(See page 15-2.)*

For answers, please turn to the Answer Key.

Introduction

You have no guarantee of how long staff members will be working at your operation. Whether your staff has been on the job for one day or five years, they must understand that food safety is always important. To make sure your operation is serving safe food, you must train your staff when they are first hired and on an ongoing basis.

Training Staff

As a manager, it is your responsibility to make sure that your staff knows how to handle food safely. You must also tell them about updates to foodservice regulations, changes in the science of food safety, and new best practices in the industry.

Your first task is to identify the training needs in your operation. A training need is a gap between what staff needs to know to perform their jobs and what they actually know.

15a Food Safety Training

All employees require general food safety knowledge. Some knowledge will be specific to the job position.

For new hires, the need might be apparent. For experienced staff, the need is not always as clear.

Identifying your staff's food safety training needs will require effort on your part. However, there are several ways to do this, including the following ideas:

- Observing performance on the job
- Testing food safety knowledge
- Identifying areas of weakness

Your entire staff needs general food safety knowledge. Other knowledge will be specific to the tasks performed on the job. For example, everyone needs to know the right way to wash their hands. However, as shown in *Exhibit 15a*, only receiving staff needs to know how to inspect produce during receiving.

Critical Food Safety Knowledge

You cannot assume new hires will understand your operation's food safety procedures without training. From their first day on the job, they should learn about the importance of food safety and receive training in the critical areas listed in *Exhibit 15b* on the next page.

Retraining

Your staff needs to be periodically retrained in food safety. You can retrain them by scheduling short training sessions, planning meetings to update them on new procedures, or holding motivational sessions that reinforce food safety practices.

Record Keeping

Keep records of all food safety training carried out at your establishment. For legal reasons, when an employee completes this training, make sure to document it.

15b   Critical Food Safety Knowledge for Employees

Personal hygiene

- Behaviors that can contaminate food
- Hand issues, which include how and when to wash hands, how to use hand antiseptics, how to use single-use gloves, when to change gloves, and correct hand care
- Personal cleanliness
- Correct work attire
- Health issues that must be reported
- Policies for eating, drinking, smoking, and chewing gum or tobacco
- Storage of dirty and contaminated clothing

Safe food preparation

- Preventing time-temperature abuse
- Identifying types of contaminants
- Learning how contamination occurs
- Preventing contamination and cross-contamination
- Handling food safely during the flow of food—receiving and storage, preparing and cooking, holding and cooling, and reheating and service
- Identifying common food allergens and methods for preventing allergic reactions

Cleaning and sanitizing

- Cleaning and sanitizing food-contact surfaces
- Identifying when cleaning and sanitizing is needed

Safe chemical handling

- Handling chemicals in the operation

Training Delivery Methods

There is more than one way to teach staff members what they need to know and do to keep food safe. As a manager, you must consider both the staff and the subject area you are teaching so you can choose the best method.

When choosing training methods, think about what would work best in your operation. Some operations use a traditional method, such as on-the-job training. Others use a more activity-based approach. No single type of training works best, because everyone learns differently. Using many methods will provide the best results.

On-the-Job Training (OJT)

Many operations use experienced staff members to teach learners while on the job. (See *Exhibit 15c.*) Learners repeatedly perform tasks while the trainers tell them how they are doing.

OJT teaches skills that require thinking *and* doing. It is good for training one staff member at a time, but it can also work for small groups. It is also good for teaching skills that require watching someone do the task correctly.

Success depends on the ability and the skill of the person doing the training. You must choose the trainer carefully. Before using OJT, you should also recognize that it takes experienced staff away from their jobs. Additionally, it is not as effective for training large groups of people.

Classroom Training

Today's workforce expects training that will entertain and teach them. This can be challenging, but it is not impossible. Using an activity-based approach to training can be very effective. People learn by doing, instead of just being told what to do. Therefore, your training should include activities that require staff to do something.

Staff should also take part in learning activities. You must create a learning environment that encourages your staff to ask questions and allows them to make mistakes in that environment. You must also make your staff responsible for their own learning.

15c On-the-Job Training

On-the-job training is good for teaching skills that require watching someone do the task correctly.

You can use many activity-based training methods to teach food safety to your staff.

- Information search
- Guided discussion
- Role-play
- Demonstrations
- Jigsaw design
- Training videos and DVDs
- Games

Information Search

Some people are curious and like to explore things on their own. You can make use of their curiosity by having them find food safety information themselves rather than telling it to them. Here's how to do it.

1 Put staff in small groups.

2 Give them questions that they must answer in a set amount of time.

3 Give them the following types of tools to answer the questions.

- Operations manuals
- Job aids
- Posters, such as the one the manager is using in *Exhibit 15d*
- Employee guides

4 Bring groups together and have them talk about what they learned.

15d Job Aids

Posters can be used to train employees and provide a reference while back on the job.

Guided Discussion

Another way to teach food safety concepts is to ask your staff questions that draw on their knowledge and experience. Your goal is to make them think and discuss their thoughts. Each time learners answer a question, you should follow with another question.

Using this approach, a training session on calibrating thermometers might go something like this.

> *Instructor:* How can you find out if a cooked chicken breast has reached the right temperature?
>
> *Learner:* Use a thermometer.
>
> *Instructor:* How can you make sure a thermometer's reading is right?
>
> *Learner:* Calibrate it.
>
> *Instructor:* How do you calibrate a thermometer?
>
> *Learner:* By using the ice-point method or the boiling-point method.

Role-Play

Many trainers use role-play to teach concepts. However, some learners do not like role-playing because it puts them on the spot. Role-play can work if you handle it the right way. Here is how to do it.

❶ Prepare a script in advance that shows the right or wrong way to perform a skill.

❷ Find two volunteers and give them time to rehearse the script. Do this early in the training session. As an alternative, the instructor can play one of the parts in the role-play.

❸ Have the volunteers act out the script.

❹ Ask the rest of the group to decide what the role-players did right and what they did wrong.

Demonstrations

Many times you will teach specific food safety tasks by showing them to a person or group. Demonstrations are most effective when you follow the "Tell/Show/Practice" model, as shown in *Exhibit 15e* below.

15e   Demonstrating a Task Using the Tell/Show/Practice Model

Tell

Tell the learner how to do the task. Explain what you are doing and why.

Show

Show the learner how to do the task.

Practice

Let the learner do the task. As extra practice, have the learner explain how to do the task before showing how to do it. Tell the learner how he or she is doing throughout the practice.

Jigsaw Design

There is an old saying that goes, "You have learned something when you can teach someone else how to do it." The jigsaw method follows this principle. Here is how to use it.

❶ Put learners in small groups.

❷ Assign a specific food safety topic to each group.

❸ Tell each group to read about their topic, discuss it, and decide how to teach it to the other groups.

❹ Take one person from each group and form new groups.

❺ Have each member in the new group teach his or her topic to the other group members.

❻ Bring the groups back together for review and questions.

Training Videos and DVDs

In the training world, there is a general belief that learners remember the material in their training sessions in the following ways:

* 10 percent of what they read

* 20 percent of what they hear

* 30 percent of what they see

* 50 percent of what they see and hear

Using videos and DVDs, as shown in *Exhibit 15f,* will help your staff see and hear their food safety training, making them more likely to remember it. Video is also very useful for teaching skills that involve motion, such as calibrating a thermometer.

If your staff is learning food safety on their own by video instruction, you should give them print materials as a supplement.

15f   Videos and DVDs

Videos and DVDs will help your staff see and hear their food safety training, making them more likely to remember it.

15g Games

Games can be used to practice principles learned in the training session and create excitement.

15h Technology-Based Training

Many operations use technology-based training to teach food safety.

Games

A game, as shown in *Exhibit 15g,* can help make difficult or boring information seem more exciting. You can also use games to practice information that has already been taught. To be effective, games must meet the following criteria.

- Easy to play
- Fun
- Meets all time frames
- Easy to bring to the training site
- Easy to change for the audience and content

Technology-Based Training

Many operations use technology-based training to teach food safety. This includes online training and interactive CD-ROMs. (See *Exhibit 15h.*) Technology-based training lets you deliver training when and where your staff needs it. It is most appropriate in the following situations.

- Staff works in different locations and/or need the same training at different times.
- It is costly to bring staff to the same place.
- Staff needs retraining to complete a topic.
- Staff has different levels of knowledge about a topic.
- Staff has different learning skills.
- Classroom training makes staff nervous.
- Staff needs to learn at their own pace.
- You want to collect specific information, such as time spent on different topics, test scores, number of tries until the training was finished, and/or problem areas.

Summary

As a manager, it is your responsibility to ensure that your staff has the knowledge and skills needed to handle food safely in your establishment.

Your first task is to assess the training needs in your establishment. A training need is a gap between what staff is required to know to perform their jobs and what they actually know. To identify food safety training needs, you can test your staff's knowledge, observe their performance, or identify their areas of weakness.

Your entire staff requires general food safety knowledge. Other knowledge will be specific to the tasks performed on the job. Regardless of their specific jobs, staff needs to be retrained periodically. Keep records of all training conducted at your establishment. For legal reasons, it is important to document that staff has completed food safety training.

Training can be delivered using a variety of methods. No single method of delivery is best for all staff members, because each person learns differently. Using several methods will result in more effective learning.

Apply Your Knowledge

Use these questions to review the concepts presented in this chapter.

Discussion Questions

① How can an establishment determine its food safety training needs?

② What are some methods that can be used to deliver training?

③ What are some situations where technology-based training would be appropriate?

For answers, please turn to the Answer Key.

Study Questions

Circle the best answer to each question.

1. **When should staff receive food safety training?**
   A   When an employee is hired, and then periodically after that
   B   Only when hiring a new employee without foodservice experience
   C   When a new *FDA Food Code* comes out
   D   Only if they request it

2. **New employees must be trained in the critical areas of personal hygiene, cleaning and sanitizing, safe chemical handling, and**
   A   crisis management.
   B   equipment handling.
   C   HACCP plan creation.
   D   safe food preparation.

3. **The manager's responsibility for staff food safety training is to**
   A   test staff's food safety knowledge.
   B   provide all staff with videos and DVDs for training.
   C   make sure that staff have the knowledge and skills to keep food safe.
   D   send all staff to a ServSafe training class.

4. **All new staff should receive training on**
   A   HACCP.
   B   crisis management.
   C   safe chemical handling.
   D   active managerial control.

5. **What is the first task in training a large group of servers to prevent contamination of food?**
   A   Assess the training needs of the servers on this topic.
   B   Make a list of possible information to cover.
   C   Provide servers with operation manuals on the topic.
   D   Put staff into small groups, based on service experience.

⑥ **In which training method does a trainer ask a series of questions to draw on the knowledge and experience of the learners?**

A Information search

B Guided discussion

C Jigsaw design

D Games

For answers, please turn to the Answer Key.

Additional Resources

Articles and Texts

Green, Laura R. and Carol Selman. 2005. Factors Impacting Food Workers' and Managers' Safe Food Preparation Practices: A Qualitative Study. *Food Protection Trends.* 25 (12): 981.

Jenkins-McLean, Terri, Chris Skilton, and Clarence Sellars. 2004. Engaging Food Service Workers in Behavioral-Change Partnerships. *Journal of Environmental Health.* 66 (9): 15.

Mitchell, Roger E., Angela M. Fraser, and Lucille B. Bearon. 2007. Preventing Foodborne Illness in Food Service Establishments: Broadening the Framework for Intervention and Research on Safe Food Handling Behaviors. *International Journal of Environmental Health Research.* 17 (1): 9.

Piskurich, George M., Peter Beckschi, and Brandon Hall, eds. *The ASTD Handbook of Training Design and Delivery: A Comprehensive Guide to Creating and Delivering Training Programs—Instructor-Led, Computer-Based, or Self-Directed.* New York: McGraw-Hill, 2000.

Web Sites

American Society for Training & Development
astd.org/astd

Conference for Food Protection
foodprotect.org

Council of Hotel and Restaurant Trainers
chart.org

International Council on Hotel, Restaurant, and Institutional Education
chrie.org

Documents and Other Resources

2009 FDA Food Code
www.fda.gov/Food/FoodSafety/RetailFoodProtection/FoodCode/FoodCode2009/default.htm

AR Additional Resources

2009 FDA Food Code
www.fda.gov/Food/FoodSafety/RetailFoodProtection/FoodCode/
FoodCode2009/default.htm

The Food and Drug Administration (FDA) publishes the *FDA Food Code*, a scientifically sound, technical, and legal document that serves as a model for regulating the retail and foodservice industry at the federal, state, and local level. The *FDA Food Code* provides a system of safeguards designed to minimize foodborne illness and to ensure employee health, as well as information on food protection, safe food, and appropriate sanitation of the food establishment. It is used as the basis for information in this textbook. Updates to the code are issued in odd-numbered years as either a supplement or complete revision.

Acrylamide Infonet
www.acrylamide-food.org

This Food and Agricultural Organization of the United Nations (FAO)/World Health Organization (WHO) Acrylamide in Food Network Web site includes formal research, surveillance and monitoring, and collaborative investigations from government agencies, research institutions, industries, and other interested parties.

American Chemistry Council
www.americanchemistry.com

Visit the food safety page of the American Chemistry Council (ACC) to learn how chemistry contributes to the service of safe food. Additionally, on this Web site, the Chlorine Chemistry Division of the American Chemistry Council, which represents the major producers and users of chlorine in the United States, provides useful Web site information about safe and responsible use of chlorine products.

American Egg Board
www.aeb.org

The American Egg Board (AEB) is the U.S. egg producers' link to the consumer. This Web site provides resources for the restaurant and foodservice industry, including ways to ensure safe receiving, storage, and preparation of eggs, as well as general information about eggs and egg products.

American Lamb Board
www.americanlambboard.org

The American Lamb Board (ALB) was created by the U.S. Secretary of Agriculture to administer the Lamb Promotion, Research, and Information Order. This Web site provides information about foodservice cuts, cooking temperatures, and food safety tips for lamb.

American Mushroom Institute

www.americanmushroom.org

The American Mushroom Institute is a trade association representing the growers and marketers of mushrooms in the United States, as well as mushroom suppliers around the world. This Web site provides information on good manufacturing and agricultural practices for mushroom growers and packers, relevant links for food safety, and mushroom-industry resources.

American Society for Training & Development

www.astd.org

American Society for Training & Development (ASTD) is the world's largest association dedicated to workplace learning and performance professionals. The society seeks to advance knowledge and techniques that successfully convert learning and capability into performance and practice. This Web site provides access to for-purchase and online resources, conferences, and educational-development opportunities for training professionals.

American Society of Heating, Refrigeration, and Air-Conditioning Engineers

www.ashrae.org

The American Society of Heating, Refrigerating, and Air-Conditioning Engineers (ASHRAE) advances technology and promotes sustainability. The organization publishes more than 100 standards and guidelines. Visit this Web site to access publications and other information relating to refrigeration and the maintenance of indoor environments.

AMS National Organic Program

www.ams.usda.gov/nop/indexIE.htm

The National Organic Program (NOP) is a marketing program within the USDA Agricultural Marketing Service (AMS). In 1990, Congress passed the Organic Foods Production Act (OFPA). This Act requires the U.S. Department of Agriculture (USDA) to develop national standards for organically produced agricultural products. These standards assure consumers that agricultural products marketed as organic meet consistent, uniform standards. Visit this Web site to access the standards and other information about the program.

Association of Food and Drug Officials

www.afdo.org

The Association of Food and Drug Officials (AFDO) fosters uniformity in the adoption and enforcement of product-safety laws, rules, and regulations for the food, drug, medical device, and cosmetic industries. AFDO also provides the forum in which regional, national, and international issues are deliberated and resolved to provide the best public health and consumer protection. Visit this Web site for information on HACCP, as well as food safety and defense.

Association of Food, Beverage, and Consumer Products Companies
www.gmabrands.com

The Grocery Manufacturers Association (GMA)-Food Products Association (FPA) represents the food, beverage, and consumer-product industries. The association works with industry leaders, policy makers, and the public to ensure that laws and regulations governing food marketing and production are feasible and practical. This Web site provides regulatory resources, publications, and food safety initiatives to support the association's role in promoting industry solutions that help consumers achieve and maintain a healthy lifestyle.

Avian Influenza
www.cdc.gov/flu/avian

The Centers for Disease Control and Prevention (CDC) provides an expert resource page on avian influenza (AI). Visit this Web site to find key facts about the virus and disease, frequently asked questions, background on known outbreaks, information for specific groups, and links to additional references and resources.

Avian Influenza
www.who.int/csr/disease/avian_influenza/en

Visit the World Health Organization's Web site for information about avian influenza (AI) around the world. Available information includes a list of frequently-asked questions, status of the global pandemic threat, outbreak summaries, guidelines and recommendations, and many other references and resources.

CDC Vessel Sanitation Program
www.cdc.gov/nceh/vsp

The Centers for Disease Control and Prevention (CDC) started the Vessel Sanitation Program (VSP) in the 1970s to protect the health of passengers and crew and to minimize the incidence of foodborne illness on cruise ships. The VSP provides the cruise-ship industry with resources and training to develop and implement effective sanitation programs. This Web site provides information on how the VSP accomplishes its mission and includes information on inspection criteria and recent sanitation-inspection scores, surveillance and outbreak investigation information, and publications and references on Norovirus and other foodborne pathogens.

Center for Infectious Disease Research & Policy
www.cidrap.umn.edu

The Center for Infectious Disease Research & Policy (CIDRAP) at the University of Minnesota functions to prevent illness and death from infectious diseases, through epidemiologic research and the rapid translation of scientific information into real-world practical applications and solutions. The center's Web site provides access to information on food safety and foodborne illness as well as news stories on bioterrorism, food security, and foodborne-illness surveillance.

Centers for Disease Control and Prevention
www.cdc.gov

The Centers for Disease Control and Prevention (CDC) is focused on American health promotion, disease prevention, and preparedness through partnerships. The CDC applies research and findings to improve people's daily lives and respond to health emergencies. This Web site provides information on disease prevention, including foodborne illness, its causes, public health impact, and methods for control.

Commodity-Specific Food Safety Guidelines for the Fresh-Tomato Supply Chain
www.fda.gov/downloads/Food/FoodSafety/Product-SpecificInformation/ FruitsVegetablesJuices/GuidanceComplianceRegulatoryInformation/UCM171708.pdf

Food safety guidelines for the fresh-tomato supply chain were developed by the North American Tomato Trade Work Group and various related trade associations. These guidelines promote further adoption of good agricultural practices throughout the fresh-tomato supply chain. This Web site provides a link to this voluntary document.

Commodity-Specific Food Safety Guidelines for the Production and Harvest of Lettuce and Leafy Greens Supply Chain
www.fda.gov/downloads/Food/FoodSafety/Product-SpecificInformation/ FruitsVegetablesJuices/GuidanceComplianceRegulatoryInformation/UCM169008.pdf

Food safety guidelines for the production and harvest of lettuce and leafy greens were developed by members of the lettuce/leafy greens industry. These guidelines provide voluntary recommendations for food safety practices to minimize the microbiological hazards associated with fresh and fresh-cut lettuce and leafy green products. This Web site provides a link to this voluntary document.

Commodity-Specific Food Safety Guidelines for the Melon Supply Chain
www.fda.gov/downloads/Food/FoodSafety/Product-SpecificInformation/ FruitsVegetablesJuices/GuidanceComplianceRegulatoryInformation/UCM168625.pdf

Food safety guidelines for the melon supply chain were developed by melon industry members, through the produce-industry food safety initiative. These guidelines provide voluntary recommendations for food safety practices associated with the melon supply chain. This Web site provides a link to this voluntary document.

Conference for Food Protection
www.foodprotect.org

The Conference for Food Protection (CFP) is a nonprofit organization that provides a forum for regulators, industry professionals, academia, professional organizations, and consumers to identify problems, formulate recommendations, and develop and implement practices that ensure food safety. Visit this Web site for information regarding previously recommended changes to the *FDA Food Code,* standards for permanent outdoor cooking facilities, and other guidance documents, along with how to participate in the conference.

Conference for Food Protection: Emergency Guidance for Retail Food Establishments
www.foodprotect.org/media/guide/EmergencyActionPlanforRetailFood Establishments2008.pdf

Produced by the Emergency Preparedness Committee of Council II of the 2004–2006 Conference for Food Protection, this document offers practical guidance for retail grocery and foodservice establishments to plan and respond to emergencies that create the potential for an imminent health hazard.

Council of Hotel and Restaurant Trainers
www.chart.org

The Council of Hotel and Restaurant Trainers (CHART) is an organization dedicated to training in the hospitality industry. CHART's objective is to provide hospitality trainers access to the industry's training professionals and solutions. Visit this Web site for upcoming conferences and resources on training and professional development.

Crisis Management: Imminent Health Hazards
www.michigan.gov/mda/0,1607,7-125--105442--,00.html

The Michigan Department of Agriculture developed emergency action procedures that outline how to plan for, prepare for, and respond to emergencies that have the potential of becoming imminent health hazards. Visit this Web site for an example of procedures developed using input from the foodservice industry and the regulatory community.

Current Good Manufacturing Practices (cGMPs)
www.access.gpo.gov/nara/cfr/waisidx_06/21cfr110_06.html

Current Good Manufacturing Practices or CGMPs are a set of regulations that take into account today's technologies and food safety hazards and address potential food safety issues. This Web site provides a link to current good manufacturing practices to control food safety hazards in restaurants and the foodservice industry.

Emerging Infectious Diseases
www.cdc.gov/ncidod/eid/index.htm

An online journal, *Emerging Infectious Diseases* represents the scientific communications component of the Centers for Disease Control and Prevention's (CDC) efforts against the threat of emerging infections. The journal relies on a broad, international authorship base to publish reports of interest to researchers in infectious diseases and related sciences and reports on laboratory and epidemiologic findings within a broader public health perspective. Visit this Web site for articles published about foodborne disease in the United States and around the world.

Environmental Protection Agency
www.epa.gov

The U.S. Environmental Protection Agency (EPA) works to create a cleaner environment and to protect the health of all Americans. The EPA's staff researches and sets national standards for a variety of environmental programs. Visit this Web site to find out the latest news and information relating to food, water, and environment safety.

Environmental Protection Agency Cross-Connection Control Manual
water.epa.gov/aboutow/ogwdw/upload/2003_04_09_crossconnection_crossconnection.pdf

This online document, provided by the Environmental Protection Agency (EPA), serves to increase awareness of the dangers of cross-connections and how they can be recognized and prevented.

FDA Food Safety
www.fda.gov/Food/FoodSafety/default.htm

As the center within the Food and Drug Administration (FDA) responsible for food safety, the Center for Food Safety and Applied Nutrition (CFSAN) promotes and protects public health by researching and implementing guidelines, policies, and standards to ensure that food is safe, nutritious, wholesome, and properly labeled. This Web site provides information relevant to all aspects of food safety and security, including corresponding guidelines, policies, and standards.

FDA Enforcement Report Index
www.fda.gov/opacom/Enforce.html

The Food and Drug Administration's Center for Food Safety and Applied Nutrition (FDA CFSAN) provides the *FDA Enforcement Report*, which is published weekly on this Web site. It contains information on actions such as recalls, injunctions, and seizures taken against food and drug products that have not met FDA regulatory requirements.

FDA Acrylamide: Questions & Answers
www.fda.gov/Food/FoodSafety/FoodContaminantsAdulteration/ChemicalContaminants/Acrylamide/ucm053569.htm

This Web site, provided by the Food and Drug Administration's Center for Food Safety and Applied Nutrition (FDA CFSAN), addresses common questions about acrylamide formation in food.

FDA Alert
www.fda.gov/Food/FoodDefense/Training/ALERT/default.htm

The Food and Drug Administration's Center for Food Safety and Applied Nutrition's (FDA CFSAN) Alert initiative is intended to raise the foodservice industry's awareness of food-defense issues and preparedness. The program identifies five key points the foodservice industry can use to decrease the risk of intentional food contamination in its operations.

FDA Food Allergens Information and Resources
www.fda.gov/Food/FoodSafety/FoodAllergens/default.htm

The Food and Drug Administration's Center for Food Safety and Applied Nutrition (FDA CFSAN) produces on this Web site information about food allergens, their management, and relevant legislation.

Food Defense and Emergency Response
www.fda.gov/Food/FoodDefense/default.htm

The Food and Drug Administration's Center for Food Safety and Applied Nutrition (FDA CFSAN) provides this Web site. Aimed at the food industry, it contains guidance, training resources, and other materials related to food defense and food terrorism.

FDA *Food Establishment Plan Review Guide*
www.fda.gov/Food/FoodSafety/RetailFoodProtection/Compliance Enforcement/ucm101639.htm

This guide was developed to provide guidance and assistance in complying with nationally recognized food safety standards. It includes design, installation, and construction recommendations regarding food equipment and facilities.

FDA Foodborne Illness Resource Page
www.fda.gov/Food/FoodSafety/FoodborneIllness/default.htm

The Food and Drug Administration's Center for Food Safety and Applied Nutrition (FDA CFSAN) provides the FDA Foodborne Illness gateway page, which contains resources related to foodborne illness. Visit this Web site to access information about HACCP, foodborne pathogens, specific government food safety initiatives, and other government sources of foodborne-illness information.

Foodborne Pathogenic Microorganisms and Natural Toxins Handbook - The Bad Bug Book
www.fda.gov/Food/FoodSafety/FoodborneIllness/FoodborneIllness FoodbornePathogensNaturalToxins/BadBugBook/default.htm

Produced by the Food and Drug Administration's Center for Food Safety and Applied Nutrition (FDA CFSAN), this online handbook, also known as the "Bad Bug Book," provides basic facts about foodborne, pathogenic microorganisms; biological toxins; and other pathogenic agents.

Guide for the Control of Molluscan Shellfish
www.fda.gov/Food/FoodSafety/Product-SpecificInformation/Seafood/ FederalStatePrograms/NationalShellfishSanitationProgram/ucm046353.htm

The Food and Drug Administration's Center for Food Safety and Applied Nutrition (FDA CFSAN) provides the *National Shellfish Sanitation Program's Guide for the Control of Molluscan Shellfish*. This Web site consists of the 2007 revision of the Model Ordinance, supporting guidance documents, recommended forms, and other related materials associated with the program. The standards and administrative practices found in the Model Ordinance ensure that molluscan shellfish produced in the United States are safe.

FDA *Hazard Analysis Critical Control Point Info Page*
www.fda.gov/Food/FoodSafety/HazardAnalysisCriticalControlPointsHACCP /default.htm

This Web site, provided by the Food and Drug Administration's Center for Food Safety and Applied Nutrition (FDA CFSAN), collects in one place many resources and guidance documents on the topic of HACCP.

Assuring the Safety of Eggs and Menu and Deli Items Made From Raw, Shell Eggs
www.fda.gov/Food/FoodSafety/RetailFoodProtection/Industryand RegulatoryAssistanceandTrainingResources/ucm192177.htm

On this Web site, the Food and Drug Administration's Center for Food Safety and Applied Nutrition (FDA CFSAN) provides information on the safe handling of shell eggs for foodservice operations.

FDA *Interstate Certified Shellfish Shippers List*
www.fda.gov/Food/FoodSafety/Product-SpecificInformation/Seafood/ FederalStatePrograms/InterstateShellfishShippersList/default.htm

The Food and Drug Administration's Center for Food Safety and Applied Nutrition (FDA CFSAN) provides the Interstate Certified Shellfish Shippers list. Visit this Web site, which is updated monthly, for shippers that have been certified by regulatory authorities in the United States, Canada, Chile, Korea, Mexico, and New Zealand under the uniform sanitation requirements of the national shellfish program.

FDA *Retail Food Stores and Food Service Establishments: Food Security Preventive Measures Guidance*
www.fda.gov/Food/GuidanceComplianceRegulatoryInformation/Guidance Documents/FoodDefenseandEmergencyResponse/ucm082751.htm

Visit this Web site for guidance on the Food and Drug Administration's (FDA) current approach to different measures restaurant and foodservice establishments may take to minimize the risk of tampering or other criminal activities to food.

FDA *Seafood Information and Resources*
www.fda.gov/Food/FoodSafety/Product- SpecificInformation/Seafood/default.htm

The Food and Drug Administration's Center for Food Safety and Applied Nutrition (FDA CFSAN) provides a wealth of seafood information and resources on this Web site. Visit this site for an overview of the FDA seafood regulatory program, information on seafood-related foodborne pathogens and contaminants, and access to seafood guidance and regulation documents.

FEMA Emergency Management Guide for Business & Industry
www.fema.gov/business/guide/index.shtm

This guide from the Federal Emergency Management Agency (FEMA) of the U.S. Department of Homeland Security (DHS) provides step-by-step guidance on how to create and maintain a crisis-management program.

Food Allergy & Anaphylaxis Network
www.foodallergy.org

The Food Allergy & Anaphylaxis Network (FAAN) is a nonprofit organization representing Americans with food allergies. FAAN's mission is to increase awareness, provide education and advocacy, and advance research on behalf of all those affected by food allergies and anaphylaxis. Visit this Web site for information on food allergens and their causes, as well as other useful food-allergy-related information.

Food and Drug Administration
www.fda.gov

The Food and Drug Administration (FDA) is responsible for promoting and protecting public health by making sure safe and effective products reach consumers; monitoring products for continued safety; and helping the public obtain accurate, science-based information needed to improve health. Visit this Web site for information about all programs regulated by the FDA, including food product labeling, bottled water, and food products, excluding meat and poultry.

Foodborne Diseases Active Surveillance Network (Food Net)
www.cdc.gov/foodnet

Together with the U.S. Department of Agriculture (USDA), the Food and Drug Administration (FDA), and ten data-collection sites throughout the United States, the Foodborne Diseases Active Surveillance Network (FoodNet) consists of active surveillance for foodborne diseases and related epidemiologic studies. These are designed to help public health officials better understand the causes, distribution, and control of foodborne diseases in the United States. Visit this Web site for data collected on the incidence of nine key foodborne pathogens, including their summary reports.

Foodborne Illness Cost Calculator
www.ers.usda.gov/data/foodborneillness

As a means to quantifying the annual economic cost of foodborne illness, the U.S. Department of Agriculture Economic Research Service has developed a Foodborne Illness Cost Calculator. Visit this Web site to access this calculator to estimate medical costs due to illness, the cost of time lost from work due to nonfatal illness, and the cost of premature death for several foodborne pathogens. The calculator allows you to alter the assumptions to determine your own cost estimates.

Foodservice Consultants Society International
www.fcsi.org

The Foodservice Consultants Society International offers foodservice design and management-consulting services. Members of this organization have specialized skills and training in developing and updating foodservice establishments.

Gateway to Government Food Safety Information
www.foodsafety.gov

This Web site provides links to selected government food safety-related information. Information regarding recent food safety news and alerts, as well as links to federal government agencies and national food safety programs from the FDA, USDA, and the CDC can be found on this Web site.

Good Agricultural Practices (GAPs): A Self-Audit for Growers and Handlers
ucgaps.ucdavis.edu

The University of California Davis Good Agricultural Practices (GAPs) for growers and handlers focus on contamination prevention, survival reduction, and cross-contamination prevention during growth, packing, and shipment of produce. GAPs can be used as a tool to assess whether or not a produce supplier has used minimum practices to ensure the safety of produce.

Hazard Analysis and Critical Control Point Principles and Application Guidelines
www.fsis.usda.gov/OPHS/NACMCF/past/JFP0998.pdf

In 1991, the National Advisory Committee on Microbiological Criteria for Foods convened to update previous documents on the topic of HACCP. The guidelines found on this Web site are the outcome of the Committee's discussions and are intended to facilitate the development and implementation of an effective HACCP plan.

Institute for Business & Home Safety Small Business Protection
www.disastersafety.org

The Institute for Business & Home Safety's purpose is to reduce the social and economic impact of natural disasters and other property losses by advocating improved construction, maintenance, and preparation practices. This Web site provides information on how to prepare for and recover your business from earthquakes, floods, fire, hurricane, tornado, and other natural disasters.

Evaluation and Definition of Potentially Hazardous Foods
www.fda.gov/Food/ScienceResearch/ResearchAreas/SafePracticesforFood Processes/ucm094141.htm

This document defines TCS food. It includes information on the process of holding food temperature, product description, pH and a_w interaction, product assessment, and challenge testing in determining whether a food is considered a TCS food.

International Association of Plumbing and Mechanical Officials
www.iapmo.org

International Association of Plumbing and Mechanical Officials (IAPMO) uses ANSI-approved processes to develop the Uniform Plumbing Code and Uniform Mechanical Code. These codes, established through scientific research, debate, and analysis, are updated every three years.

International Code Council
www.iccsafe.org

The International Code Council develops codes used to build residential and commercial buildings. Access this Web site for international building, mechanical, and plumbing codes.

International Council on Hotel, Restaurant, and Institutional Education
www.chrie.org

The International Council on Hotel, Restaurant, and Institutional Education (I-CHRIE) is the global advocate of hospitality and tourism education for schools, colleges, and universities offering programs in hotel and restaurant management, foodservice management, and culinary arts. The organization strives to unite educators, industry executives, and associations. This Web site lists available publications that promote educational opportunities in the hotel and restaurant industry.

International Dairy Foods Association
www.idfa.org

International Dairy Foods Association (IDFA) is the Washington, D.C.–based organization representing the nation's dairy-processing and manufacturing industries and their suppliers. IDFA is composed of three constituent organizations: the Milk Industry Foundation (MIF), the National Cheese Institute (NCI), and the International Ice Cream Association (IICA). Visit this Web site to access the Pasteurized Milk Ordinance, dairy-product quality standards, and regulations affecting the dairy industry.

International Food Information Center
www.foodinsight.org/

Working with a roster of scientific experts, the International Food Information Center (IFIC) collects and disseminates scientific information on food safety, nutrition, and health and translates this research into understandable and useful information for foodservice professionals. This Web site provides information on food safety, food defense, and organic food.

IRS *Business Casualty, Disaster, and Theft Loss* Workbook
www.irs.gov/publications/p584b/index.html

Provided by the Internal Revenue Service, this workbook is designed to help businesses determine losses to office furniture and fixtures, information systems, buildings, and equipment in the event of a disaster, casualty, or theft.

Managing Food Safety: A Manual for the Voluntary Use of HACCP Principles for Operators of Foodservice and Retail Establishments
www.fda.gov/Food/FoodSafety/RetailFoodProtection/ManagingFoodSafety HACCPPrinciples/Operators/default.htm

This manual, provided by the Food and Drug Administration's Center for Food Safety and Applied Nutrition (FDA CFSAN), provides the restaurant and foodservice industry with a road map for developing and voluntarily implementing a food safety management system based on HACCP principles. Developed by the FDA with input from the foodservice industry, the manual has been reviewed and endorsed by the Conference for Food Protection (CFP).

Morbidity and Mortality Weekly Report
www.cdc.gov/mmwr

The *Morbidity and Mortality Weekly Report (MMWR)*, prepared by the Centers for Disease Control and Prevention, is available on this Web site. The report contains illness data based on weekly accounts of reportable diseases from state health departments. Visit this Web site to obtain foodborne-illness data and to search report databases for synopses of actual foodborne-illness outbreaks.

Mushroom Council
www.mushroomcouncil.org

The Mushroom Council, composed of fresh-market mushroom producers and importers, administers a national promotion, research, and consumer-information program to maintain and expand markets for fresh mushrooms. Information about shipping, handling, and preparing mushrooms, as well as risks associated with the use of mushrooms harvested by inexperienced mushroom hunters, is available on this Web site.

National Association of City and County Officials
www.naccho.org

NACCHO is the national organization representing local health departments. The organization promotes national policy, develops resources and programs, seeks health equity, and supports effective, local, public health practice and systems. Visit this Web site to review community-based efforts to educate about, respond to, and track foodborne illness.

National Automatic Merchandising Association (NAMA)
www.vending.org

NAMA is the national trade association for the vending industry, including on-site, commissary, catering, and mobile vending. Visit this Web site for information regarding safe service of food via vending and catering, as well as resources on pest control, how to address foodborne-illness calls, sanitation basics, and ways to safely serve TCS food off site.

National Cattlemen's Beef Association: Beef for Foodservice Professionals
www.beeffoodservice.com

The Beef for Foodservice Professional's Web site was established by the National Cattleman's Beef Association and the Beef Checkoff program. This Web site contains information on current facts, trends, and resources on beef-safety issues and best practices. This site includes the *Foodservice Ground Beef Safety Guidelines* brochure, a food safety guide for receiving, preparing, handling, cooking, and storing ground beef.

National Chicken Council
www.nationalchickencouncil.com

The National Chicken Council (NCC) is the national, nonprofit trade association for the U.S. chicken industry, representing integrated chicken producers and processors, poultry distributors, and allied firms. Visit this Web site for consumer-consumption behaviors, product information, and research related to poultry-associated illnesses, such as avian influenza.

National Fisheries Institute
www.aboutseafood.com

The National Fisheries Institute (NFI) is the nation's leading advocacy organization for the seafood industry. This Web site contains useful information on industry and government links, nutrition and dietary health, fact sheets on fish species, and relevant seafood press releases and statistics.

National Food Service Security Council
www.nfssconline.org

NFSSC brings together foodservice loss-prevention and risk-management professionals to provide education on topics that can improve the safety and security of foodservice employees and customers. Visit this Web site to access useful resources on the topic of food defense.

National Frozen & Refrigerated Foods Association
www.nfraweb.org

The mission of the National Frozen & Refrigerated Foods Association is to promote the sale and consumption of frozen and refrigerated food through education, training, research, sales planning, and menu development. Visit this Web site for information on the proper reception, storage, and preparation of frozen and refrigerated food, including shelf-life charts, tips, and recommended food and storage-equipment temperatures.

National Institute for Occupational Safety and Health
www.cdc.gov/niosh/

The National Institute for Occupational Safety and Health (NIOSH) is part of the Centers for Disease Control and Prevention (CDC) and is the federal agency responsible for helping ensure safe and healthful working conditions for working men and women. This Web site provides access to information about NIOSH programs and training sessions, guidance documents on illness, accident prevention and safety, proper handling of chemicals, and latex-allergy prevention.

National Pest Management Association
www.pestworld.org

The National Pest Management Association is a nonprofit organization that supports the professional pest control industry's commitment to the protection of public health, food, and property. Consult this Web site to obtain information on habits and threats of specific pests, tips on pest prevention, and how to select a pest control professional.

National Pork Producers Council
www.nppc.org

The National Pork Producers Council (NPPC) is one of the nation's largest livestock-commodity organizations. Visit the NPPC's foodservice site, *www.porkfoodservice.com,* for pork-preparation tips, recipes, and consumer-consumption trends.

National Restaurant Association
www.restaurant.org

The National Restaurant Association, founded in 1919, is the leading business association for the restaurant industry, which is comprised of 935,000 restaurant and foodservice outlets and a workforce of 12.8 million employees—making it the cornerstone of the economy, career opportunities, and community involvement. Along with the National Restaurant Association Educational Foundation, the Association works to represent, educate, and promote the rapidly growing industry.

National Turkey Federation
www.eatturkey.com

The National Turkey Federation is the national advocate for all segments of the U.S. turkey industry. This Web site contains information useful to foodservice establishments, including safe purchasing, storing, thawing, and preparing information, as well as recipes, nutrition information, and promotional ideas for turkey.

North American Association of Food Equipment Manufacturers
www.nafem.org

The North American Association of Food Equipment Manufacturers (NAFEM) is a trade association of more than 625 foodservice-equipment and supply manufacturers that provide products for food preparation, cooking, storage, and table service. Use this Web site to identify foodservice-equipment manufacturers, access educational materials on such topics as equipment selection, and download other equipment-related guidance documents.

NSF International
www.nsf.org

NSF International is a nonprofit, nongovernmental organization focused on standards development, product certification, education, and risk-management for public health and safety. This organization also certifies products against the standards they develop. Visit this Web site for NSF International's food-equipment standards, as well as a listing of certified food equipment.

Occupational Safety and Health Administration
www.osha.gov

Occupational Safety and Health Administration's (OSHA) role is to ensure the safety and health of American workers by setting and enforcing standards; providing training, outreach, and education; and encouraging continual improvement in workplace safety and health. This Web site provides links to regulation and compliance documents, as well as valuable information on the prevention of workplace hazards.

OSHA *Hazard Communication*

www.osha.gov/dsg/hazcom/index.html

This Web site provides guidance on how to comply with OSHA's HAZCOM standards, including how to meet the MSDS requirement, train employees in HAZCOM, and label chemicals correctly.

Produce Marketing Association

www.pma.com

The Produce Marketing Association (PMA) is a nonprofit association serving members who market fresh fruit, vegetables, and related products worldwide. Their members represent the production, distribution, retail, and foodservice sectors of the industry. Visit this Web site for articles and publications on produce-related food safety information.

Recommendations for the Preparation of Iced and Hot Tea

www.teausa.com/general/teaassociation/foodbrewing/the_tea_manual.pdf

Based on current scientific information, these guidelines provide recommendations for safe preparation of iced and hot tea.

Risk and Insurance Management Society, Inc.

www.rims.org

The Risk and Insurance Management Society, Inc. (RIMS) is a nonprofit organization dedicated to advancing the practice of risk management. Visit this Web site to learn about risk-focused courses and conferences and to access and purchase resources relevant to risk and safety.

Risk Assessment for *Listeria monocytogenes* in Deli Meats

www.fsis.usda.gov/OPPDE/rdad/FRPubs/97-013F/ListeriaReport.pdf.

This assessment reports on the prevalence of *Listeria monocytogenes* in ready-to-eat (RTE) meat and poultry products.

Seafood Inspection Program

www.seafood.nmfs.noaa.gov

The National Oceanic and Atmospheric Administration (NOAA), part of the U.S. Department of Commerce (USDC), oversees the management of fisheries in the United States and provides a voluntary seafood-inspection service to the industry. This ensures compliance with all applicable food regulations, as well as product grading and certification services. The USDC Participants List, a reference tool for determining which fishery products have been produced in fish establishments approved by the USDC, and the U.S. standards for grading fishery products are available on this Web site.

Society for Risk Analysis

www.sra.org

The Society for Risk Analysis provides an open forum for those interested in risk management. Visit this Web site for information on risk communication and information on how to access other risk-management tools.

Tea Association of the USA, Inc.

www.teausa.com

This Web site encompasses the Tea Association of the USA, Inc., the Tea Council of the USA, and the Specialty Tea Institute (STI). Visit this site to learn about safe brewing and serving practices.

Underwriters Laboratories, Inc.

www.ul.com

Underwriters Laboratories, Inc. (UL) is an independent, nonprofit testing and certification organization for product safety. UL develops and tests products against standards essential to ensuring public safety and improved quality. This Web site provides access to UL's standards for safety, descriptions of its certification marks, and listings of UL-certified food equipment.

United Fresh Produce Association

www.unitedfresh.org

The United Fresh Produce Association represents the interests of member companies throughout the global, fresh-produce supply chain. This Web site provides access to commodity-specific guidance and other food safety documents related to fresh produce.

USDA Food Safety and Inspection Service

www.fsis.usda.gov

The Food Safety and Inspection Service (FSIS) is the public health agency within the U.S. Department of Agriculture responsible for ensuring that the nation's commercial supply of meat, poultry, and egg products is safe, wholesome, and correctly labeled and packaged. Visit this Web site for food safety information and regulations related to meat, poultry, and eggs.

Western Growers

www.wga.com

Western Growers is an agricultural trade association whose members, based in Arizona and California, grow, pack, and ship nearly one-half of the nation's fresh fruit, vegetables, and nuts. Visit this Web site to access commodity-specific guidance, good agricultural practices for leafy greens, and food-defense documents related to produce safety.

Notes

G Glossary

Note: The number(s) in bold at the end of each entry refers to the chapter in which the term is discussed in detail.

A

Abrasive cleaners. Cleaners containing a scouring agent used to scrub off hard-to-remove soils. They may scratch some surfaces. **12**

Acidity. Level of acid in a food. An acidic substance has a pH below 7.0. Foodborne microorganisms typically do not grow in highly acidic food, while they grow best in food with a neutral to slightly acidic pH. **2**

Active managerial control. Food safety management system designed to prevent foodborne illness by addressing the five most common risk factors identified by the Centers for Disease Control and Prevention (CDC). **10**

Air curtains. Devices installed above or alongside doors that blow a steady stream of air across an entryway, creating an air shield around open doors. Insects avoid them. Also called air doors or fly fans. **13**

Air gap. Air space used to separate a water-supply outlet from any potentially contaminated source. The air space between the floor drain and the drainpipe of a sink is an example. An air gap is the only completely reliable method for preventing backflow. **11**

Alkalinity. Level of alkali in food. An alkaline substance has a pH above 7.0. Most food is not alkaline. **2**

Americans with Disabilities Act (ADA). Federal law requiring reasonable accommodation for patrons and employees with disabilities. **4**

Aseptically packaged food. Food that has been sealed under sterile conditions, usually after UHT pasteurization. UHT stands for ultra-high temperature. **6**

B

Backflow. Unwanted reverse flow of contaminants through a cross-connection into a potable water system. It occurs when the pressure in the potable water supply drops below the pressure of the contaminated supply. **11**

Bacteria. Single-celled, living microorganisms that can spoil food and cause foodborne illness. Bacteria present in food can quickly multiply to dangerous levels when food is improperly cooked, held, or reheated. Some form spores that can survive freezing and very high temperatures. **2**

Bacterial growth. Reproduction of bacteria by splitting in two. When conditions are favorable, bacterial growth can be rapid—doubling the population as often as every twenty minutes. Their growth can be broken down into four phases: lag phase, log phase, stationary phase, and death phase. **2**

Bimetallic stemmed thermometer. The most common and versatile type of thermometer, measuring temperature through a metal probe with a sensor in the end. Most can measure temperatures from 0°F to 220°F (–18°C to 104°C) and are accurate to within ±2°F (±1°C) . They are easily calibrated. **5**

Biological contaminants. Microorganisms, such as viruses, bacteria, parasites, and fungi, as well as toxins found in certain plants, mushrooms, and seafood, that have contaminated food. **2, 3**

Biological hazards. Illness-causing microorganisms that can contaminate food, such as certain bacteria, viruses, parasites, and fungi, as well as toxins found in certain plants, mushrooms, and seafood. **1**

Biological toxins. Poisons produced by pathogens, plants, or animals. They can also occur in animals as a result of their diet. **2**

Blast chiller. Equipment designed to cool food quickly. Many are able to cool food from 135°F to 37°F (57°C to 3°C) within ninety minutes. **8, 11**

Boiling-point method. Method of calibrating a thermometer based on the boiling point of water. **5**

Booster heater. Water heater attached to hot-water lines leading to dishwashing machines or sinks. Raises water to temperature required for heat sanitizing of tableware and utensils. **11**

C

Calibration. Process of ensuring that a thermometer gives accurate readings by adjusting it to a known standard, such as the freezing point or boiling point of water. **5**

Carriers. People who carry pathogens and infect others, yet never become ill themselves. **4**

Centers for Disease Control and Prevention (CDC). Agencies of the U.S. Department of Health and Human Services that investigate foodborne-illness outbreaks, study the causes and control of disease, publish statistical data, and conduct the Vessel Sanitation Program. **14**

Chemical contaminants. Chemical substances, such as cleaners, sanitizers, polishes, machine lubricants, and toxic metals that leach from cookware and equipment, that have contaminated food. **3**

Chemical hazards. Chemical substances that can contaminate food, such as cleaners, sanitizers, polishes, machine lubricants, and toxic metals, that leach from cookware and equipment. **1**

Chemical sanitizing. Using a chemical solution to reduce the number of microorganisms on a clean surface to safe levels. Items can be sanitized by immersing in a specific concentration of sanitizing solution for a required period of time or by rinsing, swabbing, or spraying the items with a specific concentration of sanitizing solution. **12**

Chlorine. Commonly used chemical sanitizer due to its low cost and effectiveness. It kills a wide range of microorganisms. **12**

Ciguatera poisoning. Illness that occurs when a person eats fish that has consumed the ciguatera toxin. This toxin occurs in certain predatory tropical reef fish, such as amberjack, barracuda, grouper, and snapper. **2**

Clean. Free of visible soil. It refers only to the appearance of a surface. **1, 12**

Cleaners. Chemicals that remove food, soil, rust stains, minerals, or other deposits from surfaces. **12**

Cleaning. Process of removing food and other types of soil from a surface, such as a countertop or plate. **12**

Cold-holding equipment. Equipment specifically designed to hold cold food at an internal temperature of 41°F (5°C) or lower. **9**

Contact spray. Spray used to kill insects on contact. Usually used on groups of insects, such as clusters of roaches and nests of ants. **13**

Contamination. Presence of harmful substances in food. Some food safety hazards occur naturally, while others are introduced by humans or the environment. **1**

Corrective action. Predetermined step taken when food does not meet a critical limit. **10**

Coving. Curved, sealed edge placed between the floor and wall to eliminate sharp corners or gaps that would be impossible to clean. Coving also eliminates hiding places for pests and prevents moisture from deteriorating walls. **11**

Critical control point (CCP). In a HACCP system, the points in the process where you can intervene to prevent, eliminate, or reduce identified hazards to safe levels. **10**

Critical limit. In a HACCP system, the minimum or maximum limit a critical control point (CCP) must meet in order to prevent, eliminate, or reduce a hazard to an acceptable level. **10**

Cross-connection. Physical link through which contaminants from drains, sewers, or other wastewater sources can enter a potable water supply. A hose connected to a faucet and submerged in a mop bucket is an example. **11**

Cross-contact. The transfer of an allergen from a food containing an allergen to a food that does not contain the allergen. **3**

Cross-contamination. Occurs when microorganisms are transferred from one food or surface to another. **1, 5**

D

Death phase. The phase in bacterial growth in which the number of bacteria dying exceeds the number growing, resulting in a population decline. **2**

Degreasers. Alkaline detergents, often called degreasers, that contain a grease-dissolving agent. **12**

Delimers. Used on mineral deposits and other soils that alkaline cleaners cannot remove, such as scale, rust, and tarnish. **12**

Demonstration. Process of illustrating a skill or task in front of another person or a group. **15**

Detergent. Cleaner designed to penetrate and soften soil to help remove it from a surface. **12**

Dry storage. Storage used to hold dry and canned food at temperatures between 50°F and 70°F (10°C and 21°C) and at a relative humidity of 50 to 60 percent. **7**

E

Electronic insect eliminator ("zapper"). Mechanical device that uses light to attract flying insects to an electrically charged grid that kills them. **13**

Environmental Protection Agency (EPA). Federal agency that sets standards for environmental quality, including air and water quality, and regulates pesticide use and waste handling. **14**

Exclusion. Prohibiting foodhandlers from working in the establishment due to specific medical conditions. **4**

F

FAT TOM. Acronym for the conditions needed by most foodborne microorganisms to grow: food, acidity, temperature, time, oxygen, moisture. **2**

FDA Food Code. Science-based reference for retail food establishments on how to prevent foodborne illness. These recommendations are issued by the FDA to assist state health departments in developing regulations for a foodservice inspection program. **1, 14**

Finger cot. Protective covering used to cover a properly bandaged cut or wound on the finger. **4**

First in, first out (FIFO). Method of stock rotation in which products are shelved based on their use-by or expiration dates, so oldest products are used first. **7**

Flood rim. Spill-over point of a sink. **11**

Flow of food. Path food takes through an establishment, from purchasing and receiving through storing, preparing, cooking, holding, cooling, reheating, and serving. **5**

Food additives. Substances added to food to lengthen its shelf life. They are also used to alter food so it does not need time and temperature control. Some are used to enhance flavor. **8**

Food allergy. The body's negative reaction to a particular food protein. **3**

Food and Drug Administration (FDA). Federal agency that issues the *FDA Food Code* working jointly with the U.S. Department of Agriculture (USDA) and the Centers for Disease Control and Prevention (CDC). The FDA also inspects foodservice operations that cross state borders—interstate establishments such as food manufacturers and processors, and planes and trains—because they overlap the jurisdictions of two or more states. **14**

Food bar. Self-service buffet at which patrons can choose what they want to eat as they serve themselves. **9**

Food-contact surface. Surface that comes into direct contact with food, such as a cutting board. **1**

Food defense. Program developed and implemented by an operation to prevent deliberate contamination of its food. **3**

Food Safety and Inspection Service (FSIS). Agency of the U.S. Department of Agriculture (USDA) that inspects and grades meat, meat products, poultry, dairy products, eggs and egg products, and fruit and vegetables shipped across state boundaries. **14**

Food safety management system. Group of programs, procedures, and measures designed to prevent foodborne illness by actively controlling risks and hazards throughout the flow of food. **10**

Foodborne illness. Illness carried or transmitted to people by food. **1**

Foodborne-illness outbreak. According to the Centers for Disease Control and Prevention (CDC), an incident in which two or more people experience the same illness after eating the same food. **1**

Foot-candle. Unit of lighting equal to the illumination one foot from a uniform light source. Also called lux. **11**

Frozen storage. Storage typically designed to hold food at temperatures that will keep it frozen. **7**

Fungi. Ranging in size from microscopic, single-celled organisms to very large, multicellular organisms. Fungi most often cause food to spoil. Molds, yeasts, and mushrooms are examples. **2**

G

Gastrointestinal illness. Illness related to the stomach or intestine. **4**

Glue board. Pest-control device in which mice are trapped by glue and then die from exhaustion or lack of water or air. They are also used to identify the type of cockroaches that might be present. **13**

H

HACCP plan. Written document based on HACCP principles describing procedures a particular establishment will follow to ensure the safety of food served. See *Hazard Analysis Critical Control Point.* **10**

Hair restraint. Device used to keep a foodhandler's hair away from food and to keep the individual from touching it. **4**

Hand antiseptic. Liquid or gel used to lower the number of microorganisms on the skin's surface. Hand antiseptics should only be used after proper handwashing, not in place of it. Only those hand antiseptics that are compliant with the Food and Drug Administration (FDA) should be used. **4**

Handwashing station. Sink designated for handwashing only. Handwashing stations must be conveniently located in restrooms, food-preparation areas, service areas, and dishwashing areas. **11**

Hard water. Water containing minerals such as calcium and iron in concentrations higher than 120 parts per million (ppm). **12**

Hazard analysis. Process of identifying and evaluating potential hazards associated with food in order to determine what must be addressed in the HACCP plan. **10**

Hazard analysis critical control point (HACCP). Food safety management system based on the idea that if significant biological, chemical, or physical hazards are identified at specific points within a product's flow through the operation, they can be prevented, eliminated, or reduced to safe levels. **10**

Hazard Communication Standard (HCS). OSHA standard, also known as Right-to-Know or HAZCOM, requiring employers to tell their employees about potential chemical hazards at the establishment. It also requires employers to train employees in how to use chemicals safely. **12**

Health inspector. City, county, or state employee who conducts foodservice inspections. Health inspectors are also known as sanitarians, health officials, and environmental health specialists. They are generally trained in food safety, sanitation, and public health principles. **14**

Heat sanitizing. Using heat to reduce the number of microorganisms on a clean surface to safe levels. One common way to heat sanitize tableware, utensils, or equipment is to submerge them in or spray them with hot water. **12**

Hepatitis A. Disease-causing inflammation of the liver. It is transmitted to food by poor personal hygiene or contact with contaminated water. **2**

High-risk population. People susceptible to foodborne illness due to the effects of age or health on their immune systems, including infants and preschool-age children, pregnant women, older people, people taking certain medications, and those with certain diseases or weakened immune systems. **1**

Histamine. Biological toxin associated with temperature-abused scombroid fish (and other affected species), which causes scombroid poisoning. **2**

Host. Person, animal, or plant on which another organism lives and from which it takes nourishment. **2**

Hot-holding equipment. Equipment such as chafing dishes, steam tables, and heated cabinets specifically designed to hold food at an internal temperature of 135°F (57°C) or higher. **9**

I

Ice-point method. Method of calibrating thermometers based on the freezing point of water. **5**

Ice-water bath. Method of cooling food in which a container holding hot food is placed into a sink or larger container of ice water. The ice water surrounding the hot food container disperses the heat quickly. **8**

Ice paddle. Plastic paddle filled with ice or water and then frozen. Used to stir hot food to cool it quickly. **8**

Immune system. The body's defense system against illness. People with compromised immune systems are more susceptible to foodborne illness. **1**

Infestation. Situation that exists when pests overrun or inhabit an establishment in large numbers. **13**

Integrated pest management (IPM). Program using prevention measures to keep pests from entering an establishment and control measures to eliminate any pests that do get inside. **13**

Iodine. Sanitizer effective at low concentrations and not as quickly inactivated by soil as chlorine. It might stain surfaces and is less effective than chlorine. **12**

J

Jaundice. Yellowing of the skin and eyes that could indicate a person is ill with hepatitis A. **4**

Job aids. Materials or visual reminders used to deliver training content to employees. **15**

L

Lag phase. Phase in bacterial growth in which bacteria are first introduced to a new environment. In this phase, bacteria go through an adjustment period in which their numbers are stable as they prepare to grow. To control the growth of bacteria, prolong the lag phase as long as possible. **2**

Log phase. Phase in bacterial growth in which conditions are favorable for bacteria to multiply very rapidly. Food quickly becomes unsafe during this phase. **2**

M

Master cleaning schedule. Detailed schedule listing all cleaning tasks in an establishment, when and how they are to be performed, and who will perform them. **12**

Material Safety Data Sheets (MSDS). Sheets supplied by the chemical manufacturer listing the chemical and its common names, its potential physical and health hazards, information about using and handling it safely, and other important information. OSHA requires employers to store these sheets so they are accessible to employees. **12**

Microorganisms. Small, living organisms that can be seen only with the aid of a microscope. There are four types of microorganisms that can contaminate food and cause foodborne illness: bacteria, viruses, parasites, and fungi. **2**

Minimum internal temperature. The required minimum temperature the internal portion of food must reach to sufficiently reduce the number of microorganisms that might be present. This temperature is specific to the type of food being cooked. Food must reach and hold its required internal temperature for a specified amount of time. **8**

Mobile unit. Portable foodservice facilities, ranging from concession vans to full field kitchens capable of preparing and cooking elaborate meals. **9**

Modified atmosphere packaging (MAP). Packaging method by which the air inside of a package is altered using gases, such as carbon dioxide and nitrogen. Many fresh-cut produce items are packaged this way. **6**

Mold. Type of fungus that causes food spoilage. Some molds produce toxins that can cause foodborne illness. **2**

Monitoring. In a HACCP system, the process of analyzing whether critical limits are being met and procedures are being followed. **10**

N

National Marine Fisheries Service (NMFS). Agency of the U.S. Department of Commerce that provides a voluntary inspection program that includes product standards and sanitary requirements for fish-processing operations. **14**

NSF International. Organization that develops and publishes standards for sanitary equipment design. It also assesses and certifies that equipment has met these standards. Restaurant and foodservice managers should look for an NSF International mark (or UL EPH product mark) on commercial foodservice equipment. **11**

O

Occupational Safety and Health Administration (OSHA). Federal agency that regulates and monitors workplace safety. **12**

Off-site service. Service of food to someplace other than where it is prepared or cooked, including catering and vending. **9**

On-the-job training. Method in which experienced staff members teach learners while on the job. **15**

P

Parasite. Organism that needs to live in a host organism to survive. Parasites can be found in water and inside many animals, such as cows, chickens, pigs, and fish. Proper cooking and freezing will kill parasites. Avoiding cross-contamination and practicing proper handwashing can also prevent illness. **2**

Pathogens. Illness-causing microorganisms. **2**

Personal hygiene. Habits that include keeping the hands, hair, and body clean and wearing clean and appropriate uniforms. Avoiding unsanitary actions and reporting illness and injury are also features of good personal hygiene. **1, 4**

Pest control operator (PCO). Licensed professional who uses safe, current methods to prevent and control pests. **13**

Pesticide. Chemical used to control pests, usually insects. **13**

pH. Measure of a food's acidity or alkalinity. The pH scale ranges from 0 to 14.0. A pH between 7.1 and 14 is alkaline, while a pH between 0.0 and 6.9 is acidic. A pH of 7.0 is neutral. Foodborne microorganisms grow well in food that has a neutral to slightly acidic pH (7.5 to 4.6). **2**

Physical contaminants. Physical objects, such as hair, dirt, metal staples, and broken glass, as well as bones in fillets, that have contaminated food. **3**

Physical hazards. Foreign objects that can accidentally get into food and contaminate it, such as hair, dirt, metal staples, and broken glass, as well as naturally-occurring objects, such as bones in fillets. **1**

Plant toxins. Poisons found naturally in some plants. **2**

Pooled eggs. Eggs that have been cracked open and combined in a common container. **8**

Porosity. Extent to which water and other liquids are absorbed by a substance. Term usually used in relation to flooring material. **11**

Potable water. Water that is safe to drink. **11**

Pulper. Device used to grind food and other waste into small parts that are flushed with water, which is then removed. The processed, solid wastes weigh less and are more compact for easier disposal. **11**

Q

Quaternary ammonium compounds (quats). Group of sanitizers all having the same basic chemical structure. They work in most temperature and pH ranges, are noncorrosive, and remain active for short periods of time after they have dried. However, quats may not kill certain types of microorganisms, and they leave a film on surfaces. **12**

R

Ready-to-eat food. Any food that is edible without further preparation, washing, or cooking. It includes washed fruit and vegetables, both whole and cut; deli meats; and bakery items. Sugars, spices, seasonings, and properly cooked food items are also considered ready-to-eat. **2**

Reasonable care defense. Defense against a food-related lawsuit stating that an establishment did everything that could be reasonably expected to ensure that the food served was safe. **1**

Record keeping. In a HACCP system, the process of collecting documents that allow you to show you are continuously preparing and serving safe food. **10**

Reduced oxygen packaging (ROP). Stands for "reduced oxygen packaging." Packaging method that reduces the amount of oxygen available in order to slow microbial growth. ROP methods include *sous vide*, MAP, and vacuum packaging. **6**

Refrigerated storage. Storage used to hold TCS food at an internal temperature of 41°F (5°C) or lower. **7**

Regulations. Laws determining standards of behavior. Restaurant and foodservice regulations are typically written at the state level and based on the *FDA Food Code*. **14**

Residual spray. Type of pesticide spray that leaves behind a film that insects absorb as they crawl across it. Used in cracks and crevices like those along baseboards, these sprays can be liquid or a dust, such as boric acid. **13**

Resiliency. Ability of a surface to react to a shock without breaking or cracking, usually used in relation to a flooring material. **11**

Restriction. Prohibiting foodhandlers from working with or around food, food equipment, and utensils. **4**

Role-play. Training method in which trainees act out a situation to try new skills or apply new knowledge. **15**

S

Sanitizer. Chemical used to sanitize. Chlorine, iodine, and quats are the three most common types of chemical sanitizer in the restaurant and foodservice industry. **12**

Sanitizing. Process of reducing the number of microorganisms on a clean surface to safe levels. **12**

Scombroid poisoning. Illness that occurs when a person eats a scombroid fish (or certain other species) that has been time-temperature abused. Scombroid fish include tuna, mackerel, bluefish, skipjack, and bonito. **2**

Service sink. Sink used exclusively for cleaning mops and disposing of wastewater. At least one service sink or one curbed drain area is required in an establishment. **11**

Shelf life. Recommended period of time during which food can be stored and remain suitable for use. **7**

Shellstock identification tags. Each container of live, molluscan shellfish received must have an ID tag that must remain attached to the container until all the shellfish have been used. Tags are to be kept on file for ninety days from the date recorded on the tag. **6**

Single-use gloves. Disposable gloves designed for one-time use. They provide a barrier between hands and the food they touch. Gloves should never be used in place of handwashing. Foodhandlers should wash hands before putting on gloves and when changing to a new pair. **4**

Single-use paper towel. Paper towel designed to be used once, then discarded. **4**

Slacking. Process of gradually thawing frozen food in preparation for deep-frying. **8**

Sneeze guard. Food shield placed over self-service displays and food bars that extends seven inches beyond the food and fourteen inches above the food counter. **9**

***Sous vide* food.** Packaging method by which cooked or partially cooked food is vacuum packed in individual pouches and then chilled. This food is heated for service in the establishment. Frozen, precooked meals are often packaged this way. **6**

Spore. Form that some bacteria can take to protect themselves when nutrients are not available. Spores are commonly found in soil and can contaminate food grown there. A spore can resist heat, allowing it to survive cooking temperatures. Spores can also revert back to a form capable of growth. This can occur when food is not held at the proper temperature or cooled or reheated properly. **2**

Stationary phase. Phase of bacterial growth in which just as many bacteria are growing as are dying. Follows the log phase of bacterial growth. **2**

T

TCS food. Food that contains moisture and protein and has a neutral or slightly acidic pH. Such food requires time-temperature control to prevent the growth of microorganisms and the production of toxins. **2**

Technology-based training. Training programs delivered via a computer or other technology. **15**

Temperature danger zone. The temperature range between 41°F and 135°F (5°C to 57°C), within which most foodborne microorganisms rapidly grow. **2**

Temporary unit. Establishment operating in one location for no more than fourteen consecutive days in conjunction with a special event or celebration. Usually serves prepackaged food or food requiring only limited preparation. **9**

Thermometer. Device for accurately measuring the internal temperature of food, the air temperature inside a freezer or cooler, or the temperature of equipment. Bimetallic stemmed thermometers, thermocouples, and thermistors are common types of thermometers used in the restaurant and foodservice industry. **5**

Time-temperature abuse. Food has been time-temperature abused any time it has been allowed to remain too long at a temperature favorable to the growth of foodborne microorganisms. **1**

Time-temperature indicator (TTI). Time and temperature monitoring device attached to a food shipment to determine if the product's temperature has exceeded safe limits during shipment or subsequent storage. **5**

Toxic-metal poisoning. Illness caused when toxic metals are leached from utensils or equipment containing them. **3**

Toxins. Poisons produced by pathogens, plants, or animals. Some occur in animals as a result of their diet. **2**

Training delivery methods. Approaches for providing training to employees. This can include more traditional methods such as lectures, demonstrations, or role-play or more technology-based approaches such as Web-based training and interactive CD-ROMs. Regardless of the approach, it is important to use more than one method of delivery, because employees learn differently. **15**

Training need. Gap between what employees are required to know to do their jobs and what they actually know. There are several ways to identify food safety training needs, including observing job performance, testing food safety knowledge, and surveying employees to identify areas of weakness. **15**

Tumble chiller. Equipment designed to cool food quickly. Prepackaged hot food is placed into a drum rotating inside a reservoir of chilled water. The tumbling action increases the effectiveness of the chilled water in cooling the food. **11**

Two-stage cooling. Criteria by which cooked food is cooled from 135°F to 70°F (57°C to 21°C) within two hours and from 70°F to 41°F (21°C to 5°C) or lower within the next four hours, for a total cooling time of six hours. **8**

U

Ultra-high temperature (UHT) pasteurized food. Food that is heat treated at very high temperatures (pasteurized) to kill microorganisms. This food is often also aseptically packaged—sealed under sterile conditions to keep it from being contaminated. **6**

Underwriters Laboratories (UL). Provides sanitation classification listings for equipment found in compliance with NSF International standards. Also lists products complying with its own published environmental and public health standards. **11**

U.S. Department of Agriculture (USDA). Federal agency responsible for the inspection and quality grading of meat, meat products, poultry, dairy products, eggs and egg products, and fruit and vegetables shipped across state lines. **14**

V

Vacuum breaker. Device preventing the backflow of contaminants into a potable water system. **11**

Vacuum-packed food. Food processed by removing air from around it while sealed in a package. This process increases the product's shelf life. **6**

Variance. Document issued by a regulatory agency that allows a requirement to be waived or modified. **8**

Vending machine. Machines that dispense hot and cold food, beverages, and snacks. **9**

Verification. In a HACCP system, the process of confirming that critical control points and critical limits are appropriate, that monitoring is alerting you to hazards, that corrective actions are adequate to prevent foodborne illness from occurring, and that employees are following established procedures. **10**

Virus. Smallest of the microbial food contaminants. Viruses rely on a living host to reproduce. They usually contaminate food through a foodhandler's improper personal hygiene. Some survive freezing and cooking temperatures. **2**

W

Warranty of sale. Rules stating how food must be handled in an establishment. **1**

Water activity (a_w). Amount of moisture available in food for microorganisms to grow. It is measured in a scale from 0.0 to 1.0, with water having a water activity (a_w) of 1.0. TCS food typically has a water-activity value of 0.85 or higher. **2**

Y

Yeast. Type of fungus that causes food spoilage. **2**

AK Answer Key

1 Providing Safe Food

Page	Activity

1-2   **Test Your Food Safety Knowledge**

① True   ② True   ③ False   ④ True   ⑤ True

1-13   **Discussion Questions**

① The potential costs of a foodborne-illness outbreak include the following:

- Loss of customers and sales
- Loss of reputation
- Negative media exposure
- Lawsuits and legal fees
- Increased insurance premiums
- Lowered employee morale
- Employee absenteeism
- Need for retraining employees
- Closure

② As people age, their immune systems weaken. Changes in the stomach and intestinal tract may allow the body to keep food for longer periods, allowing more time for toxin formation. Stomach-acid production decreases with age, allowing more ingested pathogens to enter the intestinal path. Also, senses of taste and smell may decline, leading to changes in their eating habits. The food they choose may not give them enough nutrients to maintain their immune systems.

③ The three major types of hazards to food safety are biological hazards, chemical hazards, and physical hazards.

1-14   **Study Questions**

① A   ② C   ③ B   ④ D

2   The Microworld

Page	Activity

2-2   Test Your Food Safety Knowledge

① False   ② False   ③ False   ④ True   ⑤ False

2-34   A Case in Point 1

Bacillus cereus caused the illness. It is commonly linked with cooked rice. The pathogen was allowed to grow when the rice was cooled incorrectly and held at the wrong temperature.

2-34   A Case in Point 2

When the mahi-mahi was time-temperature abused, the bacteria on the fish produced the toxin histamine. Since cooking does not destroy this toxin, eating the fish resulted in scombroid poisoning.

2-35   Discussion Questions

① The following types of food have the right FAT TOM conditions that pathogens need to grow. They also have a natural potential for contamination because of the way they are grown, produced, or processed. These food items are also commonly involved in foodborne-illness outbreaks.

- Milk and dairy products
- Eggs (except those treated to eliminate *Salmonella* spp.)
- Meat: beef, pork, and lamb
- Poultry
- Fish, shellfish, and crustaceans
- Baked potatoes
- Heat-treated plant food, such as cooked rice, beans, and vegetables
- Tofu or other soy protein; synthetic ingredients, such as textured soy protein in meat alternatives
- Sprouts and sprout seeds
- Sliced melons, cut tomatoes, and cut leafy greens
- Untreated garlic-and-oil mixtures

② Time and temperature are the two FAT TOM conditions that are easiest for an establishment to control. To control temperature, you must do your best to keep TCS food out of the temperature danger zone. To control time, you must limit how long TCS food spends in the temperature danger zone during preparation.

③ Practicing personal hygiene is the most important prevention measure to prevent an outbreak of Norovirus. Other prevention measures include:

- Keeping employees with diarrhea and vomiting out of the operation
- Keeping employees who have been diagnosed with Norovirus out of the operation
- Washing hands
- Minimizing bare-hand contact with ready-to-eat food
- Purchasing shellfish from approved, reputable suppliers

④ Purchasing seafood from approved, reputable suppliers is the most important measure to prevent a seafood-specific foodborne illness.

⑤ To prevent plant toxins from getting into food, purchase plants and items made with plants only from approved, reputable suppliers. Then cook and hold dishes made from these items correctly.

2-42   Study Questions

| ① C | ③ D | ⑤ C | ⑦ A | ⑨ C | ⑪ C |
| ② B | ④ C | ⑥ A | ⑧ B | ⑩ A | |

3   Contamination, Food Allergens, and Foodborne Illness

Page	Activity

3-2   Test Your Food Safety Knowledge

① True   ② True   ③ True   ④ True   ⑤ True

3-9   Discussion Questions

① Some utensils and equipment contain metals that can contaminate acidic food. These metals include lead, copper, and zinc. If acidic food is stored in or prepared with this equipment, the metals can be transferred to the food and cause toxic-metal poisoning. It can also occur when carbonated beverage dispensers are improperly installed, which can allow carbonated water to flow back into copper supply lines contaminating the beverage with copper.

To prevent toxic-metal poisoning, only food-grade utensils and equipment should be used to prepare and store food. Installing a proper backflow-prevention device on beverage dispensing systems will also prevent the illness.

② There are several ways to keep chemicals from contaminating food.

- Store chemicals away from food, utensils, and equipment used for food.
- Follow the manufacturers' directions when using chemicals.
- Be careful when using chemicals while food is being prepared.
- Label chemical containers when transferring a chemical to a new container.
- Only use lubricants that are made for food equipment.

③ There are several measures that can be taken by both service staff and kitchen staff to ensure the safety of customers with food allergies.

Service staff

- Describe dishes so customers know how they are prepared.
- Identify secret ingredients if asked.
- Suggest simple menu items.

Kitchen staff

- Wash, rinse, and sanitize cookware, utensils, and equipment before preparing food.
- Wash hands and change gloves before preparing food.
- Assign specific equipment for preparing food for customers with allergens.

3-9   Study Questions

① B	③ C	⑤ A
② C	④ B	⑥ B

4   The Safe Foodhandler

Page	Activity

4-2   Test Your Food Safety Knowledge

① False   ② True   ③ True   ④ True   ⑤ False

4-16   A Case in Point 1

Randall made 17 errors.

① Randall did not take a bath or shower before work.

② Randall wore a dirty uniform to work.

③ Randall should have removed his watch and rings (with the exception of a plain band) before prepping and serving food.

④ Randall did not wear a hair restraint.

⑤ Randall did not report his illness to the manager before coming to work.

⑥ Randall did not wash his hands before handling the raw chicken.

⑦ Randall did not wash his hands after handling the raw chicken.

⑧ The manager did not ask about Randall's symptoms. If Randall were to report that he had diarrhea, the manager should have sent him home.

⑨ Randall did not wash his hands correctly after taking out the garbage.

⑩ Randall did not wash his hands correctly after using the restroom.

⑪ Randall did not dry his hands correctly after washing them. He got them dirty again when he wiped them on his apron.

⑫ Randall wore his apron into the restroom.

⑬ The manager did not make sure the restroom was stocked with paper towels.

⑭ Randall did not wear a finger cot or a single-use glove over the bandaged finger.

⑮ Randall did not wash his hands before putting on the single-use gloves.

⑯ Randall touched the ready-to-eat chicken with his contaminated gloves.

⑰ Randall was eating chicken while preparing food.

4-17   A Case in Point 2

① The employee should have notified her supervisor immediately when she became ill with diarrhea. Her supervisor should not have allowed her to work while ill.

4-17   Discussion Questions

① Employees must meet the following work attire requirements:

- Wear a clean hat or other hair restraint.
- Wear clean clothing daily.
- Remove aprons when leaving food-preparation areas.
- Remove jewelry from hands and arms prior to preparing food and when working around food-preparation areas.

② The following personal behaviors can contaminate food:

- Wiping or touching the nose
- Rubbing an ear
- Scratching the scalp
- Touching a pimple or an infected wound
- Running fingers through the hair

③ Bandages must be worn over wounds on hands and arms. The bandage must keep the wound from leaking. A single-use glove or finger-cot must be worn over bandages on hands and fingers.

④ Foodhandlers must follow these procedures when wearing gloves to handle food:

- Use single-use gloves. These should never be washed and reused.

- Make sure gloves fit properly.

- Never use gloves in place of handwashing.

- Wash hands before putting on gloves and when changing to a new pair.

- Change gloves when necessary:

  ○ As soon as they become soiled or torn

  ○ Before beginning a different task

  ○ At least every four hours during continual use, and more often when necessary

  ○ After handling raw meat and before handling ready-to-eat food

⑤ These health problems pose a threat to food safety and require the following action(s):

- **Sore throat with fever.** Restrict the foodhandler from working with or around food. Exclude the foodhandler from the operation if you primarily serve a high-risk population.

- **Vomiting, diarrhea, or jaundice.** Exclude the foodhandler from the operation. Foodhandlers who vomited or had diarrhea cannot return to work unless they have had no symptoms for at least twenty-four hours, or have a written release from a medical practitioner. Foodhandlers with jaundice cannot return to work unless they have a written release from a medical practitioner.

- **A foodborne illness caused by one of these pathogens:**

  ○ *Salmonella* Typhi

  ○ *Shigella* spp.

  ○ Shiga toxin-producing *E. coli*

  ○ Hepatitis A

  ○ Norovirus

Exclude the foodhandler from the operation. Notify the local regulatory authority. Work with the foodhandler's medical practitioner and/or the local regulatory authority to decide when the person can go back to work.

4-18   **Study Questions**

① A	④ B	⑦ D	⑩ B	⑬ A
② D	⑤ D	⑧ A	⑪ C	
③ C	⑥ A	⑨ B	⑫ D	

5   The Flow of Food: An Introduction

Page   Activity

5-2   **Test Your Food Safety Knowledge**

① True   ② False   ③ False   ④ False   ⑤ False

5-12   **Discussion Questions**

① Food can be time-temperature abused when it is not:

- Cooked to the required minimum internal temperature
- Cooled properly
- Reheated properly
- Held at the proper temperature

② Cross-contamination can be prevented in an establishment by:

- Assigning specific equipment to each type of food product prepared
- Cleaning and sanitizing all work surfaces, equipment, and utensils after each task
- Preparing raw meat, fish, and poultry and ready-to-eat food at different times (when using the same prep table)
- Purchasing ingredients that require minimal preparation

③ The steps for calibrating a thermometer using the ice-point method are:

❶ Fill a large container with crushed ice. Add clean tap water until the container is full. Stir the mixture well.

❷ Put the thermometer stem or probe into the ice water so the sensing area is completely submerged. Wait thirty seconds, or until the indicator stops moving. Do not let the stem or probe touch the sides or bottom of the container. Keep the stem or probe in the ice water.

❸ Hold the calibration nut securely with a wrench or other tool and rotate the head of the thermometer until it reads 32°F (0°C). On some thermocouples or thermistors, you can press a reset button.

5-13   **Study Questions**

① C	③ C	⑤ C	⑦ C
② A	④ C	⑥ B	

6 The Flow of Food: Purchasing and Receiving

Page	Activity

6-2   Test Your Food Safety Knowledge

① True   ② False   ③ True   ④ True   ⑤ True

6-21   A Case in Point 1

① Betty should have asked the delivery driver to come back later. Products must be delivered when employees have adequate time to inspect them. Deliveries must be inspected immediately. By putting the deliveries away without inspecting them, Sunnydale missed an important opportunity to identify food that:

- Was not delivered at the proper temperature
- Was damaged or mishandled
- Had been thawed and refrozen
- Had expired code dates
- Showed signs of an insect infestation

6-22   A Case in Point 2

① John had good intentions and did most things correctly. However, he did make mistakes that could result in a foodborne illness. John should have done the following:

- Notified the kitchen manager that the shipment had arrived.
- Made sure that the bimetallic stemmed thermometer he took from the kitchen had been properly calibrated, as well as cleaned and sanitized before using it.
- Cleaned and sanitized the thermometer after checking the temperature of each product. He should not have wiped the thermometer on his apron.
- Rejected the case of shucked oysters. The internal temperature of shucked oysters should be 41°F (5°C) or lower.
- Inserted the thermometer stem into the middle of the bucket of live oysters between the shellfish for an ambient reading instead of trying to judge how cold they were with his hand. The temperature of the oysters should have been 45°F (7°C) or lower.

6-23   **Discussion Questions**

① General guidelines for receiving food safely include the following:

- Training employees to inspect deliveries properly
- Planning ahead for shipments
- Planning a back-up menu in case you have to return food items
- Inspecting and storing each delivery before accepting another one
- Having the right information available, such as a purchase order
- Inspecting deliveries immediately
- Correcting mistakes immediately
- Putting products away as quickly as possible, especially products requiring refrigeration
- Keeping the receiving area clean and well lit to discourage pests

② When checking the temperature of:

- Fresh poultry: Insert the thermometer stem or probe into the thickest part of the product. The temperature should be 41°F (5°C) or lower.
- Bulk milk: Fold the bag or pouch around the thermometer stem or probe, being careful not to puncture the bag. The temperature should be 41°F (5°C) or lower unless otherwise specified.

③ Fresh poultry should be rejected for all of the following conditions:

- Purple or green discoloration around the neck
- Dark wing tips (red wing tips are acceptable)
- Stickiness under wings or around joints
- Abnormal unpleasant odor
- Temperature higher than 41°F (5°C)

④ Cans should be rejected if they have any of the following damage:

- Swollen ends
- Leaks and flawed seals
- Rust
- Dents
- Missing labels

6-23   **Study Questions**

| ① D | ③ B | ⑤ D | ⑦ B | ⑨ B |
| ② B | ④ C | ⑥ B | ⑧ D | |

7   The Flow of Food: Storage

Page	Activity

7-2   Test Your Food Safety Knowledge

① False   ② False   ③ True   ④ True   ⑤ False

7-14   A Case in Point 1

① Angie made several errors. She should not have placed the uncovered pan of raw chicken on the top shelf in the refrigerator. Nor should she have stored the carrot cake below the raw chicken breasts, since juices could have dripped onto the cake, contaminating it. Ready-to-eat food must be stored above raw meat, poultry, and fish if these items are stored in the same unit. Ideally, raw product like fresh meat, fish, and poultry should be stored in a separate unit from ready-to-eat food. All stored food should also be wrapped properly to prevent cross-contamination.

② Unfortunately, her mistakes could affect all of the food stored in the refrigerator.

7-15   A Case in Point 2

① The following storage errors occurred:

- Alyce placed the case of sour cream into an already overloaded refrigerator.
- Mary was lining the shelving with aluminum foil. This can restrict airflow in the unit.
- The temperature in the dry-storage room was 85°F (29°C), which is too warm. Dry-storage areas should be between 50°F and 70°F (10°C and 21°C).

7-15   Discussion Questions

① The recommended top-to-bottom order for storing the items in the same refrigerator is:

- Raw trout
- Uncooked beef roast
- Raw ground beef
- Raw chicken

② Live shellfish must be stored in its original container at an air temperature of 45°F (7°C) or lower. Shellstock identification tags must be kept on file for ninety days from the date the last shellfish was sold or served from the container.

③ Food can be kept safe in dry-storage areas by following these practices:

- Keep storerooms cool and dry. For optimum quality and to assure safety, the temperature of the storeroom should be between 50°F and 70°F (10°C and 21°C).

- Make sure storerooms are well ventilated. This will help keep temperature and humidity constant throughout the storage area.

- Store dry food away from walls and at least six inches (fifteen centimeters) off the floor.

- Keep dry food out of direct sunlight.

④ The first-in, first out (FIFO) method is commonly used to ensure that refrigerated, frozen, and dry products are properly rotated during storage. By this method, a product's use-by or expiration date is first identified. The products are then stored to ensure that the oldest are used first. One way to do this is to train employees to store products with the earliest use-by or expiration dates in front of products with later dates. Once shelved, those stored in front are used first.

7-16   **Study Questions**

① A	③ A	⑤ C	⑦ C	⑨ A
② C	④ D	⑥ C	⑧ C	⑩ A

8   The Flow of Food: Preparation

Page   Activity

8-2   **Test Your Food Safety Knowledge**

① False   ② False   ③ False   ④ False   ⑤ False

8-21   **A Case in Point 1**

① Here is what John did wrong:

- He failed to wash his hands before starting work and between the different prep tasks.

- He failed to thaw the shrimp properly. When food is thawed under running water, the temperature of the water should be 70°F (21°C) or lower.

- He took out more whole fish from the walk-in refrigerator than he could prepare in a short period of time, unnecessarily subjecting the fish to time-temperature abuse.

- He failed to clean and sanitize the boning knife, cutting board, and worktable properly after cleaning and filleting the fish. Microorganisms that may have been present on the fish could have been transferred to the shrimp that John prepared with the contaminated knife and cutting board.

8-22   A Case in Point 2

① Here is what Angie did wrong:

- She cooled the leftover chicken breasts improperly. Food should never be left out to cool at room temperature. Angie could have divided the chicken into smaller portions and refrigerated them or used a blast chiller.

- She subjected the chicken-salad ingredients to time-temperature abuse by leaving them out on the worktable while she performed other duties. Angie should have left the ingredients in the refrigerator until she was ready to prepare the salad.

- She pooled shell eggs when preparing the scrambled eggs. If shell eggs are going to be pooled when serving a high-risk population, such as residents of a nursing home, they must be pasteurized. This became a bigger problem when Angie undercooked the eggs.

- She failed to handle the large number of pooled eggs properly. She left a bowl of eggs near a warm stove in the temperature danger zone. She should have pooled a smaller number of eggs and kept them in an ice bath away from the stove.

- She did not cook the scrambled eggs to the correct temperature before storing them on the steam table.

- She did not clean and sanitize the worktable after she made the bacon and before she chopped the celery and cut up the chicken.

8-23   Discussion Questions

① The required minimum internal cooking temperatures are:

- Poultry: 165°F (74°C) for fifteen seconds
- Fish: 145°F (63°C) for fifteen seconds
- Pork: 145°F (63°C) for fifteen seconds (roasts for four minutes)
- Ground beef: 155°F (68°C) for fifteen seconds

② The four proper methods for thawing food are:

- Thaw it in a refrigerator at a product temperature of 41°F (5°C) or lower.
- Submerge it under running, potable water at a temperature of 70°F (21°C) or lower.

- Thaw it in a microwave oven if it will be cooked immediately afterward.
- Thaw it as part of the cooking process as long as the product reaches the required minimum internal cooking temperature.

③ There are a number of methods that can be used to cool food, including:
- Using ice-water baths
- Stirring food with an ice paddle
- Using a blast chiller or tumble chiller
- Adding ice or cold water as an ingredient

④ The rules for properly cooking food in a microwave include:
- Cover food to prevent the surface from drying out.
- Rotate or stir food halfway through the cooking process to distribute heat more evenly.
- Let food stand for at least two minutes after cooking to let product temperature equalize.
- Heat eggs, poultry, seafood, and meat to 165°F (74°C).

8-23   Study Questions

① C	③ D	⑤ D	⑦ C	⑨ D
② B	④ D	⑥ C	⑧ D	⑩ C

9   The Flow of Food: Service

Page   Activity

9-2   Test Your Food Safety Knowledge

① True   ② False   ③ False   ④ True   ⑤ True

9-15   A Case in Point 1

① Here is what Jill did wrong:
- She packed the deliveries in cardboard boxes instead of rigid, insulated carriers.
- She used the wrong utensil to fill the soup baine.
- She did not check the internal temperature of the soup before placing it on the steam table.
- She failed to make sure the internal temperature of the food on the steam table was checked at least every four hours. This would have alerted her to the fact that the steam table was not maintaining the proper temperature and that the casserole was in the temperature danger zone.

② Jill should have done the following:

- She should have kept the delivery meals in a hot-holding cabinet or left the food in a steam table until suitable containers were found or the driver arrived.
- She should have used a long-handled ladle, which would have kept her hands away from the soup, preventing possible contamination as she ladled it out.
- She should have taken the internal temperature of the soup before taking it out to the steam table.
- She should have discarded the casserole and any other food that was not at the right temperature, since she did not know how long the food was in the temperature danger zone.
- She should have made sure that an employee was assigned to monitor the food bar to ensure that customers, such as the children, followed proper etiquette.

9-16   **A Case in Point 2**

① Megan made the following errors:

- She tasted the food on the customer's plate.
- She failed to wash her hands after clearing the dirty dishes from the table.
- She failed to clean the table properly after busing it. Megan should not have wiped the table with the cloth she kept in her apron.
- She improperly scooped ice into glassware. Megan should not have used the glass itself to retrieve ice from the bin. Using a glass this way could cause it to chip or break in the ice.
- She re-served bread and butter that had been previously served to a customer. Uneaten bread or rolls should never be re-served to other customers.
- She failed to wash her hands after scratching a sore. By scratching it and not washing her hands afterward, she could easily have contaminated everything else she touched.

② Here is what Megan should have done before beginning her shift:

- She should have washed her hands after clearing the table and before she touched the water glasses.
- When cleaning tables between guest seatings, Megan should wipe up spills with a disposable, dry cloth. The table should then be cleaned with a clean cloth stored in a sanitizer solution (see Chapter 11).

- She should have used tongs or an ice scoop to get ice.
- She should have served a fresh basket of bread and butter.
- She should have washed her hands immediately after scratching the sore.

9-16   Discussion Questions

① The following practices can minimize contamination in self-service areas:

- Do not allow customers to reuse dirty plates.
- Protect food on display with sneeze guards or food shields.
- Assign an employee to replenish food-bar items and to hand out fresh plates and silverware for return visits.
- Identify all food items on display.
- Keep raw meat, seafood, and poultry separate from ready-to-eat food.

② When transporting food, protect it from contamination and time-temperature abuse during transport by doing the following:

- Use insulated storage containers capable of maintaining food temperatures of 135°F (57°C) or higher or 41°F (5°C) or lower.
- Clean and sanitize the inside of delivery vehicles.
- Check internal food temperatures regularly.
- Make sure employees practice good personal hygiene.
- Keep raw and ready-to-eat products separate during delivery and storage.

③ Ready-to-eat, TCS food can be displayed or held for consumption without temperature control (up to six hours for cold food and up to four hours for hot food) under the following conditions:

Cold Food

- It was held at 41°F (5°C) or lower prior to removing it from refrigeration.
- It does not exceed 70°F (21°C) during the six hours.
- It has a label that specifies both the time it was removed from refrigeration and the time it must be thrown out.
- It is sold, served, or discarded within six hours.

Hot Food

- It was held at 135°F (57°C) or higher prior to removing it from temperature control.
- It has a label that specifies when the item must be thrown out.
- It is sold, served, or discarded within four hours.

④ When serving food off site, you must protect it from contamination and time-temperature abuse. In addition:

- Make sure employees practice good personal hygiene.
- Ensure there is safe drinking water for cooking, dishwashing, and handwashing.
- Check internal food temperatures regularly.
- Label food with storage, shelf-life, and reheating instructions for employees at off-site locations.
- Provide food safety guidelines for consumers.
- Ensure there is adequate power for holding and cooking equipment.
- Provide adequate garbage storage and disposal away from food-preparation and serving areas.

9-17   Study Questions

① A	③ C	⑤ C
② A	④ C	⑥ B

10   Food Safety Management Systems

Page	Activity

10-2   Test Your Food Safety Knowledge

① True   ② True   ③ True   ④ True   ⑤ True

10-26   Discussion Questions

① In order for a food safety management system to be effective, the following programs must be in place:

- Personal hygiene program
- Supplier selection and specification programs
- Sanitation and pest control programs
- Facility design and equipment maintenance programs
- Food safety training programs

② The five foodborne illness risk factors identified by the Centers for Disease Control and Prevention (CDC) are:

- Purchasing food from unsafe sources
- Failing to cook food adequately
- Holding food at incorrect temperatures
- Using contaminated equipment
- Practicing poor personal hygiene

③ The four steps that should be taken when using active managerial control are:

❶ Consider the five risk factors as they apply throughout the flow of food, and identify any issues that could impact food safety.

❷ Create policies and procedures that address the issues that were identified.

❸ Regularly monitor the policies and procedures that have been developed.

❹ Verify that the policies and procedures you have established are actually controlling the risk factors.

④ The seven HACCP principles are:

- Principle 1: Conduct a hazard analysis.
- Principle 2: Determine critical control points (CCPs).
- Principle 3: Establish critical limits.
- Principle 4: Establish monitoring procedures.
- Principle 5: Identify corrective actions.
- Principle 6: Verify that the system works.
- Principle 7: Establish procedures for record keeping and documentation.

⑤ An establishment is required to have a HACCP plan in place if they perform the following activities:

- Smoking and curing food as a method of food preservation
- Using food additives as a method of food preservation
- Packaging food using a reduced-oxygen packaging method
- Offering live, molluscan shellfish from a display tank
- Custom-processing animals
- Treating (e.g., pasteurizing) and packaging juice on site for later sale
- Sprouting beans or seeds

10-26 Study Questions

| ① B | ③ D | ⑤ C | ⑦ C | ⑨ B |
| ② A | ④ B | ⑥ D | ⑧ A | ⑩ D |

11   Sanitary Facilities and Equipment

Page	Activity

11-2   Test Your Food Safety Knowledge

① True   ② False   ③ True   ④ False   ⑤ True

11-27   A Case in Point

① The people who had iced drinks at the bar became ill from the chemical drain cleaner used to clean the glasswasher drain. It is likely that the grease trap on the kitchen sink was blocked with grease. This caused wastewater (and drain cleaner) to back up into the glasswasher drain and the drain for the icemaker since this equipment shared the same piping system. Carlos had failed to install an air gap between the icemaker and the floor drain, which resulted in wastewater backing up into the icemaker, contaminating the ice. Carlos should not have tried to install and maintain the plumbing in the establishment himself. Establishments must rely on professionals to do this.

② Aside from handling a potential lawsuit, Carlos will require the services of a professional to fix the problem and will have to clean and sanitize the icemaker storage bin thoroughly before it can be used again.

11-28   Discussion Questions

① One of the most important factors to consider when selecting flooring for food-preparation areas is the material's porosity, or the extent to which it can become saturated with liquids. The *FDA Food Code* recommends the use of nonporous (nonabsorbent) flooring in food-preparation areas.

② A backup of raw sewage in an establishment is cause for immediate closure of the area, correction of the problem, and thorough cleaning.

③ To prevent backflow in an establishment:

- Install vacuum breakers or other approved backflow-prevention devices on threaded faucets and connections between two piping systems.
- Install air gaps wherever practical and possible. *This is the only completely reliable method.* An air gap is a space used to separate a water-supply outlet from any potentially contaminated source.

④ Sources of potable water include:

- Approved public water mains
- Private water sources regularly maintained and tested
- Closed portable water containers filled with potable water
- Properly maintained water transport vehicles

- If an establishment uses a private water supply such as a well rather than an approved public source, it should check with the local regulatory agency for information on inspections, testing, and other requirements. Generally, nonpublic water systems should be tested at least annually, and the report kept on file in the establishment.

⑤ The requirements of a handwashing station include:

- Hot and cold running water supplied through a mixing valve or combination faucet at a temperature of at least 100°F (38°C).
- Soap in liquid, bar, or powder form.
- A means to dry hands is required. Most local codes require establishments to supply disposable paper towels in handwashing stations.
- A waste container is required if disposable paper towels are provided.
- Signage must indicate employees are required to wash their hands before returning to work.
- Handwashing stations are required in food-preparation areas, service areas, dishwashing areas, and restrooms.

⑥ When installing stationary equipment:

- It must be mounted on legs, at least six inches (fifteen centimeters) off the floor, or it must be sealed to a masonry base.

11-28 Study Questions

① A	④ B	⑦ A	⑩ D
② A	⑤ B	⑧ D	⑪ D
③ C	⑥ A	⑨ B	

12 Cleaning and Sanitizing

Page   Activity

12-2   Test Your Food Safety Knowledge

① False   ② False   ③ False   ④ False   ⑤ False

12-25 A Case in Point 1

① Schedules do not clean dining rooms, people do. Tim had made his schedule too rigid and failed to monitor it. He should have made the necessary adjustments to take late-night banquets into account.

② Tim should enlist the cooperation of Norman, the night shift manager, to make sure the cleaning program is followed. Norman should bring problems to Tim's attention. Shift supervisors, employees, and managers must communicate effectively with one another.

③ Shifts should be scheduled to include all cleaning duties. If the banquet room closes at 1:00 a.m., the shift should extend beyond the closing time to take cleaning into account. Tim should also encourage his employees to follow a clean-as-you-go approach. In this way, the soiled tableware no longer being used by the banquet attendees could have been brought to the dishwasher before midnight.

12-25   A Case in Point 2

① The tableware can be washed, rinsed, and sanitized in a three-compartment sink until the machine has been repaired. Before cleaning and sanitizing the items, clean and sanitize each compartment and all work surfaces. Then follow these steps:

❶ Rinse, scrape, or soak the items.

❷ Wash the items in the first sink in a detergent solution at least 110°F (43°C).

❸ Immerse or spray-rinse the items in the second sink.

❹ Immerse the items in the third sink in hot water or a chemical-sanitizing solution. If hot-water immersion is used, the water must be at least 171°F (77°C). If chemical sanitizing is used, the sanitizer must be mixed at the proper concentration and tested with a sanitizer test kit. The sanitizing solution must also be at the proper temperature.

❺ Air-dry the items.

12-26   Discussion Questions

① Food-contact surfaces must be cleaned and sanitized:

* After each use
* Any time you begin working with a different type of food
* Any time you are interrupted during a task and the tools or items you have been working with may have been contaminated
* At four-hour intervals, if the items are in constant use

② Cleaning is the process of removing food and other types of soil from a surface, while sanitizing is the process of reducing the number of microorganisms on that surface to safe levels.

③ When cleaning and sanitizing items in a three-compartment sink, follow these steps:

❶ Rinse, scrape, or soak the items.

❷ Wash the items in the first sink.

❸ Immerse or spray-rinse the items in the second sink.

④ Immerse the items in the third sink in hot-water or a chemical-sanitizing solution. If hot water immersion is used, the water must be at least 171°F (77°C). If chemical sanitizing is used, the sanitizer must be mixed at the proper concentration and tested with a sanitizer test kit. The sanitizing solution must also be at the proper temperature.

⑤ Air-dry the items.

④ To store clean and sanitized tableware, utensils, and equipment:

- Store tableware and utensils at least six inches (fifteen centimeters) off the floor. Keep them covered or otherwise protected from dirt and condensation.

- Clean and sanitize drawers and shelves before clean items are stored.

- Clean and sanitize trays and carts used to carry clean tableware and utensils. Do this daily or as often as necessary.

- Store glasses and cups upside down on a cleaned and sanitized shelf or rack. Store flatware and utensils with handles up so employees can pick them up without touching food-contact surfaces.

- Keep the food-contact surfaces of stationary equipment covered until ready for use.

⑤ Factors that affect the efficiency of sanitizers include the following:

- **Contact time.** For a sanitizer to kill microorganisms, it must make contact with the object for a specific amount of time.

- **Temperature.** To be effective, the sanitizing solution must be at the proper temperature.

- **Concentration.** Concentrations below those recommended could fail to sanitize objects, while concentrations higher than recommended can be unsafe, and might corrode metals.

- **Water hardness.** The amount of minerals in your water affects how well the sanitizer works.

- **pH.** To be effective, the right amount of sanitizer must be used for the pH of the estabilshment's water.

⑥ Cleaning tools should be cleaned before being stored in a designated area away from food and food-preparation sites. When storing cleaning materials:

- Air-dry wiping cloths overnight.

- Hang mops, brooms, and brushes on hooks to air-dry.

- Clean and rinse buckets and let them air-dry.

12-26 Study Questions

  ① D   ③ A   ⑤ C   ⑦ A

  ② A   ④ C   ⑥ A   ⑧ A

13 Integrated Pest Management

Page	Activity

13-2 Test Your Food Safety Knowledge

  ① True   ② False   ③ False   ④ False   ⑤ False

13-20 A Case in Point

① Fred should have been working with a PCO and had an integrated pest management (IPM) program in place prior to his discovery of the roach infestation. While it sounds as if Fred and his staff are doing a good job keeping the establishment clean, some other measures he could have taken to prevent the infestation include:

- Screening windows and vents
- Installing self-closing doors and door sweeps
- Keeping exterior openings closed tightly
- Filling holes around pipes
- Sealing cracks in floors and walls
- Disposing of garbage quickly and correctly
- Making sure that shipments are inspected for signs of pest infestation

② Fred needs the help of a licensed PCO to help eliminate the roach infestation. The PCO may use repellents, sprays, bait, and/or traps to eliminate the roaches.

13-20 Discussion Questions

① The purpose of an IPM program is to do the following:

- Prevent pests from entering the establishment.
- Deny pests food, water, and a hiding or nesting place.
- Work with a licensed PCO to eliminate any pests that do enter.

② To prevent pests from entering an establishment:

- Screen all windows and vents with at least sixteen mesh per square inch screening.
- Install self-closing devices or door sweeps on all doors.
- Install air curtains above or alongside doors.
- Keep drive-through windows closed when not in use.
- Keep all exterior openings closed tightly.

- Use concrete to fill holes or sheet metal to cover openings around pipes.
- Install screens over ventilation pipes and ducts on the roof.
- Cover floor drains with hinged grates.
- Seal all cracks in floors and walls.
- Properly seal spaces or cracks where stationary equipment is fitted to the floor.

③ Signs of a cockroach infestation include:

- Strong oily odor
- Droppings (feces) that look like grains of black pepper
- Capsule-shaped egg cases that are brown, dark red, or black and may appear leathery, smooth, or shiny

Signs of a rodent infestation include:

- Urine stains revealed by black (ultraviolet) light
- Signs of gnawing
- Droppings that are shiny and black (fresh) or gray (older)
- Tracks
- Nesting materials, such as scraps of paper, cloth, hair, and other soft materials
- Holes in quiet places, near food and water, and next to buildings

④ Your PCO should store and dispose of all pesticides used in the facility. If they are stored on the premises, follow these guidelines:

- Keep them in their original container.
- Store them in a secure location away from areas where food, utensils, and food equipment are stored.
- Check local regulations before disposing of pesticides.

⑤ To minimize the hazard to people, have your PCO use pesticides only when you are closed for business, and employees are not on site. When pesticides will be applied, prepare the area to be sprayed by removing all food and movable food-contact surfaces. Cover equipment and food-contact surfaces that cannot be moved. Wash, rinse, and sanitize food-contact surfaces after the area has been sprayed. Anytime pesticides are used or stored on the premises, you should have a corresponding Material Safety Data Sheets (MSDS), since they are hazardous materials.

13-21 Study Questions

① C	③ A	⑤ C
② D	④ A	⑥ A

14   Food Safety Regulation and Standards

Page	Activity

14-2   Test Your Food Safety Knowledge

① False   ② False   ③ True   ④ True   ⑤ False

14-14   Discussion Questions

① The following hazards require the closure of an establishment:

- Significant lack of refrigeration
- Backup of sewage into the establishment or its water supply
- Emergency, such as a building fire or flood
- Significant infestation of insects or rodents
- Long interruption of electrical or water service
- Clear evidence of a foodborne-illness outbreak related to the establishment

② Recommendations for restaurant and foodservice regulations are issued at the federal level, regulations are written at the state level, and enforcement is carried out at the state and local level.

③ During an inspection, a manager should do the following:

- Ask for identification.
- Cooperate.
- Take notes.
- Keep the relationship professional.
- Be prepared to provide records requested by the inspector.

After the inspection, the manager should do the following:

- Discuss violations and time frames for correction with the inspector.
- Act on all deficiencies noted in the report by determining why each problem occurred, and then establish new procedures or revise existing ones. It may also be necessary to retrain employees.

④ Factors that determine the frequency of a health inspection include:

- Size and complexity of the operation. Larger operations offering a large number of TCS food items might be inspected more frequently.
- Inspection history of the establishment. Establishments with a history of low sanitation scores or consecutive violations might be inspected more frequently.

- Clientele's susceptibility to foodborne illness. Nursing homes, schools, daycare centers, and hospitals might receive more frequent inspections.
- Workload of the local health department and the number of inspectors available.

14-15   Study Questions

① B   ③ C
② B   ④ C

15   Employee Food Safety Training

Page	Activity

15-2   Test Your Food Safety Knowledge

① True   ② False   ③ True   ④ True   ⑤ True

15-11   Discussion Questions

① An establishment can determine its food safety training needs by doing the following:
- Testing employees' food safety knowledge
- Observing employee job performance
- Questioning or surveying employees to identify areas of weakness

② Methods that can be used to deliver training include:
- On-the-job training
- Classroom training
- Information search
- Guided discussion
- Jigsaw design
- Demonstration
- Role-play
- Technology-based training
- Training videos and DVDs
- Games

③ Technology-based training is most appropriate in the following situations:
- Staff works in different locations and/or need the same training at different times.
- It is costly to bring staff to one place.
- Staff needs retraining to complete a topic.
- Staff has different levels of knowledge about a topic.
- Staff has different learning skills.

- Classroom training makes staff nervous.
- Staff needs to learn at their own pace.
- You want to collect specific information, such as time spent on different topics, test scores, number of tries until the training was finished, and/or problem areas.

15-12   Study Questions

① A   ③ C   ⑤ A
② D   ④ C   ⑥ B

Notes

Index

Notes